One True Church

One True Church
An American Story of Race, Family, and Religion

Susan B. Ridgely

The University of North Carolina Press CHAPEL HILL

This book was published with the assistance of the Z. Smith Reynolds Fund of the University of North Carolina Press.

© 2026 Susan B. Ridgely
All rights reserved
Set in Merope Basic by Westchester Publishing Services
Manufactured in the United States of America

Library of Congress Cataloging-in-Publication Data
Names: Ridgely, Susan B. (Susan Bales) author
Title: One true church : an American story of race, family, and religion / Susan B. Ridgely.
Description: Chapel Hill : The University of North Carolina Press, [2026] | Includes bibliographical references and index.
Identifiers: LCCN 2025045064 | ISBN 9781469694580 cloth | ISBN 9781469694597 paperback | ISBN 9781469685335 epub | ISBN 9781469694603 pdf
Subjects: LCSH: Our Lady of Guadalupe Catholic Church (Newton Grove, N.C.)—History | Catholics—North Carolina—Newton Grove—History | Race relations—Religious aspects—Catholic Church | Newton Grove (N.C.)—Church history | Newton Grove (N.C.)—Race relations | BISAC: RELIGION / Christianity / History | SOCIAL SCIENCE / Ethnic Studies / American / African American & Black Studies
Classification: LCC BX4603.N488 O98 2026
LC record available at https://lccn.loc.gov/2025045064

This book will be made open access within three years of publication thanks to Path to Open, a program developed in partnership between JSTOR, the American Council of Learned Societies (ACLS), the University of Michigan Press, and the University of North Carolina Press to bring about equitable access and impact for the entire scholarly community, including authors, researchers, libraries, and university presses around the world. Learn more at https://about.jstor.org/path-to-open/.

For product safety concerns under the European Union's General Product Safety Regulation (EU GPSR), please contact gpsr@mare-nostrum.co.uk or write to the University of North Carolina Press and Mare Nostrum Group B.V., Mauritskade 21D, 1091 GC Amsterdam, The Netherlands.

To the generations of Catholics in Newton Grove who lived this story, and to the storytellers of Ann St. — past, present, and future.

Contents

List of Illustrations ix
Acknowledgments xi

Introduction 1

CHAPTER ONE
From Plantation to Parish 21
Antebellum North Carolina to 1870

CHAPTER TWO
St. Mark's and the Limits of a Parish's Protection 39
1870–1904

CHAPTER THREE
The Delicate Dance of Rural Catholicism in the Protestant South 65
1899–1926

CHAPTER FOUR
Maintaining Unity Through Segregation? 93
1926–1952

CHAPTER FIVE
Can Two Become One? 122
Striving for Unity, 1953–1974

Afterword 151

Notes 159
Index 187

Illustrations

FIGURES

John Carr and Euphemia Monk's sacramental record 51

Stained glass window from the sanctuary 52

Martha and Mary Delia Monk's sacramental records 56

St. Mark's School 71

Diploma from St. Mark's School 71

Sister Josita with the chickens 74

St. Benedict's Church and School 105

St. Benedict's Church interior 105

Procession of parishioners of St. Benedict's parish, 1943 112

St. Mark's parish on Easter in the 1930s 115

St. Mark's parish interior 115

St. Mark's school bus under repair 118

African American parishioners entering the first desegregated Mass on May 31, 1953 124

MAP

Map of North Carolina highlighting Sampson County and Newton Grove 2

Acknowledgments

It is a true joy to express my gratitude publicly to all the people and organizations that contributed to this book. First and foremost, I will forever be grateful to the brave and generous people who shared their stories with me for this project. You have all taught me so much about family, relationships, God, terror, perseverance, and moving forward. Thank you for being willing to answer my questions, for texting me your insights over the years, and for continually reminding me about the core goals of this work. Although I cannot thank each of you by name, your individual contributions are found in many ways in these pages. I hope they will be remembered and used for generations. I also hope you all find yourselves fairly represented in these pages. This book is dedicated to you and your ancestors.

A special thank-you to Angela Page for helping with the parish archives and making connections to the community. You are a treasure to your community. I am so grateful that this project allowed our paths to cross. I met so many other incredible people throughout my research, including Diana Zwilling and the late Monsignor Gerald L. Lewis at the Diocese of Raleigh Archives. Despite the challenges posed by the pandemic, Zwilling's resourcefulness allowed me to continue to research relatively uninterrupted. Monsignors Lewis and John Wall and Father Garneau provided an unbelievable amount of oral history and wisdom to support this work. Thank you, too, to Patrick Hayes at the Redemptorist Archives in Philadelphia, who generously helped me walk through the Redemptorist life in Newton Grove, making sure I had legible copies of letters and a firm understanding of their context. Joel Rose at the Sampson County History Museum taught me a great deal about the wider community in which Newton Grove is located. A guided tour through the museum allowed me to see and feel how the Confederacy and enslavement is being understood in the area now as well as how it was memorialized in the past. Other archivists also helped me both in person and online: Carlinthia Cox at the Archives for the Dominican Sisters of Hope, Betsy Johnson at the Mercy Heritage Center, Nichole R. Young at Fayetteville State University, and especially Rebecca Owens, chief genealogist at the Johnston County Heritage Center. Finally, I am indebted to Claire Kilgore, whose research assistance, organizing skills, and genuine interest kept this project going through the pandemic.

A Research Travel Grant from the Cushwa Center for American Catholicism launched this research and facilitated connections with many scholars, archivists, priests, and nuns who were essential to its success. A Louisville Institute Grant for Researchers allowed me to take time away from teaching to focus solely on research and writing. That support, along with Fall Research Competition support from the University of Wisconsin–Madison, was essential in giving me the time, space, and resources I needed to complete this book.

Writing, for me, is not a solitary endeavor; it requires a significant amount of communal support. I am deeply grateful to the members of my writing group, particularly Alex Hueneaus, who ensured that I dedicated at least four hours a week to writing. Lynn Neal has been discussing these ideas with me since graduate school; such a friendship is a treasure. Julie Byrne, Amy Koehlinger, and Kristy Nabhan-Warren's friendship, both inside and outside the academy, kept me afloat throughout this project and so much more. Helen Kinsella, Jordan Rosenblum, and Kathryn Lofton also supported this work in many ways. Pamela Klassen's careful attention to the introduction served to sharpen the argument. Thomas Tweed's last-minute thoughts and bibliography greatly enriched the final product, as did the anonymous reviewers' comments. My parents John and Jane (McHaney Black) Bales and my sisters Tricia Bales VanBuskirk and Elizabeth Bales read multiple drafts and listened to endless stories. David Cecelski, whose willingness to delve into the intricacies of Eastern North Carolina and offer enthusiastic support for this work, provided a much needed boost when worldwide circumstances made the completion of this project seem insurmountable.

The idea for the book began while I was taking Donald G. Mathews's Southern Religious History course at UNC–Chapel Hill, where I learned about the ever-intertwining powers of region, land, and storytelling. More recent conversations with the American Religion Workshop at Princeton University, the brown bag participants at UW–Madison, and an early presentation at the University of Texas at Austin pushed me to see this story in a wider context. The supportive and incisive critiques of Catherine Osborne and Marc Loustau, who both edited this text at different points, served to make this a much better book.

The research for this book began during my childhood summers in Beaufort, North Carolina. I spent hours rocking on the front porch, trying to escape the summer heat by getting absorbed in my mother's and grandmother's stories about their childhoods. The longer we rocked, the more likely we would be joined by neighbors and friends with whom we would swap tales late into the evening. When my dad would finally bring my sisters and me inside to bed, he would recount a "tell-story" about Blackbeard while the sweat beaded on our foreheads and dripped down our backs. Getting lost in history—family or otherwise—was our only relief from the swamp-like conditions of a North Carolina summer without air conditioning. Once the lights were off, I would spend much of the night piecing together what I had learned, reimagining how life was years ago on the family farm or in that small fishing town. Finally, I would give up and go to the kitchen for ice cubes, only to find my sisters already standing in front of the open freezer. Today, my husband Steve and my kids Millie and Andersen have similar experiences on the porch with a new set of treasured friends and my mom orchestrating it all from the rocker with the best view. This book is dedicated to all of them—to the generations of storytellers of Ann St.

Note on Language Usage

The terms used to describe African Americans have shifted significantly over time. Language that appeared in past records—such as newspapers, letters, or government documents—often served to dehumanize, stereotype, or marginalize Black individuals and communities. In this text, I do not reproduce such language in my own analysis. However, I have retained original wording in quoted historical sources to preserve the integrity of the record and illuminate the conditions under which Black people lived and resisted. In cases where quoted material includes overt racial slurs, I have modified or partially obscured those terms. This decision reflects a commitment not to replicate the harm such language continues to inflict.

Throughout this work, I use the terms *African American* and *Black* in accordance with contemporary usage. I capitalize *Black* to recognize a shared cultural and historical identity shaped by the transatlantic slave trade, slavery, segregation, and their enduring legacies. This follows the guidance of the Associated Press and other style authorities. I do not capitalize *white*, as those who identify as white do not share a similarly racialized collective history or experience of systemic oppression.

One True Church

Introduction

In the summer of 1872, seven years after the end of the Civil War, two men—one a white doctor and the other an African American farmer—walked through a cotton field mapping out the dimensions of a new clapboard church.[1] Passersby on the main road may have thought they understood this scene immediately: the wealthy white doctor was paying the poor Black farmer to build yet another Baptist or Methodist church that he would never be allowed to enter. The wealthy doctor would sit in the front pew of a fine sanctuary; the farmer would worship at a nearby African Methodist Episcopal sanctuary led by a Black preacher. Stereotypes of Southern segregation and exploitation fill in the gaps. Stereotyped stories can be accurate, at least in part. Occasionally, they aren't. And, in the case of John Carr Monk and his brother Solomon Monk, going in for a closer look reveals a semisecret world of racial and religious renegades.

These two brothers walking the land together that day would have been a familiar sight to people heading into the small town of Newton Grove, nestled in rural Sampson County, North Carolina. They grew up together on a small plantation nearby. John Carr Monk was the white son of a wealthy, enslaving landowner and had every advantage in life. His brother, Solomon Monk, as the enslaver's mixed-raced son, remained in bondage. Although he may have had advantages within the system of slavery because of his parentage, he did not have freedom of movement or any other freedom until after the Civil War. The men's lives, although radically different, were intertwined from birth and would remain so until their deaths. In the time between, they and their families came together to form an interracial, although internally segregated, Catholic congregation that would worship in the church they plotted out in 1872. As I discuss in the second chapter, once they learned about the universal Catholic Church, they sought a means for conversion so they could found this parish in opposition to the segregation of Protestant churches across North Carolina at this time.

St. Mark's, as the parish was first known, was a rarity in the "Old South"— the original Southern colonies of Virginia, Maryland, North Carolina, South Carolina, and Georgia—especially outside of port cities.[2] Sampson County itself had no notable Catholic presence before the creation of

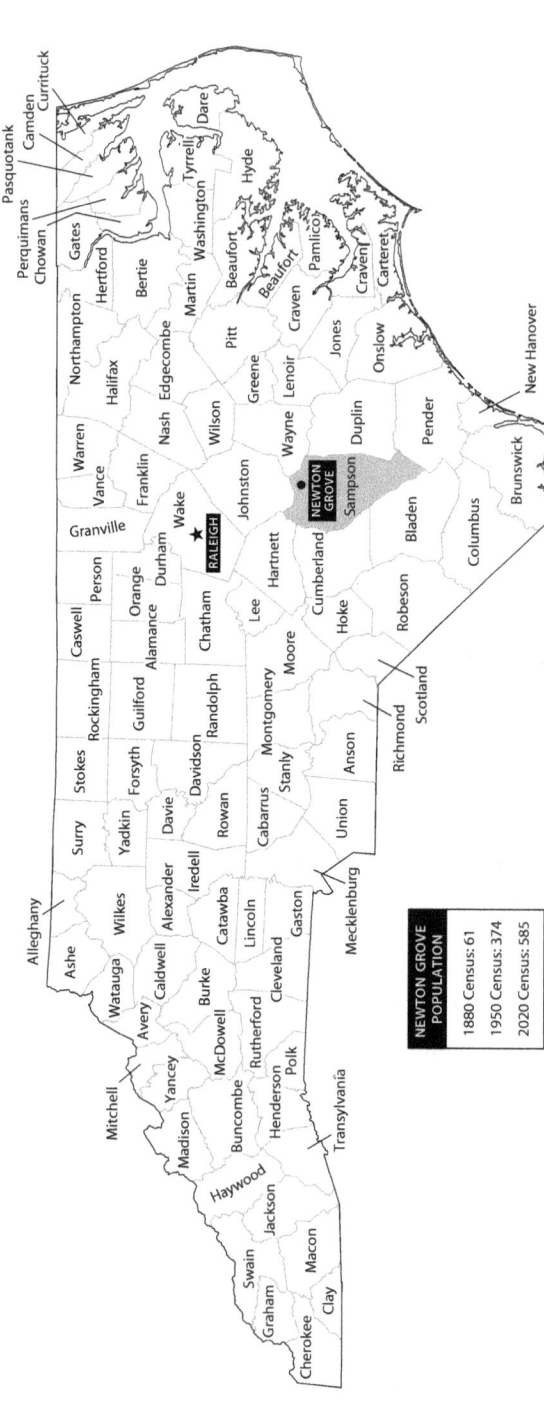

Map of North Carolina highlighting Sampson County and Newton Grove.

St. Mark's. Yet, by 1874, St. Mark's became a bustling Catholic parish full of kinfolk, both mixed race and white, who sought to codify in some way the long-established, cross-racial, mutually dependent relationships that had sustained their lives in opposition to a white supremacist regime that developed after Reconstruction that demanded these ties be erased from public view. While our contemporary minds might want to tell the story of the Monk brothers in parallel—a story in which the lives of Black folk and white folk rarely come together—attending carefully to this parish forces us to see that these neat categorizations are unwittingly performing the work of a new form of post-emancipation white supremacy, obscuring the history of this parish in all the complicated interconnectedness that created its practices and nurtured its people.

This coming together of Black and white parishioners was not easy or equal. This story is one of continual effort toward the goal of unity by Black and white Catholics, who remained on the Monks' former plantation land, land that they came to own, for the century after the end of slavery. At times, the desires of the Catholic Church aligned with those of the white and Black parishioners, allowing them to inch closer toward the goal of a truly united congregation. At other times, the aims of one or more of these constituencies were at odds with the parish's founding mission as an interracial parish.[3] Occasionally, as this history highlights, the mission was all but forgotten. And yet again and again, core members of the parish kept trying, never giving up on the possibility of an interracial Catholic parish. This story is neither one that centers success or failure nor is it unique to Catholicism, although it's set within a Catholic parish. It is a detailed investigation into the uniquely American configurations of race, religion, and family that developed in slavery and persisted through the height of integration. Looking closely at this community reveals what can be learned from their process of trying to sustain an alternative racial and religious space that is part of, rather than apart from, its community.

This parish, whose name would change many times in its history, began its life in Newton Grove as one parish with two segregated schools, as mandated by North Carolina law.[4] Until the 1930s, the parish community known as St. Mark's hosted a robust liturgical life in a sanctuary that sheltered both Black and white Catholics in a way that seemingly no other public or semi-public building in North Carolina did. The historical record confirms that by 1900 the adult congregation adhered to segregated seating for Mass, although there were occasional opportunities for the parochial school students to meet across racial lines. In response to internal and external pressures, the parish gradually split along racial lines from the late 1920s until 1939, at the very time when Catholic organizations such as the Federated Colored Catholics (1925) and the Catholic Interracial Council (1934) were forming to seek social justice and racial equality in the church. Despite these efforts to bring Black and white Catholics together, on the ground in Raleigh, the parish was split in September 1939. The diocese consecrated a Black parish on this same small slice of John Carr Monk's land 100 yards or so from the now de facto white parish, where the whole community had worshipped weeks before. This single Catholic community formally became two neighboring, racially segregated parishes. Yet what was two became one again after May 31, 1953. Bishop Vincent S. Waters, an ardent integrationist newly appointed to the diocese, remerged the formerly unified parishes amid national media coverage and local tensions. As it attempted to resist and persist in creating a single parish community, the congregation invented new practices and relied on their grandparents' traditions to survive until integration came through the public schools in the 1970s.

From its interracial yet internally segregated beginning in Reconstruction to the *Plessy v. Ferguson* decision (1896) upholding "separate but equal" as constitutional through *Brown v. Board of Education of Topeka* in 1954 that would mandate but not enforce school integration almost a year after Bishop Waters merged the parish, in some ways St. Mark's resisted yet in others capitulated to American and Catholic racial norms. As it sought to steer a course that would allow the survival of both its mission and its interracial congregation, the parish foreshadowed changes in race relations that would come to the rest of the South, and to some extent wider American society, with the civil rights movement. The Montgomery bus boycott wouldn't start until 1955 and the sit-ins at Greensboro's lunch counters until 1960. Although the integrated parish school closed in 1954 for want for pupils, parishioners had been worshipping together and attending integrated Sunday morning catechism classes for twenty years before North Carolina schools integrated in the 1970s.

What little scholarship that exists about this parish centers on its heroes, particularly its white heroes Bishop Waters of the Raleigh Diocese and, to some extent, John Carr Monk.[5] Certainly, as we will see in the coming chapters, these men risked an unimaginable amount to create an alternate model for religious communities in segregated North Carolina, one that was both Catholic and interracial in this Protestant and segregated region. A closer look at their monumental efforts, however, highlights the dangers that so many others faced to bring this parish into being. The entire community endured similar consequences to John Carr, without necessarily having his social and racialized status as protection. Unlike Bishop Waters, all the parishioners had to live and work in the wider community that saw them as religious, racial, and regional traitors to the segregated, Protestant South. They faced the anger and violence of a wider segregated society, one composed not only of outsiders but also of their own in-laws, uncles, cousins, and even siblings. The African American members took on an even greater risk, as their participation in the parish simultaneously challenged the ruling white supremacy while separating them from the larger African American community in a context in which such actions could easily mean death.

IN THE RURAL TOWN of Newton Grove today, people give their addresses by county. Within the parish they orient themselves in the world by describing where they land on John Carr's family tree. Interracial kinships are often well-known through family stories, which are shared openly in the Black community and in hushed tones in the white. Within the wider parish, Black and white members can see, if they choose to look, their family connections in the church cemetery. Christine, the indefatigable parish historian, gave me a tour of the cemetery on an early visit to the parish.[6]

"This used to be a segregated cemetery," Christine began. "White and Black. Right here is a marker." She moved further in among the stones, some crumbling, others newly cut and decorated. "The first Black person buried here was a young Monk girl. She's buried next to her parents, Solomon and Martha Monk, who were former slaves. Right across from their graves is John Carr's, which sits at the geographic center of the original parish land. Along with the Monks, you'll see Coles, Godwins, Raynors, Gregorys, and Lees repeated many times throughout this place."[7] These family names, Christine told me, were shared "across the color line." At funerals, the entire family would gather—Black and white–to say good-bye to their loved one.

This interracial familial togetherness in life and death differs significantly from other more famous recent discoveries of interracial family ties, like the hidden relationship between Thomas Jefferson and Sally Hemings or the forgotten family members that Henry Louis Gates Jr. tracked down on *Finding Your Roots*.[8] In these cases, the family ties had been lost when African American family members moved away from the plantations where they were once enslaved. The white and Black families come together for reunions today at a historical moment when embracing each other "across the color line," at least for discreet events, is largely met with celebration, not threats or violence. In Newton Grove, however, parishioners have always seen how segregation sought to destroy interracial family ties, like it divided the cemetery and its inhabitants. As the proliferation of the name "Monk" on both the Black and white sides of the church cemetery suggest, many of the parish's African American families trace their lines back to individuals held in bondage by John Carr's father, Archibald Monk; more specifically, they are related to Archibald Monk and a distant unnamed grandmother whom he raped.

Rather than focus on the Archibald Monk, the enslaver, and his actions, however, most of the African American Monks I interviewed put their energy toward giving names to the nameless tally marks on his slave census forms so they could be properly added to the family tree. They also seek to uncover and deepen other family connections with Monks, both white and Black, living and long deceased. An explanation by Archibald Monk's great-great-great-grandson, a recently retired African American man named Joseph, epitomizes the matter-of-fact way many of Archibald's Black descendants address the role enslavement plays in their family tree. Joseph, whose DNA results confirm what the African American community always knew, that he is firmly in Archibald Monk's line, said it plainly: "Sometimes in our family, we see a very fair complexion, and we're reminded where we came from and how we were treated." But he avoided offering a final judgment. "It is what it is," he concluded agnostically.[9]

In my conversation with him, Joseph, like many other folks, repeated stories of interracial family ties and how these ties were acknowledged through helping each other on the farm, using informal terms of endearment, like nicknames, or sharing regular meals in private. Others, especially white people, were less forthcoming. Still, the connection remained, sometimes waiting to be acknowledged. The deeply rooted intimacies and relative immobility of rural America shaped religious commitments, regional loyalty, and relationships across and within racial groups differently than in America's urban cities and port towns.

I knew something of these textures of Southern life from the childhood summers I spent at my grandparents' home in North Carolina where I fished alongside my great-uncle and learned to bake alongside three generations of women in a small shotgun kitchen. Yet when I went to the archives seeking evidence for exactly how race, religion, and kinship were expressed in this community, there were few surviving sources. I quickly found the only way to understand parishioners' motivations and actions was to talk with them about their experiences. My conversations taught me to situate the parish within the context of the history of the United States and the history of

North Carolina, as well as the history of the American Catholic Church and the daily needs of its members: the seasonal rounds of religious festivals, their feelings of safety in their community and their desires to educate children in a world that was tightly controlled by the dividing lines of segregation. From the interviews, I also learned about the times when those lines were crossed for practical jokes or public protest. By pairing these conversations with archival research, I was able to reconstruct this history and amplify the voices of a community of rural Catholics in Protestant North Carolina. This community included the priests who administered the parish, the sisters who taught at the parochial schools, and the everyday Black and white Catholics who filled the pews. These oral histories, when put into conversation with each other, convincingly demonstrate how one rural Catholic parish in the Protestant South can teach us to alter the standard narrative of American Catholic history, which focuses on urban centers and immigration.

As they built this standard narrative, historians initially reflected on the poverty and growing political power of the urban migrants from Europe who filled America's pews in the 19th century. More recently, scholars drew attention to Black Catholics who founded new, vibrant parishes in Northern cities following the Great Migration of African Americans out of the South.[10] In the telling of Catholic history as well as American history more broadly, however, scholars have often stuck to an image of the South's unified position on race (segregation) and religion (Protestantism).[11] While European immigrants and Black Catholics reinvented communal ties in the new surroundings of late 19th and early 20th century Northern cities, the Catholics of Newton Grove might have converted in the 1870s; yet they remained in the place of their Protestant ancestors for at least a century more. They had to navigate racial, religious, and generational change on the same land that they had occupied since before the Civil War, since the time that some of their ancestors owned their other ancestors.

Like many Americans navigating the long century after the Civil War, they turned to religion to help them find stable ground and cement fragile relationships in this seemingly topsy-turvy world. As I explain in chapter 2, Catholicism was central to their effort to create what they understood to be a truly Christian community, where Black and white parishioners worshipped in the same congregation, under the same roof, although internally segregated.[12] Both white and Black citizens of Newton Grove understood that by converting to Catholicism, they were excluding themselves collectively from a racial and regional identity that demanded division in God's body. In the

19th century, Southern Protestants separated themselves into white and Black churches, their own local communities conforming to the rapidly segregating national denominations. In contrast, the doctrine of the singular Body of Christ, as they understood the Catholic Church's interpretation of it, provided Newton Grove's new converts with a divine framework through which to maintain their interracial household connections against growing local and national hostility. Through baptism into the Catholic Church, they were creating a universally recognized spiritual kinship that would remain intact as the new regime of segregation effectively worked to erase any sign of their biological kinship. By creating and sustaining an interracial, internally segregated Catholic parish, this community affirmed their familial connections as they embraced what they believed was the sacred unity of the Christian message. Their commitment to kin and to embodying Catholicism as an alternative Christianity to the regionally dominant Protestantism kept the parish going through a time of great fear and desperation.

The parish's embrace of unity did not include an insistence on equality, nor did it extend to the parishioners' lives outside the church. Although radical for its time and place, the community did not erase racial hierarchies. This community was no utopia. Unlike later efforts that attempted to create interracial communes and communities that formed in the urban North, this parish functioned within and responded to the white supremacist frameworks set by white Southern culture.[13] As we will see, the parish had its own power structure for white members, Black members, and the parish as a whole. Still, the community met together under one roof for most of its existence, with the children in the segregated parochial schools engaged in joint celebrations and competitions. Sustaining this parish while thwarting segregation in these limited ways required being constantly attentive to the multitude of threats, both racial and religious, within the parish, in the town, and on their farms.

In this rural community, institutional segregation mattered, but it was enforced differently than in urban areas. Apart from formally segregated institutions such as schools and churches, these farm families, whether white or Black, were less likely to encounter the Colored Only signs that have come to represent this period that they saw at doctors' offices, county parks, and other public places. Although there were no markings on farms to highlight segregation's presence, its power governed every movement when Black and white neighbors were working or playing together, from who drank first to what could be said to who did what job and everything in between.

Henry, a Black man who grew up in the parish, attended the desegregated Mass in 1953, fourteen years after the parish had been formally segregated by the Catholic Church and over eighty years after John Carr Monk gathered the first interracial parish. Henry eventually became one of my most important resources in Newton Grove. He taught me about this way of life the first time we visited in his living room: "There was no sign that designated this," he explained, "but we all knew the rules." He learned from his parents where the family should sit when in the presence of white people, just as Henry's parents learned it from their grandparents. His great-grandparents navigated different rules of white supremacy under slavery. Knowing the implicit rules of each situation was essential in every generation. Breaking them would bring pain to oneself or one's family. The threat of personal and communal consequences, whether physical, social, or economic, was ever present in the lives of these parishioners who navigated between two sets of racial expectations—one at church and another in public.

Members of this parish broke the presumed link between not only Southernness and Protestantism but also Southernness and segregation. They did so by converting. Conversion gave them access to Catholicism, which they understood as a truly universal church for both whites and Blacks in Newton Grove. Catholics, according to John Carr, could belong together, sharing their traditions, theology, and sense of spiritual kinship with their coreligionists around the world. Even as they cut themselves off from the South's practice of total segregation in public spaces, they affirmed a shared Southern commitment to the value of religion, to God, to Jesus's presence in the world, and to kinship with their neighbors. It was a difficult balancing act. They had to carefully renegotiate the boundaries of segregation in ways that did not ultimately threaten the structures of white supremacy outside the parish.

In this book, I argue that the Monks' Catholic parish offered a model of Christianity that reformed and formalized, rather than erased, kinship bonds that originated in the plantation households of the antebellum period, working within a structure of freedom instead of enslavement. Cardinal James Gibbons and Mother (now Saint) Katharine Drexel supported them as they enacted a form of Catholic interracialism before it was codified by key church figures such as Daniel A. Rudd, Thomas Wyatt Turner, and Fathers John Lafarge and William Markoe in the late 1920s and early 1930s. Just as Catholic thinking on racial justice was coming to the fore, the parishioners and clergy in Newton Grove were reassessing how to ensure their community's survival, given how they embodied their commitments to the church, the South, and

Christian racial unity. As Catholic Historian John McGreevy demonstrates in *Parish Boundaries*, his work on race in Northern US Catholic communities, theories for enacting racial justice within the Catholic Church, as in other American communities, rarely translated into action before the Second Vatican Council and the civil rights movement.[14]

Decades before official action by the American Catholic hierarchy, the Catholics of Newton Grove worked to define their regional and religious identity in ways that allowed them to hold close to family and community across racial lines through the real presence of Christ in the Eucharist and the global reach of their church. Where Protestants valued local control over far-reaching denominational consistency, being Catholic meant being global and being *one* in the Body of Christ. Being Catholic also meant being bound by authorities in Baltimore, New York, and Rome rather than the local congregation. Extending financial, educational, and spiritual frameworks beyond the borders of North Carolina allowed the community to create a new future for itself, one that was not constrained by the segregated social norms of the South.

To understand how the parish strove to maintain its identity in ways that facilitated the community's survival, I analyze how parishioners, nuns, and priests wrestled with the parish's core values to build bridges with Protestant friends and family—sometimes out of dire necessity as much as pleasure—while shaping a new Southern identity that fused Catholic principles of inclusivity with Southern values of hospitality and reverence for religion. Yet in Newton Grove, the Catholic community *did* upend particular aspects of post-Reconstruction white supremacy; throughout the parish's history, they continued to push the racial boundaries *through* their commitment to their Catholic identity. These efforts to embody a different form of the God-fearing North Carolinian, in the end, stemmed from the abiding physical and familial relationships shared between the parish's white and Black members.

Doing Relational Research in Segregated America

My commitment to analyzing the complexity of this rural life comes from my own experiences as a white child whose white Southern Baptist mother, a North Carolina native, came North for job opportunities in the 1960s, married my white, Massachusetts-born father, and eventually settled outside of Philadelphia. When I first learned of the Civil War in my fifth-grade history class at Jenkintown Elementary School, I ran home to my mother for reassurance that no one in our family, no one who loved me and whom I loved, had fought to preserve slavery—or, just as bad, had donned a white sheet. She bent down to look me in the eye and recounted ancestors who fought for the Confederacy. She didn't even shy away from the shameful family rumors: "Yes, it's possible they also rode with the Klan." She ended her monologue with "You must decide if you can find a way to still accept your family. They are yours either way." The distant past and the very present collapsed in that kitchen for my mother and me the same way it did in the cemetery in Newton Grove as my interviewees recounted their own family histories. Often in family stories, the past seamlessly informs the present for the storyteller, if not for the listener.

As my mother turned back to the dishes, my ten-year-old self was bewildered. I did not expect this answer. I immediately thought not only of my grandparents and great-uncles but also of the African Americans whose names I did not know but whose work and freedom had been taken from them by folks who looked like me. I began reading what little I could find at our public library to understand their lives as well as those of my ancestors and their wider communities. All the while, I suspected that none of my other white Jenkintown friends, in 1985, were having similar conversations or were confronting America's racial past on this level of familial culpability. Perhaps they were, but none of us even dared to whisper about it publicly.

Forty years later, I don't think it's possible to resolve the tensions that make up the lives of either my ancestors or the white founders of the parish in Newton Grove. I understand that deep care for people does not absolve them from the evils they did to others. The constant wrestling and effort to delve into the complexity of one's choices motivates this book, rather than the desire for simple and satisfying conclusions. In stories about Newton Grove and elsewhere in the slaveholding and Jim Crow South, judgment too often replaces real analytical work and the difficult task of understanding others. Perhaps that is why I am drawn to stories and places like this parish, where the stereotypical reading is so obviously lacking and where the humanity of the actors, white and Black, clerical and lay, Catholic and Protestant, can still be fully realized.

To access that complexity in the case of Newton Grove, I have moved away from blanket characterizations, like "racist," of complicated people in favor of examining their actions and the consequences of those actions for the community. I assume that the white parishioners living within the framework of post–Civil War North Carolina, John Carr included, shared many, if not most, of the same racist views as their other white neighbors. Yet, they sought to form, and then worked to sustain, an interracial, albeit internally segregated, parish in the face of serious risk. These choices make such labels unhelpful, for they obscure as much as they illuminate. Further, the actions of the white parishioners need to be seen in conversation with those of the African American parishioners with whom they carved out this new communal identity. These Black parishioners joined and nurtured this parish for generations when they could have gone to an African American church only a few hundred yards from the Catholic one. The question is why. The negative consequences of joining the parish seem clear, but what were the positive ones? To assess the complexity of how race and religion intermingled across this congregation, I have sought out multiple perspectives from interviews and archival materials, bringing them into conversation with one another to get a richer view of key moments in the parish's history.

I first visited the parish in 1998 to inquire about researching their history, particularly doing interviews. I hoped to be introduced to parishioners, along with their friends and families, some who may no longer claim membership in the congregation. I read the stories in the *New York Times* about the 1953 desegregation that occurred after a decree came down from the bishop in Raleigh that parishioners should worship together once again. I was confused by how little the reporters said about the nuances of what it meant to have once had an interracial church in the South and to have been Catholic in North Carolina. Reading these reports, I wanted to know more about the life of the parish before, after, and during the desegregation and how that life was lived within particular racial and religious positionings. So, on a sunny spring day, I drove from my apartment in Chapel Hill down I-40 to Newton Grove to attend Mass and meet with the priest. I felt sure I had found my next research project. I was certain that they would want their parish's incredible story to be told in full detail. As I drove, I practiced my pitch. All my practice was for naught. When I asked the priest if I could get to know the parish better, he informed me that the congregation was not interested. I returned to Chapel Hill a bit dejected but still feeling a connection to this place and its story. In the intervening years, I honed my skills as an ethnographer, writing two books based on oral histories and participant observation. Yet this story kept tugging at me: Why was there a Catholic church in the middle of the cotton fields anyway, and how did it survive as an interracial parish for so long?

In 2017, I returned to Newton Grove. By then, three things had changed: The post–civil rights era generation had come of age; genealogy had become popular; and the parish's new priest said yes. So, I began meeting parishioners and attending Mass during several intensive summer stays in Newton

Grove. From 2017 through 2019, I spent two to three weeks each year attending Mass and other parish events, going to lunches and dinners as well as researching at the diocesan archives in Raleigh. I tried to speak to equal numbers of Black and white folks, while keeping in mind that, in Newton Grove, people are not merely white or Black, Catholic or Protestant. In their lived experience, they negotiate the feeling of being in between, a feeling that their interreligious and interracial family ties helped create. Moreover, as Marilyn and Rachel, two African American women whose ancestors were early converts to the parish, taught me, no single person in Newton Grove is the sum of their religion or race. Catholics in Newton Grove embody both characteristics simultaneously. Religion alongside race manifests through interactions just as much as it does through doctrine or law.[15] Attending to conversations that were allowed within the parish, as well as those that were not, reveals much about how a sense of identity evolved in this community over time.

Each of my face-to-face encounters with Diana Zwilling, the archivist for the Diocese of Raleigh, led to important conversations, formal interviews, and new connections, including with folks reared in Newton Grove as children who later moved away. In the 1940s, 1950s, and into the 1960s, children were taught to do as they were told. As Sister Julia Godwin, who grew up in the parish, said, "If you didn't like it and were wise, you discussed your feelings with your best friend, Jesus, and no one else."[16] Remembering childhood can be very difficult for adults trying to articulate feelings about events they experienced but kept hidden in the deepest intimacy.

Many people stopped and started and stopped again in response to my questions. I felt like they were reconstructing their interpretations through years of later experiences. They were trying to ensure that their history was properly recorded so it could be carried on by their descendants, as they had carried on Solomon and John Carr Monk's legacies. In remembering, they were constructing a "useable past," so that both they and future generations in Newton Grove could find "elements in history that can be brought fruitfully to bear on current problems."[17] As elders in their community, they told their stories with both the present and the future in mind. Yet in their stories, they are not elders; they are children, children whose knowledge of events was often limited. As David Cecelski, the noted historian of Eastern North Carolina, once told me, "In childhood, we all live in Eden."[18] Here, he referred not to actual childhoods, which can often be difficult, if not horrific, but to the way memory and the telling of memories works for many people, as people retell the past through the expectations of a particular American formulation of a carefree childhood. Moreover, as many of my interviewees recounted, the adults around them tried to protect them from many of the harsher consequences of segregation, going against the wider community's social norms and the very real struggles of agricultural life. Of course, this doesn't mean the memories are not accurate, only that they need to be understood as memories told in a particular moment in time, in their life cycle, and in the life cycle of their parish. I have tried to attend to these recollections in all their richness and fallibility. I held them up to the known facts and spliced them with archival and secondary sources for a fuller picture of events. After all, most of my interviewees spent their childhoods attending to the immediate world around them, not concentrating on how the wider context of the Roman Catholic Church or American social and political movements influenced the choices the adults around them made.

Most of my interviewees, both Black and white, spent the bulk of their time picking, canning, and cropping; they did not go into town for Cokes with friends or to restaurants. For the most part, it was the parents of my interviewees, whether Black or white, who left the farm for shopping or business. My interlocutors remembered visiting relatives' homes, church, and that's it. This is life on a farm, explained Linda, a sixty-six-year-old white parishioner: "Even before church on Sundays, we got up and worked. . . . Summer was very exhausting. . . . We were all large tobacco farmers and that's some of the hardest, dirtiest work you've ever done. It starts between three thirty and four in the morning, and you try to be in bed by ten at night, and you've had three baths in between then."[19] For these children, life centered on work—plowing, picking, cutting, barning, cooking, cleaning. This work was done with siblings, parents, and neighbors. Their time to build community came when friends helped each other bring in the crops, with canning, or with other group activities. Recounting these moments many of my interviewees spoke of Black and white families working together and affirming connections but always within the framework of Jim Crow's rural rules. It was at church where these Catholics could sit and rest. And where they could engage with each other according to their carefully designed universal church.

When COVID-19 hit, I was initially worried about how I could continue my in-person research. But actually, shifting my interviews from in-person to online helped me do more contextualizing. Although I worried that this new mode of communication would lessen the quality of the interviews, I found that the quality deepened. As good conversation partners, many folks had worried about my emotional comfort as much as they did my physical comfort when we met to speak. Sometimes my imagined thoughts about their homes, their clothes, and their town seemed to preoccupy them in the early moments of our meeting. These burdens of hospitality decreased when those with whom I spoke no longer felt the pressure to have iced tea ready or wondered if they had picked a good spot for the conversation. But with me serving as the Zoom host, my interviewees were free to talk when they wanted to and tell me more easily that they had to answer a call, go to a meeting, or give any number of other perfectly acceptable excuses that allow one to step away. Putting down the phone is a much more practiced skill than getting a guest to leave one's house. Suddenly, the burden of hosting was where it always should have been—on me.

Overall, I felt a new kind of ease in our conversations. Whereas decades ago these remote choices would have meant we couldn't look at the same image, now we were able to hit the Share button on Zoom, or interviewees texted photos while we talked. With these lines of communication open, we continued to share information long after we hit the red End button. While some contacts texted and talked frequently, others connected to me seemingly out of the blue when they remembered something or just happened upon my contact information in their phone. This ease also came from the support from younger people that interviewees often brought into the conversation to help them run "the Zoom." Technology facilitated group conversations either by accident of having a helper or by design. As Sallie, an African American woman in her sixties, explained, she needed to bring her siblings into the conversation. Soon the screen included her six brothers and sisters. "Because we have such different age groups and gaps in our family, we have had different experiences. Different perceptions about things, different things told to us."[20] Sallie and her siblings realized that in order to get the best understanding of their family history, they needed to include each person's full telling, rather than rely on internal hierarchies created by age or emotional closeness.

At first my interviewees seemed concerned when they shared feelings of ambivalence, sorrow, or other emotions that they felt might contradict my own. Some interviewees, for instance, felt their view of the seemingly triumphant events of 1953 would disappoint me. Henry, an African American man in his sixties who attended the parish through high school, answered my email with, "In reality when I think of the intent of desegregation, I am not sure that anything significant was accomplished in Newton Grove. . . . The experience was actually much more strained and reserved than having our own church, to be honest."[21] For him and for many other parishioners, integration was an important goal, but in practical terms it was more of a loss than a gain, at least in the early years. They lost a parish that felt like home only to gain discomfort. Reading this interpretation, I assured him that I wanted recollections like his, viewpoints that never made it into the archives but were essential to an accurate understanding of events.

I sought to learn my acquaintances' stories deeply and treat them with respect, regardless of what the stories revealed. The more I could demonstrate this goal, the more folks shared with me and the more I was ready to hear. In one case it took three years, with multiple exchanges, until an interviewee finally connected me to Robert, their oldest living relative who had attended Mass in the parish in the 1940s. My relationship with this elder, the family, and the other families to whom I spoke continued to grow and change over time as I shared information with them and they with me. Their research, insights, and critiques have been essential to this process of turning a segregated story into an integrated one, one that reflects their own origin stories without doing violence to their ancestors or themselves. I strive to ensure that I accurately depict these perspectives in the writing of this book (although the conclusions I reach are mine alone).

To that end I encouraged the interviewees featured in this book to read and comment on drafts of this text. I asked them to comment primarily on their own contributions and reminded them that they could not ask to change other participants' accounts. Although I knew that I was opening an opportunity for the interviewees to withdraw from the project if they did not like how they were depicted, the risk was worth it, as it helped me to maintain a transparent and ethical relationship with everyone who participated in this project. The resulting conversations were helpful, if often difficult. For many parishioners, this reading was the first time they saw the narrations of how members outside their families interpreted the community. Seeing these interpretations was simultaneously illuminating and painful.

In early drafts, some African American consultants felt strongly that I needed to do more to convey the terrors of their lives in the segregated South. Other folks, both Black and white, perceived (now corrected) missteps in family history as evidence that I was yet another person who had come to Newton Grove to fulfill my own interest. Through hours of conversation and explanation, I corrected and enriched the manuscript where I could and explained my choices to maintain the original telling where necessary. There was nothing easy about this process on either side. But it led to a richer, more accurate story. My interviewees helped me achieve this goal by showing me perspectives of particular stories that I did not have and giving me more language to describe their experiences in segregation, their impressions of the bishop, and their lives in this small farming town. This story, after all, is their story. They will live with the consequences of this book in a much more direct way than I will. Therefore, I strove to be as transparent and collaborative as I could from the very beginning of the process until the manuscript went to press.

When I met each interviewee for the first time, I shared my own history with them, along with my desire to tell the parish's story in its fullness. That is, I wanted to shift the story from one that centered almost entirely on Bishop Waters, the 1950s bishop who ordered the desegregation of the parish and its schools, to one that centered on the lives of the men, women, and children who had to live out his decree. As I listened to their stories, I learned how painful and precious these tellings were. White parishioners knew that a stranger might demonize them or their relatives for choices that they themselves were not proud of today. Still, they wanted a full accounting of their parish's unique history, one from which they could learn as well as contribute.

The concerns around a white researcher were even greater for Black interviewees. One African American woman, Marylin, for instance, grilled me before she consented to talk about attending the parish. "Church history is so often told through the lens of white leaders," I said. "I want to tell as full a story as possible, including all the people in the parish, not only the ones whose opinions are recorded in the archives."[22] Rachel, a distant cousin of Marylin's, explained her willingness to participate in this research this way: "I think it hurts people to be forgotten, to be omitted from something. When we read this history, a lot of times it's as if we [African Americans] didn't exist, and it's painful. Having a story heard gives everybody the ability to celebrate, and nobody comes to the table feeling still like not a whole person . . . and so now I'm sharing these stories with you to say that no, no, no. I'm a whole person."[23]

This desire to be fully seen and heard led many of my interviewees, both Black and white, to speak with me even though I was a religious, regional, and, often, racial outsider. Or perhaps they spoke to me *because* I was an outsider. Unlike many of them, I lived states away from my kinfolk. They taught me that their rootedness in the land here had consequences. As Sister Mary Charles, who taught at the white school in the 1950s, explained, "The thing that I noticed about it was it's like a family, and they're very close-knit. You know they're neighbors. It's all for one and one for all. All together."[24] So if someone told an unflattering story about a meddling

Introduction 17

friend in the community, they could jeopardize a needed, if seeming tangential, relationship. Such interdependent relationships in both blood and geography meant that recording the parish's history, particularly around race, could be fraught. Rachel described the tensions: "I see that [the white parishioners] doing their best to record . . . the history; I think they're trying to do it as accurately as they can, [but] I think they're trying to do it without offending white or Black families to the best of their ability. When you start doing that, things get lost. Things get lost."[25]

Beyond encouraging the sharing of these experiences, I also felt that I needed to support the various tellings of this history by guarding my own emotional responses. Virginia, a light-skinned African American woman, talked freely about the details that had been passed down about the slavery-era rapes that led to her mixed ancestry. Like Joseph who was quoted earlier on the subject, Virginia spoke in a very matter-of-fact tone. When I asked about the seeming disjuncture between the story she was telling and the style in which she was telling it, she instructed me: "You cannot go back. So, sharing my family story is what I can do. You can change today as long as you draw breath, and you can have a goal of learning and living a better tomorrow."[26] In sharing her story, Virginia, like my other interviewees, both Black and white, described her memories as facts, even when she understood that their veracity was up for debate. I received these stories as such, meaning that I understood that our conversations centered on how the community as a whole or in parts used these interpretations to thrive or fracture.

To understand the foundations upon which these stories are formed, I first focus on how this community came to be in chapter 1, "From Plantation to Parish: Antebellum North Carolina to 1870." Here, I analyze how the practices of slavery shaped relationships between and among Black and white people in Sampson County. These structures necessitated interaction between enslaved men, women, and children and their white counterparts. Within these forced interactions, other sorts of connections developed between the enslaved and free household members, who were also kin. I explore how John Carr Monk sought to find a new framework rooted in God and freedom through which to rebuild his relationships with Solomon, Martha, and their (his) family, even as white supremacists were seeking to institute near-complete racial segregation, including in the Methodist Church that they had once all shared. Chapter 2, "St. Mark's and the Limits of a Parish's Protection: 1870–1904," begins by analyzing how the community shifted from a slave economy to paid labor, tenancy, and shared work. It centers on the Black and white Monks' discovery and embrace of

Catholicism as a religion that embodied their vision of a universal, interracial church at the same time that their interracial kinship was being threatened as they were recast into strict sociopolitical categories of "white" and "Black." As the Monks managed this shift away from enslavement and toward other forms of family connection and racial hierarchy, they also had to contend with growing Klan activity. In the parish's early years, conversion to Catholicism transformed the Monk brothers and their fellow parishioners' identity. Instead of tying themselves to an increasingly segregated rural Southern Protestantism, they embraced their vision of Catholic unity enacted in both biological and spiritual kinship.

Chapter 3, "The Delicate Dance of Rural Catholicism in the Protestant South: 1899–1926," analyzes how these familial relationships continued into the next century as the parish navigated changes in agricultural techniques, race relations, and Catholic doctrine. Newton Grove's first generation of cradle Catholics, born and bred in the Church, reimagined their parish with themselves at its center. In the process, they reworked the community's foundational interracial mission. After Father Irwin left, parishioners faced the challenge of introducing a new group of priests to their community norms. They did so just when the parish's founding generation was dying.

Chapter 4, "Maintaining Unity through Segregation? 1926–1952," explores how the parish changed under the leadership of the Redemptorist Fathers, a Catholic order assigned to Newton Grove because of its specialty in African American missions, as well as the installation of a new bishop in Raleigh. Church officials were committed to separate parishes for Black Catholics and began pressuring the parish to segregate just as a new generation, who knew less about the cross-racial ties, mission, and guidelines that had held the parish together, was coming of age in Newton Grove. With internal bonds weakened, the external influences of agricultural life, Catholic teaching, and white supremacy could have greater sway in the parish. By 1939, this would mean the creation of a Black parish only 200 yards from the white one. Would the founding generation's efforts for racial unity die as this once visionary parish became a symbol of Southern segregation?

The separation was short-lived. By 1953, the bishop ordered the parishes to (re-)merge. Chapter 5, "Can Two Become One? Striving for Unity, 1953–1974," discusses the consequences of desegregation within the context of the evolving farming practices in the United States, including the parishioners' efforts to revive kinship ties across racial lines. Here, I explore the parish's continuing efforts to develop an interracial community as they worked to reconcile with African American members who had left the parish. This reconciliation work included mending ties with the bishop as well as with white members who had become alienated from the hierarchy after years of perceived neglect. The chapter ends with the integration of the North Carolina school system, the moment when the racial norms of the surrounding society finally began to match the parish's original mission.

When the parish began in the 1870s, John Carr sent a wagon out to bring African American Catholics to Mass at the county's first Catholic church. White and Black folks entering the same building each Sunday raised the community's eyebrows. A century later, white and Black North Carolinians attending Mass together wasn't noteworthy, since Black and white students were learning math together, perhaps playing sports together in public school. Moreover, they were coming and going from that school on the same bus. Thus, by 1974 it might not have been noteworthy that Black and white Catholics were being joined together in spiritual kinship as they worshipped together under one roof. Yet the fact that the parish survived this century of change as religious and racial outsiders makes it worth our attention. If we look closer, we begin to see the ways that efforts of John Carr Monk from his privileged position as a white doctor, Solomon Monk from his much more precarious position as a formerly enslaved man, and their descendants have offered those of us just passing by insight into how to create an alternative religious and political congregation without severing ties with the wider community.

CHAPTER ONE

From Plantation to Parish
Antebellum North Carolina to 1870

On my first visit to the parish, the one hundred or so white parishioners in the pews knew immediately I was an outsider. While they were puzzling over who I was, I was puzzling over why, given the parish's history, the congregation was almost exclusively white. While I was lost in my thoughts, a few parishioners strode over to me, perhaps to size me up as a prospective new member. They introduced themselves by announcing that they were "cradle Catholics," Catholics from birth. Their ancestors, they added, had converted to Catholicism alongside John Carr Monk, the parish's founder. Religious pedigrees of various sorts followed. One woman stated, "My father was a cradle Catholic, and my mother converted when I was fourteen, although she always came to Mass with us when I was a child."[1] Others, particularly men like Chris, put it more simply, flashing a smile: "I'm the only redneck Catholic most folks will ever meet."[2] He knew that, in the South, deep Catholic lineages outside of New Orleans and Maryland were nearly unheard of. There were no Catholic chapels on plantations and little recognition of pronouncements the Vatican had made about race, slavery, and the American Church in antebellum North Carolina.[3] Instead of reaching for a century's long lineage in the church, he went on to talk about his father, who converted shortly before dying. Soon enough, however, he reached back to the community's touchstone of true belonging, revealing that this "redneck's" mother, like the vast majority of other parishioners, was one branch on John Carr's family tree.

The family tree also includes John Carr's father, Archibald Monk, whom some, but not all, the parishioners mentioned that first morning. Although Archibald died before the parish's founding, in important genealogical if not spiritual ways, he links these white parishioners with their Black coreligionists and distant cousins. No members of the African American "first families" of the parish still attend Mass, so I had a different introduction to this portion of the original community. I met these former parishioners and parochial school alumni in their backyards, at the parish library, in local restaurants, and over Zoom. Still, their connection to the parish, to John Carr, and to his father had salience in their lives.

Just like their white coreligionists, African American interviewees started our conversations with their genealogies. Rachel, an engaging woman in her sixties, explained that she was Catholic on the Cole side of her family: "The way it was told to us, Solomon, who married my great-great-grandfather's sister Martha Cole [is], we believe to be, Archibald's mixed-race son."[4] These parishioners include both John Carr and Solomon Monk in their family histories. These contemporary Catholics then become, through their retellings of parish history, the parish tradition's rightful inheritors. Henry introduced himself with, "Solomon Monk, who was Dr. John Monk's half-brother, was my great-great-grandfather."[5] Just as John Carr's family was the first white family to convert, Solomon's family was the first African American family to join the parish. John Carr sponsored the baptisms of Solomon's wife and children, creating anew their connection as spiritual kinship in the Catholic Church. While many family trees, particularly those rooted in plantation economies and enslavement, center the white patriarch and enslaver, here, the sons, John Carr Monk and Solomon Monk—not the father, Archibald—stand as the foundation of the community's inheritance.

To understand how the Monk brothers came to be related and what motivated them to undergo a conversion that would allow them to worship together, we need to grasp the particular shape of slavery in North Carolina and the contours of rural life in the state after the 1863 Emancipation Proclamation. Pre–Civil War plantation households fostered kinship bonds within and across racial lines. Blacks and whites in Newton Grove acknowledging that or simply acting as if they were siblings, cousins, or other forms of kin during the period of slavery would lay the groundwork within which they could fashion new networks of influence after the Civil War. This chapter explores the details of plantation life in the area in and around Newton Grove that made such connections possible. Understanding how folks in this area structured their households, which included both enslaved and free people, helps illuminate the range of choices John Carr, Solomon, and their families made after the war, particularly their decision to convert to Roman Catholicism. Conversion helped members invent a new form of interracial community against the tide of segregation pushing Black and white Southerners apart. Today's Newton Grove Catholics continue to try to stay faithful to their family tree with the Monk siblings at the root.

John Carr Monk: The Brother Who Sought Family Unity

John Carr Monk, the parish founder, grew up on his father's Sampson County plantation alongside not only Solomon but also eleven white siblings who helped Archibald Monk establish reciprocal relations with neighboring families. John Carr eventually bought land for his own farm, the land where the Catholic parish now sits. Although this land was his by deed, it was nurtured and made fruitful by the labor of enslaved people—those he himself enslaved and those he borrowed from nearby farmers during harvest, planting, and hog-killing seasons. In Eastern North Carolina, where farms were small, planter households relied on enslaved people and neighbors to get by. Their proximity to one another meant that the white Monk family and other enslaving plantation households like the Coles' helped each other plant sweet potatoes, can butter beans, make quilts, raise hogs, and in many other ways forge a community. Familiarity led to friendship and even marriage. Marriages united the white Monks with the white Cole, Raynor, Gregory, and Lee families, just as unions between enslaved people from these households before emancipation.

Although across the South many enslaved parents and children were sold away from one another, the existing historical record reveals that nearly all of the people enslaved on the Archibald Monk farm remained there for their lifetimes or until emancipation. The enslaved people on the Monk farm, like many others in this part of rural North Carolina, had strong generational ties to each other and to the land. In these areas where plantation households were relatively stable, "kinship," says historian Steven Han, "could eventually have linked an individual slave to more than three-quarters of [a plantation's] residents."[6] Through work exchanges, marriages, and other relationships, kinship quickly knit together much of the region. For Newton Grove's Catholics, the deep roots of these family trees tied the people to the land and to each other through John Carr.

Today, John Carr Monk is both an active presence in the parish and a historical actor. His memory exists in this community on two levels: He is both an ancestor and a contemporary meaning maker. For today's descendants, his memory is a continued presence within the congregation. He is their genealogical foundation, proving to present-day kin that they are authentic inheritors of their parish; the town's entire history runs through their family tree. The living memory of the past works in the present in different ways for parishioners of both races who remember a thriving Black Catholic community in Newton Grove and those whose memories center racial tension inside and outside the church. Still, demonstrating that this ancestor might have once shared the communion rail with your family meant that you have a legitimate connection to the land and a communal belonging to Newton Grove.

Underneath it all is the land—land that was once owned by John Carr and worked by those whom he enslaved, land where owning and being owned shaped every aspect of one's life. Over time that rootedness grew into a pride of place and did not rely on legal rights implanted in laws or contracts; it relied on the nurture one put into it. Throughout the parish the land animated members' lives. As the ways the parishioners worked the land changed after emancipation, so too did the way they interacted with one another. To understand the connections that grew from and were sustained by this land, we must start at the beginning, at the farms and plantations.

Slavery and the Monk Plantation

Archibald Monk was born in 1789 in Carthage, North Carolina, about eighty miles west of Newton Grove in Moore County. His father James Monk and his mother Catherine Currie Monk had emigrated from Scotland, fleeing high rents, debt, and evictions. Once married they worked a nonslaveholding farm. Their son Archibald later moved to Sampson County to open a general store, a move that proved to be a good one for him. Four years later, on August 5, 1824, he married Harriet Hargrove, a native of Sampson County, from whom he was introduced to enslaving.[7] The following year, Archibald and Harriet welcomed their first son, William. In 1827 they would have a second son, John Carr, whom they named after his maternal grandmother Jane Carr Hargrove.[8]

As the Monk family grew, so did Archibald's political ambitions. In 1829, he began a six-year term as a member of the Democratic party in the North Carolina General Assembly. There he championed bills to support common schools, in keeping with his conviction that children should be taught at home, not in faraway boarding schools. Along with legislating to develop North Carolina's public education infrastructure, Archibald was in the General Assembly in 1831 when it quelled the white panic after Nat Turner's slave rebellion by making life much more difficult for enslaved people. Much of the white South, including Sampson County, was in an uproar after rumors spread of copycat rebellions.[9] While the alleged revolts in Sampson County did not materialize, white officials denounced twelve enslaved people as the leaders of the imagined revolts. A militia shot these men, and three others were hung.[10] There is no record of how Archibald felt about these matters. It's possible, however, that he was at least troubled by the outbreak of state-sponsored racist violence, since in 1835, while still a member of the assembly, he changed party affiliation to the less proslavery Whigs. Besides the Whig Party's stance on slavery, Archibald's advocacy for public schooling put him squarely in the camp of the party's pro-education platform.[11]

Just a few years earlier, in 1829, Archibald purchased thirteen acres of land, joining the landowning class. At about that time, he inherited his first enslaved people from his in-laws, a "gift" of human beings that he accepted despite his embrace of the Whig Party. This kind of hypocrisy was not unusual among enslavers. And it did not stop with accepting this "gift." Later he purchased enslaved people on his own. According to the 1830 census, thirteen "free white people" who were Monk family members and four "slaves" lived in Archibald Monk's household. Monk enslaved a man between thirty-six and fifty-four who worked Monk's land, as well as a girl under ten, a girl between the ages of ten and twenty, and one boy under ten.[12] The four enslaved people, the average number then for a North Carolina farmer, lived in tiny wooden slave quarters usually located just behind the main house.

One individual in the household would play an important role in the parish's founding. Although the 1830 census columns offer scant information about him—that he is under ten years old and male—oral historical and archival research reveals a bit more about his distinct identity. The boy marked as "enslaved and under ten" is likely Solomon Monk, and he was almost certainly the offspring of Archibald, perhaps with the enslaved teen-aged girl also noted on the census form. Enslavers having children with enslaved women, even children, as might be the case here, was not unusual in the antebellum South.[13] In fact, many of Newton Grove's African American parishioners today have more than just one connection to a white branch of the family tree. These acts of rape were more the norm than the exception. The birth of a mixed-race son on the Monk farm in the 1820s would have raised few eyebrows within white society, nor did it signal any changes in Archibald Monk's stance toward enslavement.[14]

Soon after Solomon's birth, Archibald began acquiring more land and enslaved people to work it, leaving him free to pursue his interests in politics, education, and medicine. By 1850, he enslaved thirteen people. That census also disclosed other local plantation owners who lived close by: Moses Cox enslaved forty-two people. His brother J. Blackman Cox owned twenty-seven people. Alexander Benton, one town over in Bentonville, owned twelve enslaved people.[15] The 1860 census revealed that just before the Civil War "27% of North Carolina's population owned slaves, and just 3% of the state's citizens owned enough slaves (20) to be considered plantation owners."[16] At the dawn of the Civil War, through purchasing more property and human beings to work it, Archibald Monk had become one of the landed elite.

The crop inventory of the Monks' farm includes peas, beans, Irish [white] potatoes, as well as their core crops of sweet potatoes and "Indian corn."[17] The 1860 census recorded that Archibald Monk's plantation grew eleven bales of cotton, the most of any farm in the area. While these statistics cannot reveal what daily life was like as part of the Monk household, they should dispel any notion we might have that the Monks lived like the fictional O'Hara family in *Gone with the Wind*, Margaret Mitchell's fanciful and racist 1936 novel and subsequent Oscar-winning movie. Popular culture has been inordinately preoccupied with this romanticized model for the lives and relationships of enslaved to enslaver in which there is a seemingly strict division between the white family and the large, enslaved communities, a model that has also been applied to Thomas Jefferson's Monticello in Virginia or George Washington's Mount Vernon. As local North Carolina historian Edward W. Phifer so aptly explains, "Generalization is often the pitfall that traps the scholar trying to analyze the many facets of slavery, an area in which minute details can be particularly revealing."[18] While the size and scope of the farm do not change the suffering and injustice of slavery, they do change the possible interactions that one might expect to see between the white family and the enslaved families that make up the household.

On smaller plantations and farms, such as the majority of those Phifer studied in North Carolina, the everyday lives of the enslavers' white family and the Black enslaved were not as separate as this summary suggests. According to historian Guion Griffis Johnson, "The prevailing system of slavery in the state [North Carolina] was that of close relationship between the master and the slave, for of the total slaveholders, fully 67 per cent worked side-by-side with their slaves."[19] By 1844 the brothers William, John Carr, and Solomon had been joined by Archibald's and Harriet's seven younger children. From the stories passed down to some of his descendants, Solomon had a meaningful relationship with his white brother, John Carr. The proximity of living quarters suggests that the two, just a year apart in age, would have known each other well, although they would not necessarily have known their shared paternity. Farms like Archibald Monk's often were located close to the living quarters of those people the family enslaved, leading to frequent interactions during work and rest hours. On these farms, Phifer writes, "The slave houses were in the yard of the slaveholder's dwelling, and younger male members of the owner's family in nearly every case played and worked in the fields year after year with slaves of their own age."[20]

To be sure, such childhood games existed within, not apart from, the plantation power structure.

The unequal status of John Carr and Solomon, as well as the other children, both white and enslaved, who called the farm home, permeated nearly every interaction. The parental expectations for Archibald Monk's white children would have been radically different than those for the enslaved children who lived out back.[21] The white and Black individuals who made up a single census household not only shared each other's names, but they also tilled the soil together. Landowners sent their white sons to the fields to work, as Bassett put it, "along with the slaves, sometimes leading the plow gang, and sometimes swinging a cradle in the harvest."[22] Still, there was nothing equal here. Farm owners' white sons would gain inheritance through their names and worked episodically. In contrast, the last names of enslaved people denoted their owner, and they were forced to labor day in and day out from dawn until dusk.[23] Even within this framework of injustice, joint agricultural work gave the white enslavers' children opportunities to develop or further relationships with enslaved laborers. Shared work, even uneven work, produced the potential for physical and emotional closeness as well as resentments when a white brother, such as John Carr perhaps, took the horns of the plough a few feet behind his enslaved half-brother, Solomon.

Whatever form of togetherness existed between the boys began to fray when formal education began. Like many farms and plantations, the Monks built a one-room schoolhouse on their land to educate their white children through elementary school. John Carr then attended Spring Valley Academy in Fayetteville, about thirty-five miles from his home.[24] Archibald expected his white sons, for instance, to attend university and hold political office while he planned a future of field and household labor for Solomon, the child he enslaved. Informal childhood relationships surely shifted as youngsters grew into adolescence and beyond. John Carr and Solomon would have remembered both their childhood connection and, as they became adults, the emerging power differential between Blacks and whites on the farm, which instilled in the African American laborers a keen sense of their subjection along with an awareness that even the smallest infraction could be punished with physical violence.

When Black descendants of Archibald Monk, for instance, recall returning to the Monk house with their white distant relatives, they felt this journey as an immersion in horrific memories of pain and punishment. One woman told me that walking in the Archibald Monk house's front door was like "a tale of two cities." "We walked in," she said, "and Archibald's [white] descendants were rejoicing: 'Oh my God, this is where great-grandma had her babies.' And I had tears streaming down my face because I said to myself, 'Where did my great-great-grandmother have her babies? You know, the ones that he forced her to have by him.'"[25]

Research by historian Alexis Wells-Oghoghomeh on how the female slaves created religious and social systems to support them in their lack of bodily safety within Southern slavery, as well as the experiences of my African American interviewees, make the discrepancies clear.[26] While white children continued the bloodline and passed down a family's prosperity, children born of enslaved mothers simply increased the enslaver's labor pool.[27] Black and white members of plantation households had vastly different and unequal opportunities and experiences. Yet they were also born and raised on the same plot of land. In these spaces, both geographic and social, they created a functioning, if deeply unequal, community.

Solomon Monk and Martha Cole: A Union That Builds a Community

Solomon appears by name in census data after emancipation, at which time he was categorized as "mulatto." Nearly everyone that I interviewed—from the oldest, a ninety-two-year-old white woman, to young Black descendants in their twenties—recognized the familial link between the white and Black Monk families. Younger white parishioners, however, did not always recognize the relationship, and when they did, they did not know the details, such as Solomon's name, his connection to John Carr, or the family he had as an adult. In contrast, these details were integral to African American family lore. Knowledge of this and other interracial connections were assumed by white people, which often meant they went undiscussed. Still, most of my white interviewees suspected there was a blood connection even if they could not name Solomon.

Among the original parish's living descendants, only Solomon's Black kin have kept his memory alive. In telling his story, they have preserved a detailed and evocative portrait of the parish's founding patriarchs beyond the name on a headstone in the parish cemetery. For them, Solomon epitomizes the enslaved community's complex internal hierarchy. Solomon worked in the house, they insist, not the fields. They believe that Archibald kept him close, perhaps out of affection as well as out of economic necessity, but his life was not without cruelty. One of Solomon's great-great-grandsons, sixty-four-year-old Henry, who has bright eyes and a businessman's authoritative but warm style, told me about how slavery's brutal hierarchies affected Solomon's progeny: "The house slaves were made up of these people like Solomon and maybe Solomon's kids . . . because they were actually [Archibald Monk's] kin."[28]

Most of the young men and women in Solomon's position remained in bondage. Every ten years, Archibald Monk told the census taker to mark Solomon as "slave." He did so like every other Sampson County planter with enslaved children. As Rachel, the African American woman in her sixties mentioned previously, suggested in her comment, it's hard to find any true sense of caring in these actions. And Archibald did not free Solomon until the Thirteenth Amendment removed all other options. This hierarchy, in all its intimacy and cruelty, also gave rise to the emotional bonds that shaped the sacred community that John Carr and Solomon gathered for their kin.

While all my interviewees emphasize that there is no way to know for sure what Solomon's life was like on the plantation, their family stories support the idea that Archibald had some kind of affection for Solomon. In sharing these remembrances, they are telling how they came to be and giving their ancestor a meaningful past. Solomon's great-grandson David recounted the story of Archibald riding his horse to Fayetteville to retrieve Solomon from slave robbers: "As if he was losing a child," he whispered, "not a slave."[29] Another descendant told me about the time Solomon Monk was sold at a livestock auction and a family friend "rode all night long to rescue him from a slave wagon in Durham."[30] While an enslaver might recapture a slave whose forced labor was economically valuable, tellers never refer to economics or labor. No, Archibald rescued Solomon, in the words of a three-times great-granddaughter, because "he worried that Martha could not take care of her children [Archibald's grandchildren] alone."[31] In a world in which the common story focuses on families being torn apart on the auction block, here, descendants tell a story of some sort of paternal love that pushed Archibald to save his son and defy societal norms. In so doing, he also saved his future grandchildren, who continue to contribute to Solomon's legacy, ensuring that he is more than a tick mark on the slave census.

Rachel described how her ancestors struggled with the hidden inequalities that pervaded pre–Civil War intimacies: "We have plantation to plantation, where the plantation owners are marrying their white children to each other . . . just beneath that is, 'I'm marrying my mixed-race children to the mixed-race children on this plantation.' Now, you've got this class of mixed-race kids that are being married from plantation to plantation as well. In an odd and very strange way, the plantation owner might be thinking, 'I'm taking care of my children.'"³² These seeming gestures of care were ways to use people and their relationships once again for economic gain. Solomon's locally recognized marriage to Martha Cole, for instance, who was enslaved by Willis Cole nearby, might have strengthened the already existing bond between the neighbors.³³ Martha was listed as "mulatto" on the 1870 census and on the parish sacramental records in 1874, meaning that Willis Cole, like Archibald, raped a woman he had enslaved, who then gave birth to Martha.³⁴ Martha was reared on Willis Cole's plantation by her yet-to-be-named mother, who might have been part of Tuscarora, a local Native American tribe, as well as African.³⁵ Perhaps their recognition of these children, whom both men kept as property, drew the families to each other, as each family chose not to hide their interracial members from the white community. Soon after the Civil War ended, however, the classification system would elide the category of "mulatto" as it shifted to the binary "white" and "Black." This shift erased the interracial connections that tied these families together.

Enslaved men, women, and children from these two plantations likely met during the labor-intensive harvest or planting seasons when local planters frequently lent enslaved people to each other to increase productivity. The movement of people back and forth between farms was not unusual and led to the development of affections that resulted in marriages, like that of Solomon Monk and Martha Cole. The economic logic of the slave system dictated the practice: "The only relationship that mattered was mother to child," writes historian Steven Hahn, "because it was the way that slavery was inheritable."³⁶ These white conventions, however, did not constrain the many ways that African Americans maintained familial relationships under the brutality of enslavement. Although it's likely Solomon and Martha continued living on separate plantations after marriage, they would have maintained their tie through having requests granted to work for each other's enslaver or to have family visits. However they happened, it's clear that they did spend time with one another, since the couple had one child born during the Civil War, while they were both still enslaved.

Emphasizing the maternal line was central to the economic logic of slaveholding, yet the enslaved themselves often constructed their identities differently. Hinton Cole, Martha's brother, for instance, switched between the surnames Cole and Monk depending on where he was working. Two couples, Hinton and his wife Sarah Elizabeth Williams and Martha and Solomon Monk, originated a line of descendants with a strong connection to each other, to the land, and to Newton Grove.³⁷ But Solomon and his children converted to Catholicism and joined the parish, while Hinton and his family did not.[38] In the 1870s, Hinton's family would follow the regional norms by joining an all-Black Protestant White Oaks Disciples of Christ Church. Only a small slice of Archibald Monk's immense household converted to Catholicism. Why remains a beguiling mystery. Descendants of the converting families have chosen to live in this mystery by remembering Solomon and John Carr's boyhood connections, their play, and their laboring, as well as their unequal status. They honor the legacy and mystery of their outlier rural Catholic identity by identifying with the brotherly bond that, they believe, persisted despite the realities of slavery and segregation's brutal efforts to separate the races. And they believe that, in part, it was this relationship that eventually spurred John Carr to take the unusual path he did.

John Carr Monk Sets Himself Apart

In the tumultuous years surrounding the Civil War, John Carr Monk staked a risky claim for the Union, even emancipating the people he owned. He started on this dangerous path with a seemingly innocuous step: In 1848, he became a teacher and followed in his education-activist father's footsteps. Two years later, in 1850, he moved to Philadelphia to attend medical school. Archibald occasionally tended to neighbors' wounds and minor illnesses, using a combination of book reading and folk remedies; in contrast, John Carr Monk would learn to practice medicine in one of the nation's most prestigious medical schools, the University of Pennsylvania. At the medical department of the University of Pennsylvania, he was joined by a number of other Southern landowners' sons since it was becoming customary at this time for the landowning class to use educational credentials to become a Southern "gentleman." John Carr studied medicine with 650 southerners, which made up 51 percent of the student body between 1850 and 1853.[39]

Here, as Christopher Willoughby argues in his compelling work, *Masters of Science: Racial Science and Slavery in US Medical Schools*, these medical students would have learned a white supremacist racial science. The faculty at Penn's medical school wrote the textbooks and taught the lectures that argued anatomical differences between white and Black people into existence. Northern medical schools, the University of Pennsylvania chief among them, Willoughby found, attracted southern students because they taught that racial differences—from supposed discrepancies in skull size and leg length to presumed differences in disease tolerance—were embodied and meaningful. Professors used tactile lectures and visual aids from museums to "satisfy prospective physicians' curiosity and prejudice."[40] By the time John Carr entered medical school, these teachings were accepted as scientific fact. For the students at Penn and other medical schools, these supposed differences in anatomy constituted scientific evidence for white supremacy and the permanent subjugation of people of African descent. If John Carr's lived experiences growing up on slaveholding plantations had caused them to doubt slavery's justness, his time in the classroom served to provide him, and his classmates, with a scientific rationale for the cruel practice.

Simultaneously, outside the lecture hall, these aspiring young men fell in easily among the elite promenading down Chestnut Street or picnicking in Fairmount Park. A large population of African Americans lived in this strictly segregated city. The wealthiest Philadelphians had a reputation for being sympathetic to southern mores and sensibilities.[41] As historian Daniel Kilde argues, "Parents and young men craved entry into Philadelphia's high society because such acceptance confirmed the family's place within the American aristocracy."[42] John Carr attended classes along with social gatherings like society parties and church services. We know this because other southern medical students left personal diaries. The young men wrote about trading advice about navigating Philadelphia's high-society abolitionism as enslaving southerners. They even gossiped about which churches and ministers were likely to offer abolitionist sermons and thus were best to avoid on Sunday mornings. Evidently, being a southern enslaver required good sources of information and deft avoidance to be a polite presence in Philadelphia society. While John Carr didn't immediately take up the mantle of abolition—either then or later when he returned to his slave labor–based North Carolina plantation— it's certain that he was aware of the abolitionist debates occurring in the city. When he returned to Newton Grove, John Carr brought with him the proslavery teachings he learned in the classroom and whatever antislavery ideas he might have gleaned in sermons.

By the time John Carr graduated from medical school on April 3, 1852, Solomon was twenty-six. The age-mates' relationship had certainly changed from their childhood days on the plantation, especially now that John Carr had become Dr. John Carr.[43] In contrast, the only record we have of Solomon from this year is a chit mark on the national census, one of fourteen such marks for the enslaved men, women, and children on the Monk plantation.[44] In 1854, John Carr followed in his father's footsteps as one of fifty Whig delegates to the North Carolina Democratic Convention. This political position both cemented his high standing in Sampson County and prepared him for the negotiations that would be coming soon when the Civil War broke out.[45]

The following year, John Carr married Euphemia Alice Eason, daughter of Col. John and Elizabeth Eason. Col. John Eason had been an officer in the Whig Party of Johnston County, which may have been where he was first introduced to John Carr, perhaps through Archibald.[46] For John Carr, the aspiring gentleman, it was a strategic match; the Easons had a plantation worth one and a half times as much as Archibald's land and enslaved more than three times the number of people in 1860.[47] Often, marriages between Archibald's white children and those of other landowners also solidified business connections. They created recognized blood ties between the Monk family and the wealthy Hargrove family (in Archibald's case) and the Gregory family (in the case of his other son Henry Clay Monk). Similarly, Rufus, the brother who helped John Carr start the parish, married into the Royal family, while sister Margaret became a Benton; the Benton plantation, for which Bentonville was named, neighbored the Cole plantation where Solomon's wife Martha and her brother Hinton were enslaved. Through these marriages the community knit itself together into a vast extended family.

Within the next six years, John Carr fulfilled the social expectations of his class, his in-laws, and his father by enslaving eight people to work his growing farm. With their forced labor, he managed a successful 576-acre plantation with a net worth in 1860 of about $19,000 ($700,000 in 2024 dollars).[48] Yet, his heart was not in farming, particularly once the war began. For in that same year, North Carolina voted to remain with the Union. A year later, after the Battle of Fort Sumter, John Carr stood for election as a delegate to the state convention to consider secession for a second time. This time, he was the only Unionist candidate.[49] He received only one vote in the election. The vote was cast by a voter in Sampson County, most likely himself. The state legislature voted for secession, 81 to 23. On May 20, 1861, North Carolina became the last state to secede from the United States. Secession brought increased pressure to Southern farmers who could no longer rely on Northern goods and customers for their agricultural products. Keeping farms running once the war began was essential to the survival of Southern families. Many Sampson County farmers went to great lengths to generate crops and profited mightily while agricultural prices were high. Even Archibald sold large amounts of grain to the Confederacy.

John Carr, in contrast, stopped producing cash crops during the war and ceased participating in the economic and labor system that made them possible. He took the remarkable step of emancipating the people he owned.[50] Over the course of the war, he shut down his plantation except for a few subsistence crops and turned his attention to medicine. As a doctor, John Carr was exempt from military service. Even though he was a noted Unionist in the area, he offered hospitality to Confederate troops from Newton Grove and the surrounding area as they marched into battle, according to a story in *The Fayetteville Observer* from June 10, 1861. The community built a table eighty feet long to seat the soldiers. Before the communal dinner, according to *Observer*'s reporter, John Carr told the crowd that "the ladies prepared this feast for the independent Blues [a Confederate militia], who were going to fight the battles on behalf of their honor and fire-sides."[51] His brother, Claudius Buchanan Monk, a lieutenant in the Confederate Army, accepted this welcome. John Carr then sent him off in good style, despite his misgivings about North Carolina leaving the Union.

His choice in hosting this dinner may have been to separate his convictions about the larger political situation from expressing his love for his brother. As the article suggests, the men were also fighting for their own families. Hosting the dinner demonstrated support for the community, although he disagreed with North Carolina's position in the war. This action would be the first of many in which John Carr would live his own convictions in a way that would allow him to continue to serve his family and friends whose political convictions he did not share.

John Carr, like everyone else in Newton Grove, eventually found himself struggling to survive the war's devastations. He lost his brother Claudius, whom he had hosted at the community table, at the Battle of Spotsylvania. Another brother, Henry, was wounded twice, first at Cold Harbor and then Gettysburg.[52] In 1865, General William Tecumseh Sherman's soldiers pillaged Sampson County. Union Blues descended upon Bentonville and Newton Grove after their infamous March to the Sea. This battle, the bloodiest in North Carolina, occurred between March 19 and 21 and inundated the area with 60,000 Union troops and 20,000 Confederate troops.[53] It was a slaughter, an intimate one for John Carr and his neighbors. The fighting took place just five miles from his house.[54] John Carr's farm fell behind Union lines, meaning he would not have reached the Confederate wounded until the battle's end. Surely, though, he could smell the gunpowder smoke and hear the cannon blasts that foreshadowed the devastation he would find when he finally did arrive at the field hospital. Upon arrival there, he would have participated in what Col. William D. Hamilton of the 9th Ohio Cavalry described in a grisly report to family back home: "A dozen surgeons and attendants . . . cutting off arms and legs and throwing them out the windows, there they lay scattered on the grass."[55] This battle, the last full-scale action of the Civil

War, played a key role in bringing an end to the war, but it also left Sampson County's residents traumatized and full of loathing for the North.

To ensure his army was well fed while his enemy suffered, Sherman sent troops down every dirt road. They left vandalized and pillaged farms for miles around the battlefield. Family letters from nearby plantation owners and other stories recount how "the Northern troops killed the cattle, stole the mules and horses. In fact, they took Grandpa's horses and carriage and rode by whooping and hollering, that he might see what they were doing."[55] This psychological warfare—total war's victory by humiliation—led soldiers to destroy family heirlooms and build bonfires of Confederate dollars in addition to making off with food stores. Many families went to great extent to save what they could, such as the man who "hid his money in the [bee]hive for safe keeping."[56] Other folks buried jewelry and money in the family graveyard. For the white community, in particular, this near annihilation by the North felt personal as they recalled the looks of joy on Union soldiers' faces as they rode away on family horses or watched their brothers and uncles stripped naked at gunpoint.[57] When Sherman's army finally marched out of Sampson County, he left an entire region of starving and destitute families trying to regather the pieces of fractured legacies and lineages. The stories they preserved about these depredations created immense and lasting animosity toward the North.

In 1867, with the horrors of the war still fresh, John Carr Monk seemed to renounce the South and its ideals when he joined the Republican Party. He certainly alienated his neighbors by changing his political affiliation to a party that was supported by the North and overwhelmingly African American in its membership. John Carr's reason for making this fateful decision, which was described as "a crime" in this "particular section of the South," is lost to history.[58] The difficult consequences he faced, in contrast, are possible to reconstruct. The words of Rev. William E. Cox from nearby Pitt County, North Carolina, describing his father's decision to join the Republicans, offer some sense of what life might have been like for the Monks: "One who did not live in the South . . . can hardly understand and appreciate the depth and intensity of feeling in the South toward the North in general and the Republican Party in particular. There was still fiercer intensity of that feeling toward a [white] Southerner who opposed the Confederacy and aligned himself with the Abolitionists and the Republican party. That, in the eyes of the [white] rank and file in the Confederate States, was 'the unpardonable sin.'"[59]

Committing the "unpardonable sin" of supporting freedom for enslaved people like Hinton, Martha, and his half brother Solomon meant accepting the label "scalawag"—and the abuse that came with it. John Carr's neighbors hated him, if Cox's description of his father's fate is any indication: "Social ostracism, persecution, slander, and all sorts of indignities were heaped upon him by kinsmen, neighbors, friends and others, to the day of his death."[60] John Carr surely expected his neighbors' revulsion, yet he had the courage to follow his convictions. John Carr probably faced physical violence and intimidation, too. Cox's father, for one, had the windows of his offices smashed, patients refused to come to him for treatment, and former friends and colleagues shouted, "black Republican," "ni**er lover," and "carpet bagger" at him.[61] If his story was anything like Cox's, John Carr was now, for all purposes, an enemy in his community.

John Carr took a major step away from his natal Southern values when, at the start of the Civil War, he chose to become a Unionist who voted against secession. He demonstrated that he was antislavery by freeing his slaves during the war. With the end of the fighting, he joined the party that had supported Lincoln's Emancipation Proclamation. Republicans also supported the Thirteenth Amendment that abolished slavery. Republicans had done for the country what John Carr had done for those he himself had enslaved. Yet the cost to the South, to his own community, to his own family must have been brutally demoralizing. The archives remain stubbornly silent on John Carr's feelings about what he went through in the next few years. However, one can imagine that watching the dissolution of the relationships supported by the plantation system and the resulting bankruptcy of North Carolina would have been devastating.

The destruction of the plantation system threatened white political and social control; in the process it seemed to erase the different forms of intimate relationships between the enslavers' white family and those he held in bondage. Freedom combined with a new social sensibility that pressed for the near complete separation of white and Black persons, for example, meant John Carr would need to find new ways to sustain a connection with Solomon and other African American kin who were once enslaved by his father and neighbors. The year after the ratification of the Thirteenth Amendment, the North Carolina Assembly began circumscribing African Americans' rights. The three postwar amendments to the United States Constitution, which Republicans hoped would protect the rights of the newly freed African Americans, did little to change North Carolina politics. Former Confederate soldiers held positions of power; they designed a new form of white supremacy that could function within the country's new legal conditions that forbade slavery. In 1866 the state legislature passed "Black codes" to legislate the relationship of white and Black North Carolinians. These laws made interracial marriage illegal; limited movement through vagrancy provisions; sentenced Black men to death at the whim of white men's accusations about rape; and allowed former enslavers to hold Black children who had been "orphaned or left destitute by the war" in "multi-year apprenticeships." Legalized involuntary servitude continued in North Carolina, leading a representative from the Freedmen's Bureau to bitterly complain that the state's Black codes told Black citizens they are "inferior and must be so kept by law."[62]

Nonetheless, in the years of Reconstruction that followed the war from 1865 to 1870, and for perhaps as much as a decade beyond, African Americans saw glimpses of increased opportunity and equality. Across the South, according to historian Eric Foner, Black citizens "reunited families separated under slavery, established churches and schools, claimed the rights of free labor, pressed for civil equality and the vote, and demanded access to land."[63] Hinton and his family, as well as Martha, Solomon, and other newly freed peoples associated with the Monk farm, began to purchase land around the former plantations where they were once enslaved.

The African Americans who would join John Carr in founding Newton Grove's Catholic parish used Reconstruction to acquire land of their own, often from the very individuals who had enslaved them. Although deeds and legal documents are scarce, oral histories and census data reveal that Archibald Monk and Willis Cole's mixed-race children received parcels near the land given to their white half siblings. Just after Archibald Monk died, the 1870 census takers wrote that Solomon Monk "works on a farm" and located his home next to Martha's brother Abram, who also "works on a farm."[64] The next census in 1880 lists each of them as "farmer," not "farm laborer" or "works on a farm." Along with gaining land, Solomon had also moved further down the road from Martha's brother onto land that the Cole family had likely given or sold to him.[65] By 1888, records show that Hinton and Sarah Cole sold Solomon and Martha Monk additional land for $200.[66] Through Martha, the Cole family served as an important source of support and status for Solomon, who was well on his way to using his new freedom to become a prosperous and prominent community figure.

Old ties like the affinal bond between Solomon and the Cole family remained strong even into Reconstruction; it fostered new forms of Black prosperity but just as importantly served to keep white and some Black North Carolinians in the area. As one of Solomon's descendants, Joseph, who spends his free time doing genealogy with distant cousins, both Black and white, admonished me, "Don't ever let them tell you we [African Americans] didn't have nothing. After the Civil War, we bought land. In some places, white folks died with white heirs but left land to Black offspring. Some of us had a lot." Not surprisingly, however, "it got taken from us."[67] Through unfair lending practices and the division of farmland to large numbers of children, some of the grandchildren of freedmen and women who procured their own land in the years after the Civil War would become sharecroppers. As we'll see in the next chapter, while the Civil War had ended slavery, Reconstruction was a short-lived idyll. The coming structural racism of the post-Reconstruction period, enforced by the Ku Klux Klan and other terrorist groups, brutalized African Americans in an attempt to erase this progress.

As North Carolina, like much of the South, endured economic collapse after the Civil War, the stability and security brought by these interracial familial and extrafamilial relationships were especially important to men like John Carr, who continued to rely on Black neighbors for farm labor. Further, he had been exposed by his Northern education to both scientific racism and abolition, which seemed to come together for him in an ideology that allowed him to counteract efforts to sever his community ties while maintaining a power differential between the races. He began to negotiate these challenges both through the Bible and perhaps through the pulpit. This post–Civil War journey came together for John Carr in a remarkable way that transformed the interracial family into which he was born into a single, segregated congregation that was publicly recognized and long lasting despite changes in societal expectations around family and race. He did so not as a biological father but as the founder of a parish — one that sought a membership for Black and white townspeople. John Carr was extending what he knew of his own family and church life during the enslavement period, adapting it to this new religious household he was trying to create. This household, like many before the Civil War, would include all races, including members who were tied to the community by common cause, if not by blood. Here, as in his birth family, hierarchy would remain.

Exactly what it meant to share this spiritual tie across the races was unclear. What was clear, however, was that in this time of postwar segregation, baptism into the Catholic Church made the bonds between parishioners legitimate in the eyes of this church, even as it drew suspicion and anger from surrounding Protestants. In this spiritual family, the connections established by the plantation household continued to exist long after newer means of implementing segregation and white supremacy made that kind of interracial public interaction a dangerous anomaly.

CHAPTER TWO

St. Mark's and the Limits of a Parish's Protection

1870–1904

As different as John Carr Monk's life and decisions were from the white men around him, we're still left wondering: How did this isolated country doctor with no formal theological training and no knowledge of Catholicism decide that converting to that tradition was the solution to his problems with segregation? His journey begins with an act of renunciation. He abandoned his family's home congregation, Goshen Methodist, when the members voted to segregate. They forced African Americans in the congregation to join a local African Methodist Episcopal Church.[1] John Carr Monk stood as the sole white member to publicly protest the decision, and he became a traitor among his neighbors by repudiating their belief that racial segregation was a divine responsibility.

After the vote, John Carr frequently talked about his desire to find a nearby church that would support his vision of Christian unity. He found none. As the story goes, shortly after the Goshen vote and when John Carr was still grappling with this loss, his brother, Rufus, came across a text by the Catholic archbishop of New York City, John McCloskey. McCloskey's Sunday homily to a group of diverse immigrant Catholics, "Church Unity and Churchmen's Duty," came out in a special New Year's circular in the *New York Herald*. But John Carr didn't read it until much later because McCloskey's impassioned plea for unity in the Church only reached him by accident. In a gesture that would forever change the history of Newton Grove and North Carolina—if not the Catholic Church in America—Rufus picked the piece of seeming trash out of a pile of papers used to protect medicine bottles during shipping and handed it to John Carr, who read: "God is one, Christ is one, and the Church is one."[2]

Archbishop McCloskey might well have been reminding the Irish and Italian immigrant communities in America that although they tended to resent one another, they were, in fact, part of a single church. Nonetheless, John Carr heard a prophetic statement addressing his concern about the complete racial segregation of his local churches, when the archbishop stated: "No matter whether you're not in unison either in national or personal feeling . . . rich and poor, high and low can come together, it matters not from how distant climes they come nor what may be the costumes they wear . . . they are all blended and united together into a harmonious whole in faith."[3] As he read, John Carr must have seen his longing for unity—togetherness for himself and his extended family—in McCloskey's imagery. This "harmony" the archbishop emphasized stood in sharp contrast to the racially divided Protestant churches, churches that separated Christian from Christian and brother from brother for political reasons.

Archbishop McCloskey closed his sermon saying, "If there are DIVISION and DISCORD (and there are) that is not God's work—'an enemy hath done this.'"[4] While McCloskey was speaking to New York City's divided Church—split between national factions of European immigrants—Monk took an interpretive leap and heard these words as a call for racial reconciliation. Here, Monk believed, was a Church where such differences didn't threaten unity; people embraced these differences as parts of a "harmonious whole," in McCloskey's words. The Catholic Church was true to its catholic—that is, universal—name. McCloskey understood this universality to refer to the Church's global reach, not an insistence on racial unity. Without a priest to guide their interpretation, however, John Carr and his compatriots were free to apply the archbishop's words to their context to create their own local Catholic theology. Contrary to the Southern sense that segregation was God's design, Archbishop McCloskey said that unity is God's work; division, the devil's.

According to his descendants, John Carr turned to friends like Enoch David Godwin, then a Presbyterian, to talk over what he'd learned.[5] These conversations centered on their interpretation of Catholic theology rather than the Church's actions in America. They read unity within the context of the racially segregated South and knew immediately what the archbishop meant. They did not have a catechism or a Catholic neighbor from which to get the Church's current position. If they had, they might have heard that the American bishops called for greater outreach to African Americans in the South the year after the Civil War's end. This appreciation of white bishops for the souls of Black worshippers might have been meaningful. Even more meaningful would have been knowledge of the existence of interracial Catholic parishes, with internally segregated seating, flourishing across New Orleans, where both Black and white worshippers had deep family roots in the Church. As historian Bentley Anderson writes, "From 1718 through 1890s, New Orleans parish churches were racially integrated. . . . The fact that the races were under one roof reflected the concept of a catholic (i.e. universal) community."[6] The New Orleans model in this early period, at least until the *Plessy v. Ferguson* decision in 1896 made segregation a constitutional framework for race relations, could be seen in other places in the former colonial South. John Carr and his neighbors, however, would not have known that, in their earliest decades, they were not alone in understanding that Catholicism facilitated, even necessitated, racial unity. Nor would they realize that they were one of the few interracial parishes that outlasted *Plessy*.

John Carr and his neighbors had no way of knowing this history. They knew little about the American Catholic Church's overwhelming support of the Democratic Party and the party's ideological allegiance to white supremacy. "Most Catholics remained staunch Democrats," historian Leslie Woodcock Tentler explains, "even as Democratic regimes in the South kept black men from the polls, imposed legal segregation, and turned a blind eye to mounting violence against an increasingly isolated black population."[7] Serendipitously, John Carr didn't know any of this, which freed him up to develop his own idiosyncratic reading of the Catholic theology of unity and universality. For him and other potential converts around Newton Grove, Catholicism offered a welcoming doctrine within which they could redefine themselves as Christians and counter the segregation being imposed at Protestant institutions all around them.

Father Mark Gross was overseeing the Wilmington parish in Bishop Gibbons's absence when he picked up a letter from John Carr Monk seeking information about the Catholic Church. John Carr chose Wilmington, 100 miles from Newton Grove, because as a "seaport town . . . there was a chance there might be a priest there."[8] He was right, but Gross was still surprised by this inquiry, written by an unknown country doctor from a county the priest had never set foot in. He passed John Carr's letter to his superior, Bishop James Gibbons of Richmond, whose area of oversight extended to North Carolina. Bishop Gibbons would eventually be elevated to cardinal, though he was already a major figure in American Catholicism, so much so that in 1870 he was attending the First Vatican Council in Rome.[9]

Bishop Gibbons later recalled that upon returning to Wilmington, his assistant handed him a letter "addressed 'To any Catholic Priest of Wilmington, N.C.'"[10] John Carr was driven and desperate. He waited barely three days to send his plea after Rufus showed him McCloskey's homily. Desperate, perhaps because he was so deeply stung by the Goshen congregation's vote to expel its Black members and so clearly alone as the only white member to vote against it, he wrote to find a priest who he hoped would help him learn more about the Catholic Church that he read about in the newspaper, a religious community that seemed to embrace all God's children. Such a church could restore the mixed racial religious services of the past in Newton Grove, where all his neighbors and members of the Monk household could worship together in one building.

Cardinal Gibbons replied to John Carr's letter when he returned from Rome, sending a list of books for him to read and promising to introduce him to a priest as soon as possible. This positive response no longer exists, but it's clear that Gibbons either explicitly or implicitly endorsed John Carr's understanding of the universal Catholic Church as a church that supported white and Black members worshipping under one roof, in a single parish.

IN THIS TELLING — and the same story is told almost verbatim by newspapers, journal articles, and current parishioners alike — John Carr focused on the unity of the Catholic Church in integrating diverse ethnic and racial populations throughout the world. And yet unity, for the Catholic Church, and very likely for John Carr, did not mean racial equality. Although the congregation would be interracial, power would not be evenly divided among Black and white parishioners or laity and clergy. Unlike the Protestant church he left behind, the Catholic Church would not hold votes, giving each person — each man — a say in the affairs of the Church. Rather, the Catholic Church's hierarchy emanated from the authority of the pope, whose role was like the patriarch of a global family. Gaining a place to build a multiracial community meant losing autonomy over how the community would be shaped. John Carr, however, probably knew little about the Catholic Church's structure at this time, as he was focused squarely on the chance it offered to sustain and sacralize his interracial relationships. This church united kin of all races within God's congregation.

Equality and community were separable concepts at this time. John Carr would have had little direct experience with racial equality during his early life. Further, his medical school training in Philadelphia would have reinforced the idea that there was a biological need for such stratification. John Carr lived in an America, and more specifically, a Southern world, both before and after the Civil War, where patriarchy in family life and the racial hierarchy of the white population were in evidence everywhere. Nonetheless, by aligning himself with the Catholic Church he insisted on his version of racial unity — at least in religious life — amid an intense region-wide push for near complete segregation. His actions set the newly formed Newton Grove parish and its founder on an uncharted path, a path that would set it apart from other Catholic communities as well as from its Protestant neighbors.

The Backlash Against Reconstruction

Conversion transformed John Carr Monk's white southern identity—one that was beginning to be tied to both Protestantism and segregation—into a white southern Catholic identity, which centered on kinship in Christ despite a racial hierarchy of white leadership and power in the Catholic Church. These elements of inclusion and hierarchy, tied as they were to a global Church rather than a regional denomination dictated by local norms, opened new avenues of connection for the Catholics of Newton Grove. For John Carr and those who joined him, the benefits of this new community, including their understanding that they were enacting God's will, outweighed the economic, social, and physical threats from the broader Protestant white community.

While John Carr took certain administrative steps, the process of both conversion and building the church went beyond mere bureaucratic tasks and the buying of tools and materials. He became a lay theologian and creative religious entrepreneur who cobbled together an innovative religious community that offered a different model for southern identity. In joining this congregation, Newton Grove's Catholic parishioners drew on regional concerns for family and God in a way that was in conversation with, but wholly different from, their white Protestant neighbors. Rather than establishing separate buildings and denominations for each race, the parish embodied a version of the unified Christian family that they read about in the Bible. At St. Mark's Catholic Church, as the parish would be known, Black and white Catholics worshipped in the same house, under one roof, and practiced baptism to become part of the same spiritual family, the one Catholic Church.

From the end of the Civil War through the early 1870s, Reconstruction seemed to offer a chance for Black Americans to achieve racial equality with their white neighbors. The Fourteenth (1868) and Fifteenth (1870) Amendments granted newly freed African Americans citizenship, equal protection, and, finally, suffrage for all men regardless of race. While many newly freed African Americans left the South, others felt tied to the land on which their ancestors had worked and died and where their children had been born. In the years immediately following the war, many of these families in North Carolina joined millions of other Black families across the South as landowners. Sociologist W. E. B. DuBois estimated that by 1875, Black families owned three million acres of land in the South, a number that would grow over the next three decades until reaching approximately 16 million acres by

1910.[11] The Monks, the Coles, and many of their neighbors were a part of this Black land-owning class. As Virginia recounted during our conversation, "My great-uncle gave my dad his land, which he [my great-uncle] inherited from his father, who was 'mulatto.' And his father inherited hundreds of acres from [a white person] on the Wills Cole Plantation."[12] Men like her grandfather could live freely near their white and Black family members to build a future of their own, relying on their own farms and labor for prosperity rather than working under white oversight.[13] Freedom also meant a reorganization of relationships between the freedmen and women and their former enslavers as well as a new relationship with the land for all members of the plantation household. For many white North Carolinians, this moment of reorganization brought great fear as Black men and, to some extent, women began taking new roles in the community as owners, voters, and power brokers.

The Republican Party offered a political home to both landowning and nonlandowning African American men. Republicans had supported emancipation and rights for African Americans. With President Andrew Johnson's 1865 appointment of Republican William Woods Holden to North Carolina's governorship, African American men looked forward to active participation in state and local government. Holden's election to a full term in 1868 solidified their hold on these new opportunities as he continued to appoint African Americans to positions in his administration. Meanwhile, in the run-up to the 1868 election, Black leaders held freedman conferences across the state to encourage voter registration and recruit African Americans for state and local office. The election elevated Black men into political offices for the first time across the whole of Eastern North Carolina.[14] The threat of Black voters and their potential to further upend the white supremacist structures that survived Southern surrender filled the white community with fear.

However, African American progress was short lived. In 1870, North Carolina Republicans lost statewide elections to a prosegregation coalition. White citizens sought to enforce white supremacy by intimidation, fear, and violence.[15] White supremacist and terrorist groups like the Ku Klux Klan thrived and embodied many whites' fervor for segregation.[16] These groups had a common purpose, as historian Scott Reynolds Nelson argues: "[to] drive Black voters away from the polls, while threatening whites who voted Republican."[17] Vandalism and murder were used systematically to politically silence African Americans and white Southerners who pushed back against this new system of societal control.[18]

But segregation had a religious element that scholars sometimes overlook. White ministers and their congregations, like Newton Grove's Goshen Methodist Church, ensured that their religious communities sanctified this "organizing principle" of white supremacy.

Historian Donald G. Mathews put it most strongly: Segregation itself was religion, as he argued in his study of Southern lynching celebrations.[19] John Carr's vote against segregating Goshen did not simply put him in opposition to a burgeoning racial system. In his neighbors' eyes, he was apostate, a heretic, a rebel against God's will.

John Carr Monk, now a Republican, put himself further at risk for violent Klan retribution.[20] By 1870, approximately 40,000 North Carolinians had joined the Klan and other white supremacist groups. Governor Holden described these groups first as merely political, but then he admitted that their "character was changed, and those secret Klans began to commit murder, to rob, whip scourge, and mutilate unoffending citizens."[21] After Klan members murdered State Senator John Stevens, the governor declared martial law in Alamance and Caswell Counties. The Klan and similar organizations threatened, intimidated, and killed African Americans as well as whites who subverted their efforts to ensure that the South was comprised of racially segregated communities dominated by a white elite. Eventually, in 1871, reactionary North Carolinians grew powerful enough to persuade state congressional Democrats to impeach Governor Holden for trying to suppress the Klan's reign of terror.

In the fall of that year, after a crackdown by the federal government, Klan activity waned throughout the state, but not in Sampson County. In Clinton, twenty miles from Newton Grove, night riders ransacked every cabin in an African American neighborhood, raping several women and threatening everyone in earshot as they searched for Menus Herring and Gabriel Rialls, two Black men who had testified against the Klan.[22] On September 23, 1871, Herring was ambushed and executed. Rialls and those with whom he traveled sought warrants for the arrest of the killers. The government officials sent to find the Klan members received no support from the locals in their search. Although they were unsuccessful in that effort, by the end of the year, Klan members were confessing to their participation in this campaign of terror.[23]

In 1872, when John Carr converted to Catholicism, Klan activity had greatly diminished in North Carolina, in large part because they had achieved their objectives. Even though Holden's Republican lieutenant governor took over for him and held the office for another term, his ability to implement

Republican policies was limited by conservative Democrats in the state congressional houses.[24] Although ostensibly Republican led, the lived reality in North Carolina was one of increasing segregation and diminishing African American presence, let alone input, in public life. Within this context, John Carr sought to create his unified church.

Although there are no recorded lynchings in Newton Grove, the Klan did terrorize people there, and talk of murders and rapes elsewhere certainly spread the fear.[25] This fear likely kept African Americans from formally converting in the early years of the parish when baptism would have required standing next to and being touched by a white priest and sponsor in a public or semipublic setting. For they knew actions that allowed them to mix with white folks in any way could lead to their murder and the torture of their loved ones, as had happened with Menus Herring.

White Catholic families, too, had their horror stories about the Klan, but these stories did not end in murder, rape, or the destruction of their community. Sister Julia leaned forward in her chair, eyes wide and determined as she told me family lore that included the Klan burning a cross on her family farm. Her great-grandfather, Enoch Godwin, was the intended target. "The Ku Klux were going to kill him because he came into the church with John Carr," she explained. "The [Protestant] ministers . . . came to his house and told him they wanted him to come back to the church. He said, 'I'll never go back to your church because you're supporting wrong.' He had to go down to the pigeon place and hide in the woods to keep them from finding him."[26] Eventually, he climbed inside a barrel and stayed there for twenty-four hours until relatives found him and took him to Raleigh for safety.[27] He and others were willing to persevere through this menacing to join and sustain an alternative model of Christianity that they believed more closely reflected God's will as it maintained key interracial connections.

By 1876, many African Americans from Newton Grove had decided to respond to this rash of extralegal violence—as well as the legal discrimination that state legislators were enshrining into the civil code—by voting with their feet. Historian Frenise Logan writes about these "exodusters," rural Blacks departing the South, in the November 14, 1889, edition of the *New Bern Daily Journal*: "At Kinston yesterday the town was crowded with negroes anxious to shake the North Carolina dust off their shoes and try their fortunes in some other state. It is said that there were about 1,500 enthusiastic 'exodusters' in the town. . . . The train could not accommodate all who wanted to go."[28]

While many newly freed men and women left rural North Carolina, other folks chose to stay because they had land and support networks that they were not willing to leave behind. The Black residents of Newton Grove felt the strong push and pull. They owned their land and had century-long community relationships. They resented the rural South's cash-poor economy and felt battered by repeated farm crises in the early 1900s. Freedom and landownership combined with the arrival of the Klan strained the relationships between Black and white interrelated families. Where once these families were universally understood to be a part of the same household and thus responsible for each other in various socially prescribed ways, now families were expected to reject one another. White supremacy insisted that they dissolve any remaining meaningful supports that tied white and recently freed people to each other, replacing them, perhaps, by building bonds with community members of the same race. This process ignored the lifetime of connections that reinforced the sense of obligation within these extended interracial families. John Carr's conversion to Catholicism sought to reimagine these interracial familial relationships in a way that ran counter to the Klan's plan.

A Catholic Church in the Protestant South

Outside of Texas, Louisiana, and other places where original settlers were also Catholics, the story of southern religion has been primarily a Protestant one. However, Newton Grove shows that important innovations in American Catholicism were also occurring within small Catholic parishes in overwhelmingly Protestant regions as well. In 1820, at the time Irish immigrants began flooding the Northeast, there were so few Catholics in Georgia and the Carolinas that a single diocese in Charleston oversaw the Catholic population of these three states.[29] More than forty years later, in 1868, North Carolina was separated from the Diocese of Charleston and made a Vicariate Apostolic, which meant the state was a Catholic territory where the hierarchy of the Church was not yet fully established. Bishop James Gibbons took over responsibility for North Carolina's scattered Catholic groups and delegated pastoral responsibilities to a young priest, Father Mark Gross, who traveled the state serving Mass in living rooms and backyards as well a few small parishes. Besides Father Gross, North Carolina was also served by a few priests and nuns who were members of religious orders sent from Catholic communities outside North Carolina. The parishioners of St. Mark's hoped that one of these priests might be assigned to be their full-time pastor, a person who could say Mass and perform the sacraments regularly as well as help them build relationships with the wider Catholic world from which they had long been isolated. The parishioners would find, however, that for every benefit, financial and otherwise, that these priests, these outsiders, provided through their connections to the Catholic world beyond Newton Grove, they also got in the way. As they brought structures and practices of the wider American Catholic Church to the parish, they simultaneously brought opportunity and acted as obstacles that prevented parishioners from addressing the unique requirements to sustain a rural, interracial, internally segregated parish in the segregated South. Survival within this context took continual and nuanced negotiation with both Catholic and white southern tradition that outsiders learned only through difficult trial and error.

Of course, the priests' and nuns' ignorance of southern mores was not entirely their fault. Neither the Vatican nor the American Catholic Church offered clear guidelines for how to minister in the area. After the Civil War, at the 1866 Second Plenary Council of Baltimore, the bishops who gathered from every part of the United States promised new approaches to Catholic missions in the South. Participants worried over how to handle the South's growing culture of segregation, especially since the Church had identified missions to African Americans as a priority. But they ended the council without taking a stand on segregation, leaving it to individual priests to decide on an appropriate response.[30] In effect, though, priests were left on their own, with no guidance from either official dictates or their bishops.

This was a blessing in disguise. In the absence of top-down instructions and guidelines, the nascent Catholic community in Newton Grove had the ability to shape its own Catholic culture in its early years. Along with racial inclusiveness, to survive, the parish also needed to be ecumenical to some degree. Newton Grove's first Catholics adopted a different approach to Protestantism than their coreligionists, who viewed the parish as a respite from Protestant America. In Newton Grove, Protestantism was central to the warp and woof of parishioners' lives and remained so after they converted. John Carr set the example when he sold two acres of land in 1876 for one dollar to the Schools Committee of Westbrook Township for "the purposes of a colored school and for colored preaching and for no other purposes whatsoever."[31] This land was meant to house an African American public school and White Oak Disciples of Christ Church, a Black Protestant congregation founded by Hinton Monk's brother-in-law. While the deed was intended to create a school, there is no historical evidence of a public African American school there until 1910, and even then, it does not seem to be associated with the church. Instead, obituaries of former members of White Oak list the neighboring Johnston County public schools for education.[32] Whatever school did exist would have relied on the community's scarce funds for its first thirty years. With funding dependent upon white approval, a school-age population, and faculty that was needed in the field, offering consistent schooling would have been difficult, if not impossible, for the African American public school system in North Carolina. Moreover, these retellings make clear that students had to find their own way to school either by foot or by horse and buggy. Nonetheless, with John Carr's efforts in supporting the Black community here and with other parish efforts to support the Protestant community, Catholics demonstrated that they shared a strong sense of family and devotion to God that connected them to their kin and neighbors regardless of their religion, even if their denominational identity set them apart. Newton Grove's Catholics developed a more generous approach to Protestants than did their coreligionists in other places.

A good number of white family members and friends converted that first year; many more folks, both white and Black, became part of the community but were not immediately baptized. Father Michael Irwin, the parish's second residential priest, once wrote that John Carr's brother was one of these fellow travelers: "Julius did not join, but came to the church regularly for forty years, walking four miles to Mass every time the priest came for a Sunday."[33] Despite his dedication, Julius waited until his dotage to convert, which meant that in the eyes of the surrounding community, he was still Protestant. Many other extended family members attended Masses or other church events regularly without changing their affiliation. They married into the parish with little resistance and only converted when age inspired a desire to be buried next to their Catholic spouses. For these Catholics, being part of the Catholic Church meant having parishes that were ecumenical and interracial to some degree, even though the Vatican and the American bishops had neither adopted a position against segregation nor encouraged outreach to Protestants.

Out of necessity, nearly all of these recently converted Catholics were married to Protestants. To accommodate these interfaith families and combat anti-Catholicism, the parish had to be much more inclusive than a parish comprised solely of Catholics living within a specific geographical boundary might have been. St. Mark's parish was not a Catholic enclave; it was a porous community that was open to all North Carolinians who wanted to participate in parish activities, even if Catholic doctrine forbade them from taking the Eucharist. While this extension of Southern hospitality helped the parish survive by undercutting anti-Catholic sentiment, it also exposed this parish to danger. Parishioners and priests knew, or would quickly learn, that their neighbors would sanction them for any misstep, sanctions which could be costly to some and potentially deadly to others.

Recognizing Household Bonds through Conversion

So many times, in so many conversations, I heard African American parishioners try to make sense of John Carr's decision. Scratching their heads or shifting in their chairs as they puzzled through his momentous choice, they wanted to make it clear to me that it was more than his sense of Christian justice that led John Carr to take this courageous stand to abandon his Protestant faith. His desire to worship with his mixed-race brother Solomon helped spur this bold move. As Henry, one of Solomon's third great-grandsons, recounted: "He couldn't take Solomon, who was his half-brother or his other [mixed-race and African American] kin, to church with him. So that's . . . how the church at Newton Grove was formed."[34] With Solomon now living as a free person on his own farm, church served as the one place where the brothers could display their bond, where they could be united in faith. John Carr sought a church that would sanctify his kinship to the Black people in his family and theirs to him. Rather than understanding Black and white worshipping under one roof as sinful, in his new understanding of Catholicism, it was an embodiment of the Universal Church.

Bishop Gibbons baptized John Carr into the Catholic Church on October 27, 1871, at his diocesan seat. Having been born in Maryland in 1834 and having spent part of his youth in New Orleans before the Civil War, Gibbons likely comprehended some of John Carr's understanding about race and the Catholic Church as well as what he would face as a Catholic convert in North Carolina.[35] In a memoir written forty years later—that he recalled the encounter at all is a testament to the powerful impression that John Carr made—Gibbons describes their subsequent conversation. "He came to Wilmington to make a profession of faith. I baptized the family and learned, with the deepest interest, of the circumstances that had led to his conversion and of his hopes in regard to the community in which he had lived all his life as a prominent physician." He finished the account by declaring that God himself accomplished John Carr's conversion, writing, "the finger of God touched here."[36] Of course, John Carr would also have stood out in Gibbons's memory for his missionary successes, bringing hundreds of friends

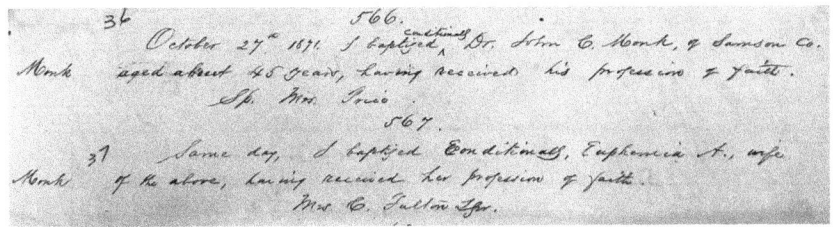

John Carr and Euphemia Monk's sacramental record of their conditional baptism by Bishop James Gibbons at St. Mary's Church, Wilmington, North Carolina, October 27, 1871. Courtesy of the Diocese of Raleigh.

and family into the Church, which North Carolina's Catholic hierarchy had not been able to do. Gibbons continued, offering some insight into why so many converted: "[He was] highly respected and as a physician had access to every family in all that region. His zeal to enlighten the people was surpassed only by his solid piety and good example."[37] For Bishop Gibbons, this missionary zeal was paramount. What the Bishop did not choose to remember—or perhaps never learned—was how much damage John Carr did to his status by converting.

The enthusiasm with which Bishop Gibbons recalled this conversion obscures the costs for John Carr and his family. Father J. H. O'Rourke, SJ, a Jesuit missionary priest who traveled through Newton Grove in the 1870s, left a personal record about the aggressive gossip that followed John Carr after he became Catholic. In a 1905 letter entitled "A Month in North Carolina," O'Rourke wrote, "Directly the news of his conversion reached Newton Grove, the Protestants took alarm and determined to settle with the newly made Papist, who had disgraced their town." The town took John Carr's conversion to be an offense against the collective, not an individual choice. He had tainted the entire town, rejected societal norms, and infected the community with a seemingly foreign religion. O'Rourke also remembered the town's effort to bring Monk back in line: "At once the Doctor and his wife were ostracized and excluded entirely from all social intercourse by his former friends, his lucrative practice fell away, and he was reduced to some straights to support his then young and growing family."[38]

John Carr and his family did not quail before the character assassination and economic pressure. Instead, they hosted the priest on his first visit to Newton Grove, displaying the doctor's dedication to the Catholic Church amid the intimidation campaign. This show of strength brought the first threat of violence, according to O'Rourke: "The first time the priest visited

St. Mark's and the Limits of a Parish's Protection

Stained glass window from the sanctuary memorializing John Carr Monk's baptism and Cardinal Gibbons's recognition of the sacrality of the parish land. Courtesy of Our Lady of Guadalupe Parish.

Newton Grove, it was with considerable difficulty that the more coolheaded men of the town succeeded in protecting him from the violence of the mob."[39] John Carr's standing in the community could no longer protect him or his guest. With a priest physically present in their town, there was great fear that the Protestant men of Newton Grove would reach their breaking point and that avoidance and verbal threats would turn into punches. Luckily, such violence did not occur. Having successfully protected the priest, the congregation needed to learn how to protect themselves in a lasting way.

The new community relied on the relationships of trust that had been built between them on their farms and plantations decades earlier. In the beginning, converts came from within John Carr's family and close circle of friends. Within a few months of John Carr's conversion, his sister Catherine and her children, as well as his neighbor John T. Gregory, who would later marry Amanda Godwin (Enoch Godwin's daughter), joined the Church. They all heard Father Mark Gross celebrated the first Mass at the Monks' house on March 4, 1872. Father Gross returned about once a month to say Mass for the new converts. In between monthly Masses, the congregation likely met on their own in parishioners' homes, with African Americans preparing for baptism at a later date, once they could do so safely.

Seeking to encourage this fledgling Catholic community against the town's opposition, Bishop Gibbons soon made his own visit to Newton Grove in March 1872. He persevered through an uncomfortable journey including a rare snow and sleet storm. "The next morning being Sunday, I celebrated Mass in John Carr's house and preached there later in the day to an earnest audience. The religious interest was profound. It promised to become, as it truly did, a movement of the whole district toward the Catholic Church."[40] John Tracy Ellis, Cardinal Gibbons's biographer, has argued that this work in Newton Grove gave "heart and courage to Gibbons to continue his efforts in spite of all difficulties."[41] John Carr had done what Catholic missionaries could not—with Gibbons's support he had converted North Carolinians. But just as important, he had offered his family a way to hold true to a Southern identity. He had inspired them to draw on the strength of neighborly interdependence to create an opportunity—exceedingly rare in the post–Reconstruction South—to build a community of Blacks and whites.

Attendees have also left us sumptuous catalogs of the meals the Monks offered after Mass. In their recollections, the food seems just as important as the ritual. "Barbecue, roast, pork ham, eggs, sweet potatoes, collards, pickles, molasses, corn bread, wheat bread, butter, milk, preserves, and all kinds of country good-things would quickly disappear," wrote one relative. The families stayed long into the afternoon for "religious discussions."[42] Eating together after receiving the Eucharist and engaging in theological conversation infused this typical pork-heavy North Carolina meal with Catholic significance. This meal epitomized Southern hospitality's conventional approach to pairing savory and sour: three meats, two vegetables, pickles, and bread. Through the nonverbal yet deeply persuasive sensory dimension of taste, the Monks demonstrated that Catholics did not lose their Southernness with conversion.

Since there is no mention of African American attendees at these gatherings, it seems very likely that only white parishioners were present. The presence of Black people in typically white settings, like at a white man's dining table, would have been noted. Their absence, which would be assumed, would not. For Martha and Solomon Monk, this exclusion must have angered or at least disappointed them. Surely they would have hoped that John Carr would have fully included them in the congregation after taking such a stand for religious racial unity among his white neighbors. From the beginning, this unity had strict limits. It was designed to resist complete separation while still accommodating discrimination, racial hierarchy, and internal segregation that survival seemed to necessitate. After all, they sought to create a lasting religious community, not a momentary symbolic disruption to the status quo.

The absence of African Americans from this home meal, however, does not mean that they were not a part of the community, to the extent that southern norms would allow it. During the period before the parish had a church building, African Americans likely met for catechism to prepare for conversion as part of the Sunday school John Carr supported and may have joined white Catholics for Mass or conversations, particularly if it were held in a protected area, such as a backyard. Racial unity was critically important to those who converted, so it stands to reason they would want to embody that unity in some way even when the official Catholic community was all white. Nevertheless, no written trace remains to tell how the community might have accomplished this goal before it was sanctioned through conversion into the Catholic Church. Parish records reveal, however, that as soon as the community had a church building of its own, African American members of the Monk family were prepared to join.

The first Black converts—Solomon's wife Martha Cole Monk and three of her children—joined the church in October 1874. And as in the case of Julius Monk, Solomon did not convert for another five years. Despite this fact, one can be fairly certain that he would have followed the pattern of most of the other folks who joined later than their spouses, yet, in the meantime, attended at least occasional Masses and other parish events with his wife and children. Martha linked two prominent households: Cole and Monk. Her conversion occurred inside St. Mark's Church one month after Bishop Gibbons consecrated it on the land given by John Carr. Since no African Americans had converted in the two years prior to the building of the church, it seems likely that having the physical church offered the security and privacy needed for Black people to be formally joined with their white coreligionists. Their baptisms could take place inside a communal building, rather than in John Carr's home. Perhaps the intimacy involved, with the white priest touching the Black convert's head, would have pushed the boundaries of segregation too far if they had occurred in a white home. Or perhaps the fear created by Menus Herring's murder remained in the Black community, reminding everyone about the costs of transgressing racial norms in Sampson County. After more than two years of quiet from the Klan and within the protective walls of the church, Martha Monk and her children felt safe and ready to join the church. In the South, where there was respect for the sanctity of churches, folks might have taken some solace in the fact that they would be safe inside the sanctuary.

Moreover, the design of St. Mark's offered a physical nod to parishioners' segregated practice within the building's four walls. The church had a large staircase in the front that led to a large blank wall where one might expect a stately front door. Instead, parishioners found a small door on either side.[43] This two-door system, so common in the South, whether marked for a particular race or not, alerted Protestants outside the building that seating in the sanctuary would conform to the norms of segregation, even if the Black and white parishioners were defying convention by meeting together. According to parishioners' stories about the community's earliest days, the African American families came in through the door on the left and the white families through the right. There are no extant notations about who sat where. Still, the doors created the expectation that what happened in the sanctuary followed the rules of how to be a Catholic within, not apart from, the racial structures of the segregated South.

While in other segregated spaces in Newton Grove, part of the point of separation was the erasure of Black presence, here parishioners saw one another throughout the Mass. Yet the parish did follow segregationist custom during the Mass. White families received the Eucharist before the Black families, for example. However, each would have seen the other while passing to and from the altar. In North Carolina, where segregation meant keeping Black people invisible to whites unless they were acting in service to them, even this seemingly modest biracial practice boldly challenged the status quo, although Catholics hid this challenge behind a facade of social conformity. Through this careful public/private negotiation, the parish was able to protect African American parishioners like Martha Cole Monk as they formally joined the community.

On October 18, 1874, John Carr Monk and his wife, Euphemia, took the step of publicly acknowledging their intimate bond with Solomon and Martha by standing before the congregation as baptismal sponsors for Solomon's

St. Mark's and the Limits of a Parish's Protection   55

Sacramental record for Martha Monk. Notice that Rufus Monk, a brother of John Carr and Solomon, stood as sponsor for her. Twenty-eight days later, John Carr and Euphemia sponsored fourteen-year-old Mary Delia. ("John A." must be "John C." because there was no other John Monk in the parish at this time.) Courtesy of the Diocese of Raleigh.

youngest child, Mary Delia.[44] Mary Delia was approximately fourteen at the time. As part of her baptism, the Monks agreed to help raise Mary Delia in the church, acting as a mentor to her. Although John Carr sponsored white children and families, the existing records show Mary Delia to be the only African American person he sponsored in baptism. His brother Rufus Monk had sponsored Martha and three of her other children the month prior. The baptismal certificates that recorded these sponsorships created a formal connection between these white uncles and their Black nieces and nephews. Here in the postbellum segregated South, where an African American person looking a white person in the eye could get that person lynched, baptism united the white and the Black Monk family in spiritual kinship with real-world responsibilities to one another.

Along with their bonds to each other and to the church, African American Catholics' high status within the Newton Grove community likely helped them get ahead while negotiating everyday interactions with potentially hostile white neighbors. Early converts came from a more prominent place than many other formerly enslaved persons. Father James Garneau, a beloved pastor of Newton Grove's Catholic community in the 1980s, remarked in one of our discussions that "the early Black parishioners were landowners. They were a particular subclass of the Black community."[45] That subclass not only owned land, but they also had direct kinship with their white coreligionists.

What was true of the Black parishioners was also true of the white members who, after all, came out of the same plantation households, but with more rights to ownership, education, and upward social mobility. Collectively the parishioners often found such mobility and economic advancement through their family inheritances and from their newly formed Catholic alliances. Their Catholic connections enabled them to access funds and personnel from outside the region to build and run their schools, especially at a time when their neighbors saw the parish as a threat and its integrated membership as anathema to God's plan.

Although it would take a generation to build the networks that would give parishioners a leg up, the paths were being laid. Early African American parishioners like Betsy Lee Robinson and John Robinson, whose grandchildren sat in the church's first pew, did not pass down stories about why they chose to convert, but they did leave memories of John Carr. When he wasn't farming for himself, John Robinson worked for John Carr. His wife Betsy helped Euphemia rear Catherine, the youngest of her three daughters, after John Carr's death in 1877. Most likely, the doctor and his family introduced the Robinsons to Catholic teachings while he worked.[46] Eventually, the Robinsons had fourteen children whom they reared in the Newton Grove parish. John Carr even helped the children get to Mass on Sunday morning, according to Henry, one of the Robinsons' living descendants. "[John Carr Monk would] take his horse and wagons and come around and pick them up and take them to church." In another conversation, the Robinsons' great-grandson, who also grew up in the parish, expressed his own astonishment. "It was absolutely amazing that he would do that," he blurted out. "I mean, he cared that much."[47] Caring and connection being demonstrated publicly by a white Man for his Black coreligionists broke the racial codes of the time and, given Henry's reaction, perhaps for our time as well. When John Carr died, the parish continued his practice, ensuring that as many parishioners as possible had safe and reliable transportation to Mass.

While nothing remains that speaks directly to the daily relationships he had with other African American parishioners (or, more broadly, if the Monks combined spiritual connection with material support for one another), John Carr's transportation was key to getting the parish off the ground. Muddy ruts served as rural roads in 1870s rural North Carolina. Having a sturdy wagon meant a safe and relatively speedy trip to church, which in turn meant less time away from the fields.[48] Further, this transportation seemed an extension of what the Robinsons might have received at John Carr's first nondenominational Sunday school. It was a visible, yet discreet, defiance of segregation. The parish's displays of racial inclusion and other efforts to represent the Catholic concept of unity in the Body of Christ were always done in quiet; parishioners sought safety (and in some ways comfort and perhaps respect) by not drawing attention to these practices.

Although the Monk and Cole families formed an early core in the parish, new converts continued to join throughout the first fifty years. By 1881, at least twenty-eight white families from Newton Grove had been baptized into the Catholic Church. Four Black families had also been baptized and it's likely more were attending but had not yet converted. Almost every one of these families either had or would soon have between eight and fifteen children, so the addition of even one new family meant a lot to the parish. As one of Archibald Monk's white great-great-granddaughters explained: "Daddy had ten brothers and sisters and there are thirty-two of us grandchildren." Her relative's conversion added forty-two new Catholics to the community in the span of a generation.[49] All of these families had to make the same choice as John Carr: to disassociate themselves from the segregated Protestant churches and the families who attended them. All of the families faced some version of the isolating and hateful consequences for that decision as well.

Within the first five years of the parish's founding, many African Americans with family in the Catholic Church were attending Masses at St. Mark's as well as occasional events at the Disciples of Christ Church since they could not attend the whites-only paraliturgical events at St. Mark's. This occasional participation at White Oak did not give parishioners of St. Mark's access to the political activity and self-determination that the Protestant congregants shared. Choosing Catholicism meant being excluded from a center of power. They would not hear the sermons or participate in church societies of mutual support and equality. Conversion put them in a vulnerable position in the wider Black community. They could not be rooted equally in both the Black and Catholic world.

At this time the Catholic Church considered attending a Protestant church a mortal sin. Out of deference to Catholic teaching, parishioners probably would not have gone to Sunday services, but they attended social gatherings like picnics and concerts. For many African Americans, being part of both communities provided a way to stay connected to their wider family, who had remained in their Protestant churches. Although the parishioners were frequently seen as traitors for choosing this white church, the parish's outreach to the broader Newton Grove community—in terms of support for education and infrastructure—often, but not always, helped to ease interfaith family tensions. This tradition of outreach to the community had been established by John Carr and then taken up by the priests who followed him. It was a necessary act of pastoral care to blunt anti-Catholic sentiments in Newton Grove.

While all the new converts, both Black and white, had Protestant family, including Protestant spouses, no white Catholics reported hearing of their Catholic relatives attending their family's Protestant churches. Many did remember that their Protestant family came to the Catholic Church, often for de facto white-only picnics and other entertainment that accompanied Mass or a weekend mission led by a visiting priest. For while the wider community gradually and begrudgingly accepted, with segregated seating, interracial Mass attendance in the privacy of the church, they would not accept such flouting of segregation on the public church lawn.

Within the first decade, however, the tensions caused by the establishment of a Catholic church in a Protestant community began to soften as non-Catholics started to appreciate the Christian devotion that both they and their Catholic neighbors shared. By 1886, for instance, the *Goldsboro Messenger*, one of the area's local papers, informed the community that "music at the Catholic Church was such improved on the second Sunday by the addition of two male voices. The choir now consists of Mrs. Monk, her daughter, the organist, well known in Goldsboro circles, and Messrs. Godwin and Gregory."[50] These white members of the Monk, Godwin, and Gregory families were well known not only to the parish but also to those who mingled in Goldsboro's society circles. In rural Newton Grove, Catholics were among the town's well-established lineages, not recently arrived immigrants trying to build a new life like they were in so many American cities. Like all Christians in Newton Grove, Catholics sang to organ music just like their Protestant cousins. Moreover, when this singing became more artful, it was favorably reported in a regional newspaper, alongside prosaic announcements about the upcoming Methodist Sunday school convention.[51]

However, what went unsaid in this newspaper article, as it usually did in reporting social highlights, was that the St. Mark's choir was all white. Unlike at White Oak, which was all Black, African American parishioners could not take public roles or leadership roles in the choir or at the altar. Still African American (and white) folks from the countryside around Newton Grove converted. The *Salisbury North Carolina Evening Sun* included a favorable note about St. Mark's submitted by an unnamed "N. C. Baptist." "The membership is now between 200 and 300, and they have a priest who spends his entire time among the people," the paper reported. "This is the only Catholic Church we know of in the State. They are working hard educationally and religiously."[52] Actually, St. Mark's was then the eleventh Catholic Church in North Carolina, but to the Baptists in Salisbury, North Carolina, located far from any ports, Catholicism was clearly a new religious tradition, and despite being an anomaly, the letter implies it should be respected. Tensions lessened, and respect for Newton Grove's Catholics grew despite the inclusion of both Blacks and whites in the St. Mark's congregation. St. Mark's held onto this hard-won and tenuous respect by segregating in other parts of church life: Priests and lay leaders were all white, and so too was the choir that received that favorable community review.

Some Protestants took to public forums to make the case that even such seemingly limited transgressions of Southern norms must end. In an 1879 letter to the editors of the *Raleigh Christian Advocate*, for instance, Newton Grove's Mr. Isaac Williams warned that "the Roman Catholics are planting themselves in that community. They have already built them a church and will do the cause of truth and true religion great damage unless, we rally to the help of these struggling members and friends of the Church."[53] If readers of this letter took direct action against the parish, it does not appear in the surviving history. Nonetheless, the public nature of this letter served as a reminder to readers and parishioners alike that Catholics should be understood as invaders taking hold of longtime residents and turning them away from Protestantism. Every townsperson had the responsibility to bring these newly converted Catholics back into the religious and social norms of the community. Some readers, for instance, might have used the same tactics they used against John Carr when he converted—social and economic exclusion to demonstrate the consequences of turning against the community. Letters like this one and their corresponding actions offered menacing instruction to the parishioners attending St. Mark's. Their decision to embrace a new white Christian Southern identity, which tolerated a much higher degree of racial togetherness, was a threat to the community and would spark threats in return. This togetherness, however, had its limits.

While Cardinal Gibbons continued to laud the Catholics of Newton Grove long after he left North Carolina, few Catholics who had not lived as religious outsiders in the state recognized the unique character and dedication of the parish. Traveling priests invited to give sermons and other visitors viewed the Newton Grove Catholic congregation through the lens of broad stereotypes of hardscrabble, rural country folk, stereotypes that distanced the parish from the American Church's urbane core. Catholic clergy used this stereotype to justify and structure their own missionary work in the community. Father Francis X. Mueller, C.Ss.R., reported on his 1875 visit to give a series of Masses:

> The first Sunday I preached between 12 and one o'clock, and it was, in the shade and draft, 81 degrees. I was bathed through and thought with perspiration . . . a gentleman walk[s] up to the altar . . . brings me out a large pitcher of water, bows to me, bids me to take a drink. I at first refused; he places the pitcher on the altar back of me and knowing that this good and methodistic people would not think strange of me, grasped the pitcher and took a gulp of water . . . Big strapping farmer boys, rusty old coats and heavy boots, hats on walking into the little church as if they were going into a barn . . . They eyed me as if I were an elephant sent by Barnum for a curiosity show. But they are willing and anxious inquirers after the Faith, and eventually the whole section of the county will become Catholic.[54]

Father Mueller's form of disciplined and true Catholicism, in his eyes, was as foreign to this parish as elephants. To him, their commitment to come to Mass after sweating in the fields desacralized the sanctuary, turning it into a barn. Moreover, the parishioners' hospitality made them Protestant rather than generous. Father Mueller's missionary optimism proved to be mistaken. Rural curiosity did not turn North Carolina Catholic. His paternalism did not dissuade the parish from embodying a Catholicism that recognized the needs of its parishioners and priests in the agricultural South. Despite frequent misunderstandings of Catholic visitors from cities throughout the Northeast, the parish would continue to develop its thoroughly Catholic, racially unified, if internally segregated, and comfortably southern identity.

Institutionalizing Catholic Unity

Immediately upon the parish's founding, John Carr Monk began making preparations for a parochial school. In 1875, he asked Margaret Robinson to teach at Newton Grove's new lay-run Catholic school, the first in North Carolina.[55] Robinson knew the trials of being a Catholic in North Carolina well. She was the child of Irish immigrants who had built a home chapel in nearby Goldsboro to maintain their Catholic faith. Since the area lacked parochial schools and a strong parish life, her parents ensured she received a strong Catholic education by sending her to Notre Dame Academy in Baltimore. Later in life, Robinson's daughter recounted her mother's stories of John

Carr's generosity that helped the parish's educational mission get off the ground. "The school came in for a full share of his interest," she recalled in a letter to a parish archivist, "finding pupils, paying tuition of many and providing clothing for some of the needy."[56] At a time when only wealthy children received education, an education in the form of private tutors at home, with John Carr's generosity, the parish could offer accessible and inexpensive education to the wider white community.

Although there was no official parochial school for African Americans until 1900 when the St. Francis School was founded, the parish offered Sunday school classes where they received some instruction. In these early years, the community did the best they could to meet the needs of the African American parishioners, for there was little guidance from the Vatican or the American Catholic Church on this issue. By the 1880s, priests serving Newton Grove had greater clarity, as the Third Plenary Council in 1884 offered guidance for how to minister to African Americans. The Council called for the creation of an annual collection from each diocese to fund the evangelization of Native Americans and African Americans. Along with generating funds for this evangelization effort, it also spurred the founding of religious orders with a distinct mission to serve these communities. Recognizing white Catholics' own prejudices against African Americans and Native Americans, the Council insisted that the church set up separate parishes and schools for racial minorities.[57]

As an interracial, internally segregated parish by local design, it ran counter to the Catholic Church's developing missionary program. By the end of the 1890s, Father Edward, OSB, the parish's first resident priest, reached out to orders interested missionizing to African Americans, orders that had formed in response to the Baltimore council's call for outreach. He hoped that the orders' funds, earmarked for this missionary work, could be used to support both the white and Black members of his rapidly growing parish in Newton Grove.

Father Edward found a receptive partner in Mother (now Saint) Katharine Drexel, a nun who had grown up in Philadelphia in a prominent and devout Catholic banking family.[58] As a child, Drexel had governesses, went to private schools, and enjoyed the finery and social niceties of Philadelphia's high society. Her family also ran a weekly Sunday school and food pantry for the poor. Upon her father's death, she received a large fortune that she used to continue her family's charitable work. But by 1889, she felt an even greater calling and decided to enter a Pittsburgh convent run by the Sisters of Mercy.[59]

Father Edward would have known Drexel by reputation as an enthusiastic promoter of Catholic missionary work in African American and Native American communities. Drexel traveled widely to Indian missions and read avidly about the massacre at Wounded Knee, which occurred while she was preparing to take her vows in Pittsburgh. Inspired and concerned, she decided to leave her order and found a new group, the all-white Sisters of the Blessed Sacrament.[60] Along with the usual commitment to poverty, chastity, and obedience, she added another vow: "to be the mother and servant of the Indian and Negro races according to the rule of the Sisters of the Blessed Sacrament; and not to undertake any work which would lead to the neglect or abandonment of the Indian and Colored races."[61] At a time when the interracial parishes in New Orleans were being segregated through the building of Black parishes, Father Edward found an enthusiastic patron in Drexel, who wanted to use the Sisters of the Blessed Sacrament as a way to donate her inheritance to support education and evangelization for African Americans. Over her lifetime, Drexel donated $20 million to Catholic schools including, at Father Edward's urging, several grants to St. Mark's. Her first of many donations to St. Mark's came in 1900 to support the Black Catholics in the parish. Over the course of the next twenty-seven years, Katharine Drexel and the Sisters of the Blessed Sacrament donated over $10,000 to the parish.

Donations from Sisters of the Blessed Sacrament came with the condition that African American and white parishioners have equal access to the sacrament of the Eucharist, by which she meant that African Americans must sit on the main level with their white coreligionists in seats that were equally close to the sacrament, not set off in the back of the church, in a balcony, or far to the side. At St. Mark's, for example, she helped fund a remodel of the church that would allow African American parishioners to sit in the small row of pews that ran down the left-hand side of the sanctuary. The white families could sit in either the middle row of pews or along the right-hand side of the church. At Mass, as one older parishioner recalled, "all the Black families sat on the left side and the white people sat on both the middle and right sides [of the sanctuary]. . . . The Robinsons would sit in first [pew] on the left side, and then the Coles behind them, and then I think behind us, the Monks, sometimes the Royals and this family whose last name was Cox. Similarly, in the white pews, the Godwins sat in the front pew, while the Smiths sat a few pews behind."[62] Here, segregated seating meant sitting side-by-side, in full view of each other and of the altar. North Carolina law prohibited creating similar spaces where Black and white school children could learn under the same roof. Where possible, however, Katharine Drexel expected equal access and biracial, if not truly interracial, activity. For the first time in the parish's history its interactions were being directed in part by someone within the Catholic hierarchy instead of a descendant of John Carr Monk.

The parish gave up their autonomy for Drexel's financial support, support that enabled the parish to grow into what fellow North Carolinians would call the "Catholic City." This period of parish building officially began in 1904 with the arrival of Father Michael Irwin. Nearly twenty years after John Carr's death in 1877, the parishioners would find themselves in constant negotiation with their Protestant neighbors, their clergy, and the Sisters of the Blessed Sacrament as they tried to maintain their racially unified, internally segregated Catholic Church amidst the expected religious and racial norms.

CHAPTER THREE

The Delicate Dance of Rural Catholicism in the Protestant South

1899–1926

From its beginning, the parish's mere existence threatened Southern racial and religious norms. As the parish grew, bringing in new members and even attracting Protestant children to its new schools, so did the perceived menace in the minds of many white Protestant adults. One night in 1918, the white girls sleeping in their dormitory on the second floor of the convent awoke to a commotion outside. They peered down from the windows onto a group of Klansmen on horseback with guns drawn. The nuns quickly ordered the terrified girls under the beds. The priest appeared at the scene with a shotgun as the threats continued. Some children slipped from their hiding spots, their curiosity getting the better of their fear and the nuns' command. But the men menacing their school were not anonymous, despite their white sheets. The girls recognized the shoes of their Protestant uncles poking out. "Is that you Uncle Joe?" one girl called out.[1] Others followed, also calling out to their relatives by name. With the element of anonymity destroyed, the hostile group retreated.

St. Mark's managed to avoid violence that night, and the children's terror gradually eased. But Newton Grove's Catholics knew it was a brief reprieve. The threat of white violence, even from relatives, persisted. The parishioners, both Black and white, chose one side of their family and a shared faith over their designated racial classification and the kin who chose to abide by regional norms. Such a decision, they knew, would have consequences. As the parish grew from a small group of converts to a campus with dormitories for boarding students, the parish also learned to be vigilant about the local rules of segregation and ever mindful that the next group of Klansmen might shoot first.

One year after this incident, the American Catholic hierarchy would once again have to address the question of how to nurture Black Catholics. The statement that resulted from their 1919 meeting denounced "all attempts at stirring up racial hatred." The Catholics of Newton Grove were working to maintain their interracial community in a moment when race relations were so violent and volatile that the Vatican requested that the US bishops call for an end to lynching in America.² This chapter explores how the parish attempted to negotiate local attitudes towards race using the theological and financial resources of the Catholic Church as it tried to build—tenuously and always under threat—its own version of a racially inclusive community. They had new resources at their disposal, including the priests and nuns who even took up arms to defend their Catholic charges that night on the church lawn. But the presence of ordained clergy was a mixed blessing, for the parishioners now had to confront the policies of the Catholic clergy more directly, including some new rules and teachings from their resident priest, Father Michael A. Irwin, as well as demands from afar in the form of the expectations of Katharine Drexel and other donors. These outside voices, from those both within and without the Catholic hierarchy, had their own ideas about how the parish should enact its vision of unity, expectations which often conflicted with the parish's efforts to maintain its interracial identity while conforming to local segregationist norms. Unlike in the Northeast and Midwest where segregated neighborhoods justified racially homogenous parishes, obscuring the influence of white supremacy in parish life, St. Mark's had to confront regional and national racial mores daily and directly when deciding where to build a school when to begin the school year, and on what occasions the parish's pupils could gather across racial lines. Transgressing the boundaries of these mores meant that hostility and violence against individual parishioners or the community was always a possibility.

Despite these constant fears, the parish did more than persist. It continued to grow. This chapter also explores how Catholicism gave the parishioners distinctive tools—tools their Protestant neighbors did not have—to navigate the rural South's post–Civil War segregationist society. In Newton Grove some townspeople welcomed the church and the opportunities it offered to worship with household members across racial lines along with the consistent educational opportunities for their children, including financial support for high school and college degrees. Instead of resisting the new religious identity brought by Catholicism, these Newton Grove residents welcomed it. They infused their Catholic identity with St. Mark's own Southern style, partly because the latter was their commonsense way of life but also so that the parish could survive. Although these parishioners found a fragile peace within the Newton Grove community, the parish constantly feared that non-Catholics might breach this accord. They worried that the regional or national moods toward race relations might shift, just as they worried about random acts of violence from outsiders passing through town. This constant sense of dread, however, did not cause the Catholic community to cower.

Together they sought to rear their children to be faithful and dedicated Catholics, who understood their faith bound them to their Black and white coreligionists both. This chapter ends by exploring two case studies: Beatrice Cox and her quest for education beyond St. Francis's school and Dolores Jackson's efforts to join the Dominican Sisters. Conforming to certain racial norms of the broader Newton Grove community helped assure their neighbors that, although they were modeling an alternative communal structure for worship, they were not threatening the broader dictates of white supremacy that governed life outside the parish.[3]

A New Catholic Inheritance: Education and Infrastructure

After more than two decades of itinerant pastors, including Father Thomas Fredrick Price, the first native North Carolinian to be ordained into the priesthood, the parish finally welcomed its first resident priest in 1899. Father Edward Meyer, OSB, offered consistent pastoral guidance that the parish had never had before. At the same time, Meyer clashed with members over practices that differed from Catholic norms. He wrote to Katharine Drexel, who had helped him in his previous missionary efforts to African Americans, that parishioners gave him an enthusiastic welcome. "Both colored and white seem to be jubilant," he gushed, "because they have a resident priest. I also think that the colored people here are very different from those in towns and cities." What he meant by this difference is unclear, but perhaps it was the openness to Catholicism that he found striking, for he added, "My first visit was to a poor colored woman who is dying with consumption. She is a Baptist, but I hope I can receive her into the church before death."[4] The parish's welcoming attitude toward the neighboring community—including forms of reciprocity that pushed conventional boundaries of Catholic belonging—offered Meyer new opportunities to minister to Protestants and African Americans.

At the same time that St. Mark's was welcoming new converts in Newton Grove, Father O'Rourke, SJ, a visiting Jesuit priest, described how racial divisions, combined with the region's overwhelming anti-Catholic sentiment, thwarted all missionary efforts in North Carolina. In his 1905 letter to his community in Woodstock, New York, he explained, "Time and again when non-Catholic missions were held for the white people, and the negro was admitted, the whites immediately left the church and refused to attend the lectures. The only means of getting a hearing for the truths of faith from the white people of North Carolina is to exclude the Blacks."[5] Given this context, unbeknownst to the growing Catholic community in Newton Grove, the prevailing wisdom was to create separate missions for Black and white Catholics in the state. And yet, in just a few years, the interracial, if internally segregated, St. Mark's flourished with over 200 white Catholics and 80 Black Catholics worshipping in the same church each Sunday. Moreover, the parish continued to grow.

As he helped nurture the parish, Father Edward ventured into territory—both physical and pastoral—far beyond Father O'Rourke's focus on telling parish members about the truths of the faith. He had begun soliciting Katharine Drexel's help to missionize to Black Catholics in North Carolina and Virginia in 1897, just six years after she founded her religious order and the year after *Plessy v. Ferguson* deemed segregation constitutional. He wrote Katharine Drexel in 1900 to discuss the $1,500 that she had sent to him for a rectory and Black school at St. Mark's, telling her, "There are a few model Catholic families (colored) here and this helps the cause very much."[6] Within this context, it's clear that these model Black parishioners not only went to weekly Mass but also supported the parish financially. Many parishioners, both white and Black, supported the parish through labor or in-kind trades. In contrast, the Black Catholics whom Father Edward knew had money and, most likely, land and genealogical ties that united them with the founding Monk family. They made the parish stand out, at least in the eyes of outside supporters like Drexel. It may have been this local Black financial support as well as the deep connection that the Black community had to the parish that helped keep Katharine Drexel donating.

Father Edward used Drexel's money to start Newton Grove's African American parochial school, which was the only private educational institution of its kind in Sampson County.[7] Although Sampson County had twelve private schools for white children, the closest one for Black students was about ten miles away. None of these schools had the geographic reach of a parish school where children might come to board from as far as fifty miles away.[8] By the early 1900s, when the schools associated with St. Mark's parish were getting established, there was no uniform public schooling in North Carolina for either its white or Black children, and most religious schooling taught only basic skills and Bible lessons. While the parish met the state requirements of segregated schools by having the two separate buildings on the same land, they were supported by the same single parish, St. Mark's.

Five years after the school began, Father Edward and the Bishop decided to seek out religious sisters to teach at the schools. Soon they negotiated with the Dominican Sisters of the Holy Rosary, a white order based in Newburgh, New York, to provide nuns for the Newton Grove parish. At St. Mark's white nuns would be teaching both the Black and white children. He might have chosen differently and invited the Oblate Sisters of Baltimore or another segregated Black order to run the parish schools. This would have aligned more closely with local custom of having Black teachers for Black students, but it would have put him at odds with the local community.[9]

The white community in Newton Grove would accept a white teacher for its white children but certainly not a Black teacher, even if she were a nun. That being the case, Father Edward, in fact, had no other choice if the parish schools were to thrive. Black families had to accept white teachers, whatever their desires might have been; their children would not have an education otherwise. The choice of the all-white Dominican order, then, maintained the regional norm of white leadership over Black communities, but it was not a comfortable fit. The parish's interracial structure, even with its internal segregation, was not only at odds with the surrounding community, but it was also at odds with the norms of the American Catholic Church, where schools, religious orders, and parishes were implicitly, if not explicitly, segregated. With a framework of parishes rooted in geography, white urban parishes were de facto segregated because of racially homogenous neighborhoods that resulted from lending practices and redlining, like most urban parishes in this period. Black parishes, by contrast, were explicitly created as racial parishes where religious orders with a specific mission to African Americans could pastor. These structural barriers kept the church from modeling the kind of unity that John Carr Monk sought. They also made it difficult for the Catholic hierarchy to minister to the parish founded on that principle; neither the nuns in the schools nor the priests on the altar had experience with this kind of interracial community.

Father Michael A. Irwin, who administered the parish from 1904 through 1928, built the infrastructure to support what many in the area called the "Catholic City" of Newton Grove, completing twenty-two major building projects in his twenty-four-year pastorate. Coming from the Vicariate-Apostolic of North Carolina, Father Irwin understood that creating Catholic institutions with impressive buildings sent a message to onlookers about the strength and stability of the parish and, by extension, the American Catholic Church. He fit the parish-builder model of the priesthood that was gaining steam across North America during this period. Under his leadership, Newton Grove's Catholic parish was transformed from an unremarkable rural space of undifferentiated cotton and cornfields into a visually Catholic place through the erecting of stone statues of Mary and the creation of St. Mark's Parochial School with its attendant dormitory and convent. Slowly, the neighbors began to adjust to a Catholic vocabulary for these buildings. They learned a convent was where nuns lived. A shrine was for Mary's statue. A rectory housed the priests. As with the parishes in the Northeast and Midwest, this "brick and mortar" period served to announce a Catholic presence to neighboring Protestants, but much more importantly, it demonstrated to all North Carolina's Catholics that the tradition had a firm, stable footing in the state. As it did so, it infused the area with the sacred. Saints' names and visible markers like steeples projected sacredness and permanency for this newly founded community and effected an important shift from the parish's precarious early years in which parishioners faced the threat of violence when they were not overseeing the parish's day-to-day workings.[10]

Born in Virginia, Michael A. Irwin was a lifelong Catholic, yet his views were shaped as much by American politics as by the global Catholic Church. He began his working life as a secretary for a member of the US House of Representatives ten years before deciding to join the priesthood. He left his job because his views as a Southern Democrat conflicted with his congressman's staunch Republican positions.[11] Ordained at Belmont Abbey near Charlotte at age twenty-eight, Father Irwin cut his teeth setting up Catholic institutions. He worked alongside Father Fredrick Price, who would cofound the Catholic Foreign Mission Society of America, better known as the Maryknoll Fathers, building mission chapels, schools, a rectory, and other institutions to support North Carolina's Catholics. In 1904, the archbishop named him the full-time resident pastor of St. Mark's parish, where he quickly put this experience to use.

As pastor he used the fundraising skills that he had learned under Father Price to reach out to prominent Catholic philanthropists. In 1911, he wrote an extended essay in a fundraising journal dramatizing his little outpost parish's struggles and successes, hoping that his story would tug at the heartstrings of influential Catholic donors. "This spiritual darkness is at its greatest in North Carolina, and that too among a people who are in many other respects intelligent and well-meaning. Here, I mean to refer only to their ignorance of our holy religion. No Christian knows less about Catholicity than our Southern people, but when won and thoroughly instructed no one makes better Catholics."[12] In keeping with the First Plenary Council of Baltimore's 1852 recommendation that every parish have its own school, Father Irwin immediately set about stabilizing the parish school so that he could form Newton Grove's children into strong Catholics.[13]

St. Mark's School building. During the Depression this building was rented out and classes were held in the church. Courtesy of Our Lady of Guadalupe Parish.

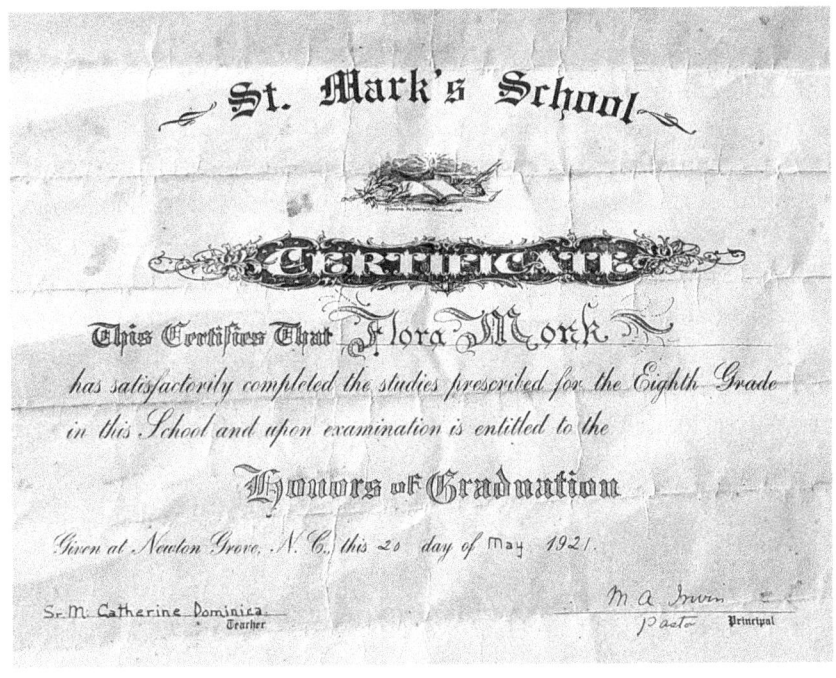

Diploma from St. Mark's School. Courtesy of Our Lady of Guadalupe Parish.

Since North Carolina's Constitution mandated segregated education, Father Irwin would need two school buildings on his property.[14] Building a school for African American students set the parish apart from most other white-run institutions and Christian communities in the South. Government and church groups rarely attended to the educational needs of Black children, in part because they wanted their limited resources to benefit white children. They also harbored economic anxieties that education would encourage African American youth to seek work outside of farming and other forms of manual labor. Undaunted by these prejudices and fears, Father Irwin set himself to the challenge of finding double the funds so that he could buy an extra set of everything, from the buildings on down to the pencils—one for the white school and one for the Black.

As soon as Father Irwin took control of the parish, he began searching for a white schoolteacher for the white Catholic school that John Carr Monk had founded. He followed that search with one for a Black schoolteacher. Across this rural county, parents needed a school nearby or one with boarding capacity (which Newton Grove would soon have for white students) to educate the children. He, like the bishops in Baltimore, recognized that a school would serve to anchor the parish and protect Catholic children from the anti-Catholic sentiment widespread in the nation's public school system. Providing for all of Newton Grove's children, both Protestant and Catholic, would give the parish a way to introduce itself to the community by helping its children rather than converting citizens.

With the nuns' arrival in 1907, Father Irwin could also shift St. Francis's School for African American students from a lay teacher to women religious. Sister Josita Cavagnaro, OP, an Italian American nun from East Rutherford, New Jersey, took charge of the Black school and eventually its dormitory. She remained their primary teacher and dorm mother for fifteen years. Her letters mostly deal with the mundane but occasionally also reveal poignant yearnings. For instance, in one letter home she asked her mother to send ten pounds of spaghetti, one pound of dried mushrooms, and one gallon of olive oil—"the real Italian kind." Filling this list would both stock the pantry and help with her homesickness. North Carolina offered none of these familiar flavors. In the culinary realm, like all others, Newton Grove was a distant and strange land for Sister Josita and the other Dominican sisters. Although her young boarders brought their own food for the week, even seeing, and perhaps smelling and tasting, such exotic ingredients would have opened new worlds of possibilities for her students. After a big snowstorm, she reported to her family in New York: "I had a ride on a homemade sled with 3 seats drawn by two mules. Just think of it!"[15] As she brought new experiences into the children's lives, they did the same for her, teaching her how to sled, country style. She balanced her desire for adventure with her desire for her students to have a complete and current education.

Sister Josita's students at St. Francis's seemed to have felt her concern and connected to her personally. A few later named their own children in her honor, as did some of the white pupils at St. Mark's School. One of her pupils, Mamie Robinson, recalled decades later that she had the special privilege to introduce Sister Josita to the town: "Two or three times a week [Mamie] walked five miles [from her family's farm] to Newton Grove where she took Sister out in Father Irwin's horse and buggy through the country (causing a great deal of excitement because the people had never seen a nun. . . . And to see a fourteen-year-old girl and a nun flying around the countryside driving a bay horse and buggy was really something!)"[16] The parish gave Mamie, who relatives described as a "force of nature," the important, if potentially dangerous, task of acting as a liaison between Sister Josita and the community. This young African American girl would likely have had to endure the stares and taunts of white townspeople as the buggy drove by. She might have also heard exclamations of disgust, confusion, or surprise from Black community members.

Sister Josita, the city girl from East Rutherford, may well have experienced the same surprise while getting to know the unfamiliar culture of Newton Grove where she was tasked with such things as feeding chickens. Her letters and the stories show that she took differences in stride, even when others' shock turned into apprehension. When Dominican Sisters arrived in their full habits, it might have announced that the parish was here to stay, but it also announced to the broader Protestant community that Catholicism was something foreign, something very different indeed.

Fear of this difference did not subside easily. In 1908 the parish hosted two Christmas tree parties: one to which all white people were invited and a second in front of St. Francis's School "for the Colored people to which all are invited."[17] Here the parish sought to build community among the white and the Black societies of Newton Grove without offending the community norm of segregation or causing friction among the parishioners, who seem to have abided by a rule that all nonliturgical events would be separated by race. Three years later Father Irwin reported to Mother Drexel: "We are flourishing here, but have been going through a period of persecution for several years past. The coming of the Sisters 6½ years ago aroused the latent bigotry of the backwoods people and particularly because one of them [Sister Josita], a white

Sister Josita with the chickens. Courtesy of Our Lady of Guadalupe Parish.

woman, volunteered to teach the colored [children]."¹⁸ But fear was also a fundraising opportunity. He concluded the report with an appeal to Drexel to help him buy a neighboring farm for an African American boarding school.

It was not an easy ask. Father Irwin, again, tried to persuade Drexel to make an exception to her integrationist principles. Integration was not the only way to help Black Catholics, he insisted, and in fact, it would put the Newton Grove parish at risk. He offered her an acceptable but inexpensive alternative proposal: to build a boarding house for Black students. "I intended it to be a plan to board girls principally—and *small* boys—not large ones."¹⁹ While Father Irwin might have hoped to educate all African American boys, he knew that such action would endanger the students, their white house mother, and the whole Catholic parish. Here again he sought to manage this interracial parish within the framework of the segregated South, not to overturn that structure. In a truth so widespread that it remained unspoken, their neighbors believed that such arrangements went against God by inviting interracial romantic relationships or, worse, rape. Within the framework of Southern segregation, the separation of white women from Black men, even Black boys, was essential.

Realizing that Katharine Drexel might put her principles over the practical realities of maintaining a biracial parish, Father Irwin included, "Only yesterday a highly respectable colored man told me he would send his children to our school if they had any place to board . . . There is a very high prejudice against our Sister Josita, who teaches the Colored school, and even if I had sisters to take charge of more colored work, I could not let them sleep out among the blacks for some considerable time and owing to the danger of total ruin to the white school following such a course. I am between the devil and the deep sea."[20] Such action would end both schools, for these were not two separate communities, but one. So, a transgression like having white nuns care for Black boarding students would threaten the entire parish, including the white parishioners.

Father Irwin called on Drexel's reasonable side. She might have been able to push the boundaries in her hometown of Philadelphia, but in a rural community like Newton Grove, governed by segregation and populated primarily by Protestants, a single white woman in nun's habit who taught African American children was vulnerable. And, to be sure, the young people she cared for were at terrible risk. The community had experienced what happened when these tensions turned into action, like when the "night riders," threatened the white schoolgirls who boarded on the convents' second floor, the event that began this chapter.[21] Father Irwin was not the only member of the parish who found himself between the "devil and the deep blue sea." The reality of aligning themselves with a church that stood against strict segregation meant that all parishioners had to watch their step. They passed the stories about the "night riders" on to their children to ensure that the next generation would remember to follow the spoken and unspoken racial rules for the community to insure the parish's survival.

MAINTAINING TWO SCHOOLS with boarding facilities in a country parish became a constant financial challenge. Newton Grove's rural economy was cash poor, so it quickly became community practice to pay tuition and parish offerings in kind. Sister Josita reported, in shock, about the unfamiliar kinds of payment she began receiving after taking up teaching in Newton Grove: "Tuition is paid in foodstuffs, and harvest time usually finds the good Sisters with a surplus of whatever is then in season. Farmers drop in with their contributions of sweet potatoes, etc., and at 'hog-killing time,' of pork, until the Sisters are often at a loss to know what disposition to make of them."[22] The nuns insisted on cash for their salaries, which posed a problem for the parish. Some months they went without pay, relying on whatever Sister Josita received from Mother Drexel's foundation, which often provided their only cash resources. The sisters often went without, since Sister Josita had to split these donations between her compatriots and the buying of school necessities for the African American children. Drexel's archives include appeals from Sister Josita for new textbooks and then for new editions several years later, both of which Drexel provided.[23]

Since the white children of St. Mark's received their books on a regular schedule from the diocese, not from Drexel's order, there was no need to write special appeals, so no records remain of these exchanges. Did some of the books Sister Josita acquired for the African American St. Francis's School end up in the desks of the white students at St. Mark's? It is difficult to know. This practice would have reversed the flow of resources that emerged once segregated public schools in North Carolina were established a decade later, in 1917, only to largely be put on hold during the Depression.[24] It's reasonable to expect that the schools did trade books since, although they were housed in separate buildings and segregated, they shared personnel as well as other resources. Like in other aspects of the parish, there was an element of John Carr's Catholic ideal within the system that remained hidden from outsiders.

The two Catholic schools that Father Irwin maintained for the parish to address the community norms of segregation were key to drawing families, Protestant and Catholic and Black and white alike, to the parish. Seven years into his tenure in 1911, Father Irwin reported that the parish had grown to serve four hundred white Catholics and sixty Black Catholics. The parish, which drew parishioners from neighboring counties as well as the town, was now nearly six times bigger than Newton Grove, which posted just seventy-three inhabitants in the 1910 census.[25] In fundraising appeals and other profiles describing his work, Irwin emphasized the schools' religious and intellectual curricula. "Besides a solid English course, Latin grammar, vocal and instrumental music are also taught. The school children constitute the choir of the church and are able to render in good style in Gregorian chant including the Requiem Mass with all its parts." Few white schools in the area could claim to teach Latin or to prepare children to do more than excel in their assigned roles on the farm. Not only was the education superior, but Father Irwin was also quick to note that "the school entertainments are the wonder of the country around and invariably draw non-Catholics in large numbers."[26] Father Irwin leveraged his connections outside the region to bring in movie projectors for curious crowds of townspeople as well as plays performed by touring theater companies.

By the 1920s, Father Irwin wrote an essay expressing his pride at the parish's thriving schools. The boarding school facilities, which he called the "Dormitories," had transformed a modest Newton Grove community of converts into a strong Catholic parish: "Having half of the children of the parish here with us at the Dormitories for five days each week, the other half walking to school from their homes, we are able to do things that are found difficult even in large parishes." With the two boarding schools, the parish could offer the children a truly immersive Catholic experience as they ate, slept, learned, and played alongside the priests and nuns. While allowing for constant modeling of proper Catholic behavior, this boarding arrangement also insulated the children from the daily influences, questions, and slights of Protestant family members and neighbors.

In his essay, Father Irwin went on to highlight how the parochial schools gave both Black and white children the same opportunities as Catholic children elsewhere. He described how they were enmeshed in Catholic liturgical time, participating in the weekly High Mass, regular religious festivals, and processions during Holy Week. He concluded, "The generation now advancing toward manhood and womanhood is indistinguishable from the best Catholics anywhere in their manners."[27] Newton Grove, he believed, was a credit to the South and its tradition. The children, in particular, were growing well suited to become emissaries, if not missionaries, to others of their race and in their region.

Individual Flourishing as Catholic Mission

As children born into the parish ("cradle Catholics") came into adulthood in Newton Grove, particularly the children of the founding families, Father Irwin and others tried to give them a leg up with their outside Catholic connections. Irwin placed young children in Catholic orphanages if their families couldn't care for them. Young adults he got into convents and seminaries if they felt called to Catholic ministry. Still others went on to colleges and universities after graduating from the parish's parochial schools. While there were many universities and colleges nearby, schools like North Carolina State, which provided agricultural and engineering education, only admitted white students until the 1950s. Most institutions of higher education available to African Americans were normal schools that prepared students for teaching careers.

In August 1927, for example, Father Irwin wrote to the bishop to find a place for two orphaned white girls from the Sutton family. The girls were descendants of Enoch Godwin, one of John Carr Monk's good friends. Enoch was also the father-in-law of J. T. Gregory who converted during Cardinal Gibbons's first visit to Newton Grove in 1872. Father Irwin wrote a letter of recommendation to the Sisters of Mercy requesting that they make space for the younger girl at the Catholic orphanage in Belmont, North Carolina. The Bishop also went to St. Mary's Industrial School during a trip to Baltimore, Maryland, to entreat them to offer her older sister a scholarship.[28] The priests' connections with Catholic institutions beyond the parish helped him find stability and at times advanced education for the children, just as it provided financial resources for the parish far beyond what the local population could give.

Amelia, a white woman in her mid-eighties, recounted that her mother, Jane, came from a small town nearly fifty miles away from Newton Grove to attend the parish school because it would place her in a network of Catholic educational institutions that offered advanced training beyond what could be found in her town. Jane's five younger siblings joined her when they became of school age. Amelia explained, "They didn't have the schools down there [in that small town] like they had here. So, she came here and went to school, and then when she finished school in Newton Grove, she . . . went over to church [to ask what to do next]. They sent her to Belmont. So, she, actually, went there to school. She got a pretty good education there."[29] While other students might have ended their formal education, Amelia's mother continued on. Not only that, but Amelia also proudly told me that her mother excelled at Sacred Heart Academy in Belmont, a secondary and finishing school run by the Sisters of Mercy. In fact, Jane's Newton Grove teachers had set her up for success with a strong recommendation to the Belmont teachers, who were familiar with Newton Grove because they belonged to the same religious order that staffed St. Mark's. Just as involvement in the parish led some young women like Sister Julia to take religious vows, it allowed others like Jane to pursue secondary education.

Amelia's reference to Jane's "pretty good education" was much more than most young people outside the parish could hope for. Amelia's father, she recalled, "was a little bit envious of her being able to go to school over there," and Amelia remembered sadly that it had caused tension in the family. Amelia's father's education had ended with his graduation from the parochial school, while his wife had taken advantage of these unprecedented opportunities. The snide comments he made throughout their marriage, she said, revealed his jealousy.

However, he seemed to find some solace in the fact that he and his wife remained solidly rooted in Newton Grove. After all, even after attending high school and more, Jane had returned to marry, raise her children on her husband's family farm, and attend the family parish. Like Jane, most students would have had few opportunities after eighth grade had they not had access to Catholic institutions outside of Newton Grove. White boys from the parish, however, also found their way to Belmont to attend the Benedictine Belmont Abbey College, which served North Carolina's Catholics as a combination monastery, junior college, and high school. By 1915, Black students in the parish had access to Xavier University in New Orleans. Katharine Drexel had founded Xavier to train Catholic school teachers. Even though many of these students would have returned to Newton Grove after finishing their schooling, not all of them did. The broader Catholic world provided the parish's young people, especially African American students, a productive life beyond the parish. Education offered not only a way up, but also a way out.

African American parishioner Beatrice Cox, who was described by those who knew her as exuding pride, self-confidence, and respectability, understood that the network of Catholic educational institutions offered her a path beyond St. Francis's School. With the support of her parents, particularly her mother, Beatrice was determined to make that network work for her. Her mother, Lula Monk Cox, Solomon and Martha Monk's daughter, became St. Francis's School's first teacher in 1900.[30] The five years with Lula at the helm was the only time in the school's history that the African American students were instructed by an African American teacher. Lula clearly passed her love of learning on to both her students and Beatrice.

When Beatrice turned six, she began attending St. Francis's School along with her mother and her many cousins. Beatrice and the other students learned and played together in a thoroughly Catholic space through their elementary and middle grades. After eight years of walking across the fields adjacent to the parish that her father both owned and worked to attend St. Francis's, Beatrice aspired for more. African American farming families like hers rarely had the resources to send their children to secondary school. They lacked the transportation needed to get from the farm to the classroom. Even more importantly perhaps, they needed the children's labor to keep the farm running. Education would need to happen in a more informal way, in the spaces in between work and through the agricultural tasks being done, not in a classroom, following a curriculum. Knowing the burden education placed on her family, after her graduation, Beatrice bravely asked Father Irwin and Bishop Hafey's financial assistance to continue her studies. She hoped to attend the Institute of St. Francis de Sales, a Sisters of the Blessed Sacrament boarding school for African American girls in Rock Castle, Virginia. Although her letter to the bishop was lost, she clearly made an impression on him by reminding him of her accomplishments at St. Francis's and her ability to act as a positive ambassador for the faith going forward. The bishop lost no time writing to the Sisters on her behalf. When Beatrice received her acceptance to the Institute, Mother Superior Julianna reached out to the bishop to ensure him that she and the other sisters would support Beatrice's drive and ambition: "We shall do all in our power to prepare Beatrice for her future vocation in life, and to make of her an ideal Catholic young lady."[31] The bishop sent $40 (just over $700 in 2024 dollars) for her first semester's tuition.

The fact that Beatrice went to the bishop demonstrates that the tuition was an unimaginable sum for her own family to pay. The family faced falling cotton and tobacco prices that plunged the state into a depression in the 1920s, a decade before the rest of the country joined it during the Great Depression. After Father Irwin left the parish, Beatrice continued to reach out to the bishop to ensure that he maintained his interest in her education. She wrote him frequently to thank him for his support and to keep him informed about her progress. In turn, he ensured that she received the education she wanted. "I wish you to assure Beatrice Cox," he reminded the Sisters, "that I will care for her tuition at Rock Castle during the coming year, as during the past. I feel that she is deserving of assistance and will be of valuable aid to the colored people in her section in the future."[32] Whether it was Beatrice's own devotion to the church, her heritage, her hard work, or a combination of the three that made Beatrice deserving, we don't know. Surely all three played a part, since the bishop offered this assistance neither to Amelia's father nor to many other children.

Before her final year, Beatrice reached out to thank the bishop for his help, but she also took a moment to promote her own success. "Last year I received the first honor medal for the highest average in the school," she wrote. "It is very pretty, and I was very tickled to get it. And I often think about it was all due to you."[33] In 1931, Beatrice asked Bishop Hafey to fund the next step of her education at the State Normal School in Fayetteville. He agreed to contribute $100 a year until she earned her degree. Her parents, she assured him, were "going to try to bear the rest of my expenses."³⁴ Again she graduated with "the highest average during [her] two-year course" of study. She told Bishop Hafey that "being the only Catholic girl in my class made me feel that I should do all in my power to do my best and stand ahead if I could." Beatrice clearly fulfilled the bishop's, as well as her own, desire that she show the Protestant teachers and students how high achieving Catholics could be. She had become a model Catholic woman, infusing all the actions in her life with her devotion to the church.

In her graduation letter to the bishop, she sought his advice about signing a contract to teach in Red Springs, about 200 miles from Newton Grove in central North Carolina. She wasn't sure if she would find a Catholic Church there. She wanted to be sure she could stay Catholic, especially since she had seen many leave Newton Grove only to stop attending Mass. "I could say my Mass prayers and go to Fayetteville on some weekends to Mass," she insisted. "I think our little parish has something to be thankful for."³⁵ Beatrice, like many African American parishioners of her generation from Newton Grove, never returned to her hometown. She stayed in Fayetteville where she taught elementary school and served as the corresponding secretary of its alumni association in 1943 and 1944.

But Beatrice did not abandon Newton Grove. Although she regularly attended St. Ann's parish, a historically African American parish in Fayetteville, she returned for her wedding to Harold Watkins in 1947. When Beatrice died in 2002, at the age of ninety-two, her family held her funeral at St. Ann's, the African American Catholic Church in Fayetteville, and a graveside service in Newton Grove. She is buried in the cemetery at her childhood parish alongside her mother, father, aunts, uncles, and cousins. Her gravestone, neatly carved out of white granite, is surrounded by the proud burial markers of the parish's first generation of Coxes, Coles, and Monks.³⁶ Beatrice's story is one of many African Americans who were immensely benefitted by the education provided by St. Mark's in Newton Grove despite the challenges imposed by segregation. Although they left Newton Grove to pursue opportunities elsewhere, like Beatrice, they never forgot the Newton Grove community and the Catholic church that nurtured them in their youth.

AT THE SAME TIME Bishop Hafey was placing his check for $40 into an envelope and mailing it to Virginia for Beatrice, Father Irwin was seeking to further Dolores Jackson's dreams to become one of the Dominican Sisters of Newburgh. Having been taught by these Sisters at the parish school in

Newton Grove, she applied to join this New York–based order. However, the Dominican Sisters were all white women, primarily German and Irish. Although the order never made its policy of segregation explicit, when Dolores applied to join the order was aiming to remain white.[37] One of nine children, whose parents converted after their older children began attending the parish school, Jackson grew up on a family farm in walking distance to St. Mark's and was a lifelong parish member. In the loopy teenage writing of her spiritual autobiography, Sister Dolores Jackson, OP, wrote upon joining the convent: "My mother took me over to the convent and Sister Josita placed me on the altar in the Sister's chapel. When she put me back in my mother's arms saying, 'Now, Mrs. Jackson, she belongs to us.' My conviction has always been that I received my vocation with my Baptism."[38] Dolores worked with Sister Josita on Saturdays cleaning the church grounds with her classmates. She recounts telling her mother as a middle schooler that she would "never commit a mortal sin," and as a teenager she even refused to dance. She was already thinking about her First Profession, the first step toward entering the order, and worried that even attempting the Charleston would give the strict Mother Superior a reason to block her at the convent's doors.

When Dolores did knock on the convent's door in 1927, it was not her actions but her race that almost derailed her plans. Upon her arrival at the convent in upstate New York, Mother Superior Blanche wrote to Father Irwin for assurance that the rumors that Dolores "has negro blood in her veins—on her mother's side" were false.[39] For if they were true, Dolores must leave the convent. Like the leaders of other American Orders, Mother Blanche enforced the code of white supremacy by keeping her order segregated and white, even though working with African American lay people was part of her order's mission.[40]

Father Irwin responded with an argument that is hard to read, even though it apparently convinced this northern Mother Superior who was very much concerned with racial purity:

> Ignore it and forget it and hush it up forever, I say, because one of the fruits of the coming of the son of God in human form was to lift up the poor from the dung hill and to place him with the princes of the people. Mother—it is possible that a pure and holy maiden who has not a moral but a social defect of only a 1/32 or at most 1/16 [African American blood]—should be unacceptable in an order of Religious

when she never has been unacceptable such in a Catholic School among proud Southerners?[41]

In other correspondence that found its way into the archive, Father Irwin does not use this language about "a social defect" and white purity. It's difficult to tell whether he was building common ground with the Mother Superior or if this rhetoric was part of his unarchived everyday conversations. No matter the strategy behind the statement, Father Irwin clearly knew, and perhaps accepted, the racial hierarchy of the day. Nonetheless, his response highlights that St. Mark's parish, even with its commitments to racial inclusion, still understood and worked to a large degree within the racial framework of the segregationist South. Father Irwin didn't challenge the racial context of the Mother Superior's argument: He took her premise in stride that there was something lesser or suspect about African American ancestry. Forty years after the start of the parish, racist elements of its biracial beginnings were already being hushed up to advance both individual and parish goals.

We can also gain insight into Dolores's place in the complexly integrated community of St. Mark's from the fact that Sister Josita placed Dolores on the altar in her baptism story. Since the conversation revolves around Dolores's unawareness of her African American heritage, she probably sat on the white side of the church. The older generation, however, probably knew about her interracial background. In such a small town, it would be nearly impossible for shifts in racial identity to go unnoticed. Father Irwin's coded discussion of Dolores's Black heritage acknowledged the racist "one drop rule": At that time, any fraction or amount of African American blood constituted one as Black. He insisted Dolores is "a pure and holy maiden," despite this "defect."

He leveraged the New York–based Mother Superior's sense of Northern superiority and enlightenment over the South. It was a strategic move to ensure that she would embrace Dolores, and indeed Father Irwin won the day. Dolores remained in the convent and achieved her dream: a high school diploma from the convent school, Mount Saint Mary's. Later, she matriculated to Villanova University. After spending a decade in the North, Sister Dolores was still, as Sister Jeanette Redmond stated in Jackson's funeral homily in 1985, "a southerner. She spoke with a drawl and professed a desire, coupled by the blessing of the Congregation, to serve the people of the South." For most of her fifty-nine years in religious life, Sister Dolores played cards with, read to, and in other ways ministered to her fellow Southern Catholics.[42] Sister Dolores knew the challenges of being a Southern Catholic and the importance of having a supportive community to help you navigate them.

Anti-Catholicism, Racism, and the Solidification of a Southern-Style Parish

This distinctive southern-style parish risked and at times even provoked the broader community's anti-Catholic prejudices. The threat level from white Protestants, particularly outsiders who were ignorant of local habits of cooperating across churches, ebbed and flowed over the decades. Despite such hostility, Father Irwin hatched ambitious plans to expand the parish's built footprint. As early as 1914, he began a funding campaign to support the expansion of St. Mark's. His first move was to approach Katharine Drexel, even though he knew she would only support the project if it benefitted the African American parishioners as well. The renovation, in his words, would create a "solid and permanent church that will seat twice as many (and twice as many colored too) as the present church."[43] Along with making room for more parishioners and demonstrating to onlookers that the parish was growing, the addition also improved the conditions for the white school children. For years the parish had raised cash by renting out the white students' school facilities for events while holding classes in the sanctuary. Low cash reserves were a constant problem in this cash-poor economy. Irwin included designs for a new cruciform building, highlighting how this expansion would provide the parish with a visible monument to Catholic pride and permanence, even as it also provided the congregation with space to grow.

As he completed this wood-and-stained-glass announcement of Catholicism's presence in the rural South, Father Irwin noted in other writings that anti-Catholic persecution in the area was increasing. No longer content to threaten nuns and publish offensive screeds, locals were now destroying property. "Nearly all the chapels have been attacked by some wicked people," he reported in a missionary appeal. "A favorite diversion would be to knock out the window lights [panes]."[44] These threats and acts of vandalism continued to grow as the anti-Catholic impulse in the state and the country took hold.

Despite the increasing fears, the priests worked to ensure that the parish could embody its religious and racial identity in its efforts to educate all children, but only by acknowledging the necessity to maintain the segregation demanded by the broader Newton Grove community. Surrounded by these threats, the parish had to find ways to uphold its biracial mission. Katharine Drexel had helped Father Irwin purchase two houses on a nearby plot of land for the African American school in 1911, greatly increasing educational access for Black students.[45] However, it also raised the ire of many white townsfolk. North Carolina would not mandate public education for Africans Americans for another two years. The state's rural public education system was limited in general, and those schools that did exist were severely underfunded. St. Francis's, with its professionally trained staff and classroom amenities, stood out and attracted attention. Some white folks in the community surely feared that an education at St. Francis's School would lead its African American students to outperform their white counterparts or question the rules of segregation or would simply provide the students with economic possibilities outside of farming and menial labor. Through St. Mark's School, the parish also provided excellent education opportunities for white students, and Father Irwin wisely did not restrict that education to Catholics. But Irwin and the parishioners were always working to maintain this precarious balance between goodwill and resentful anger.

Further, Father Irwin recognized that priests and donors from outside the South, like Katharine Drexel, were likely to underestimate the potentially lethal consequences of unsupervised school recess. The white children could play "before the convent gate," while the Black children played "in the priests' front yard." This segregation was important, as Father Irwin stated in his private note to the priests, but it was not something that he wanted publicized. "Tell this privately to teachers," he wrote in the priests' daily diary of events, keeping it out of public view. When he corresponded with Katharine Drexel or other donors, he never referred to the true menace that the priests felt doing even the most mundane tasks. Twenty-five years into his tenure at St. Mark's, Father Irwin knew what donors wanted to hear, just as he knew the boundaries of integration within which the parish had to operate to educate their students without raising the ire of the white community. The children could only play in the shadow of the separate church buildings and with the oversight of the priests and nuns. Handing over authority, even temporarily, to individuals who were ignorant of the tacit agreement between parish and community put everyone in peril, especially the African American children.

Dread ran like a throughline across multiple volumes of Father Irwin's house notes. Well into the 1920s, alongside banalities about lessons taught and meals served, he wrote panicked accounts about threats of white violence. He would not step away from Newton Grove without leaving strict warnings. "Tell teachers on no account to leave children in the schoolhouse or on the school grounds without the presence of a teacher," Father Irwin cautioned a priest who filled in while he was on vacation. "White children may play before the convent gate—waiting for teachers—Col. Children as usual in the priests' front yard. This is *important*.—Tell this privately to teachers."[46] Both in class and at play he was desperate to make sure the Black and white children would be segregated. This was key, in his view, to keeping the parish's part in the unwritten agreement it had negotiated with the white Protestant neighbors. Parish adults knew how risky it was to have a group of white children playing on the same property as Black children within sight of the road, where passersby from outside the community—whose children were not benefitting from the schools—might happen to glance over. The parishioners knew: Anyone could see. Anything could happen. Ensuring that the children were separated in play demonstrated to any potential vigilante that the parish was observing the rules of segregation. Even though they were Catholic and had both Black and white children playing nearby each other in public, the parish did not intend to court a white Protestant backlash by openly flaunting regional norms.

The looming threats to the parish made Father Irwin plead with increasing urgency for money to build a separate hall for Black parishioners. He planned to name the building for St. Benedict the Moor, the patron saint of African Americans. Of course, he also knew the title would mark the space as segregated and, in so doing, would thus designate St. Mark's as white. It was another act of outward compliance to lessen the likelihood of violence by outsiders. Internally, such a hall would mean that African Americans, whether Catholic or Protestant, could gather to deepen their bonds with each other, while in turn strengthening their connection to the parish and the church.

These changes could only improve Black attendance at Mass and at the parochial school to a limited degree, though. At this time, farming families across the region—including Black farmers—were struggling against an outside threat of another sort. By the end of 1922, Newton Grove farmers were panicked over a tiny gray boll weevil pest, newly spreading in the area. With its long snout that bored holes in unripened cotton buds (bolls) to lay eggs, the boll weevil was laying waste to the area's main cash crop.[47] In 1919, motorized gins had been spooling cotton from dawn to dusk all winter, but by 1929, production had declined so much that local farmers had barely a month's work to do after the November close of the harvest season. In those ten years in Sampson County where Newton Grove was located, production dropped from 35,326 bales to 29,109 bales.[48] This 18 percent drop of devastated farmers who were already barely surviving on thin profit margins. Black farmers, who were more likely to be sharecroppers in debt to white landowners, were hit especially hard and often struggled to pay the landowner the share he demanded. Starvation conditions spread across North Carolina. Landowners also felt the pinch when they had no crops to sell.[49] The parish felt these economic effects, too. Many parish families could no longer afford tuition, and others abandoned their weekly offerings as the economic depression of the 1930s came early to the rural South.

The financial crisis caused a rift between the parish and its Northern benefactors, including the order that supported the nun-teachers. In 1922, the sisters surprised Father Irwin when they refused to return from their summer retreat in New York. Sister Josita and two other sisters had been diagnosed with tuberculosis, and the remaining nuns complained of exhaustion and demanded rest and recuperation at home in their Newburgh convent. Upon seeing the sisters, particularly Sister Josita, so ill, the Mother Superior wrote a letter to Bishop Hafey announcing the removal of the Dominican sisters from Newton Grove. In it she blamed Father Irwin for not improving Newton Grove's harsh conditions. Sister Josita died shortly thereafter in September 1923.[50] Her death, combined with the Mother Superior's criticism, stung Father Irwin so badly that three years later, in a letter to the Mother Superior, he mentioned Sister Josita's previous complaints and took special care to rebut them one by one.

In the same year, he took his argument all the way to the bishop of Baltimore: "On the whole the health of those Sisters [crossed out words, illegible] who came here in ordinary condition was good. Sister Josita after 13 years of labor fell into a decline and died of T.B. in Hawthorne N.Y. [Sept. 1923] after 2 years of enforced rest. She was admirable in life and in death. Her devotion to Sister Norberta, O.P, [the Superior] undoubtedly hastened her end. She is the only one we have lost in 15 years out of a community of five or six some of whom were always delicate."[51] Certainly life in Newton Grove presented intense physical challenges. The South's summers were hot and humid, and the parish did struggle with rudimentary living conditions, not to mention the tense atmosphere of anti-Catholicism and white supremacy. Yet it's also true that Father Irwin tried to meet the sisters' needs, if only to keep his schools running.

Once the sisters did not return, Father Irwin had the difficult task of finding replacements. Their suffering in Newton Grove was now well known among other Catholic religious orders. His students were also being lured away by local public schools, as he told his bishop in a September 1922 letter: "Public school education may be somewhat innocuous in the cities; it is not so in the country. Around Newton Grove, within a ten-mile radius, there are several large public schools and high-schools recently erected. All of which are located near Protestant churches. In these schools, secular instruction is pretty good, but the spirit is anti-Catholic, and, in a few years, it would gravely hurt our children."[52] Many public schools' curricula reflected Protestant churches' anti-Catholic bias, if not their outright mission to convert Catholics to the "true faith." Father Irwin went on to grumble about increased access to public education in the state; infrastructural improvements, he noted, had also decreased the demand for his boarding schools. "Roads are now good," he complained, "and streams are spanned by concrete bridges."

The question of how to maintain a Catholic culture in Protestant North Carolina loomed large for Father Irwin as anti-Catholicism began reaching its peak. By 1925, Southern journalists frequently vented anti-Catholic spleen on newspaper front pages. These grievances were so harsh that Father Irwin felt moved to respond in print, writing lengthy letters to the editor to correct the authors' errors.[53] For example, in response to a visiting minister's two-column-length article in the *Sampson Independent*, entitled "Foreign Hordes Are Threatening American Ideals," the newspaper gave Father Irwin four entire pages for his reply, entitled "Rev. Irwin Sets Forth His Views."[54] Nearly fifty years after the parish's founding, community leaders still had to argue for Catholics' rightful place in the county.

TO HELP SUPPORT the African American community, Father Irwin argued tirelessly for funds to build St. Benedict Hall, which he imagined as a space for African Americans to gather on parish grounds. He developed multiple designs, each with different flourishes, such as a portico and tongue-and-groove shutters. In 1921, he wrote his diocesan bishop to explain his proposal for a space to seat 250.[55] This was almost five times the number of their Black parishioners then. Irwin pictured social gatherings like those offered to the white community: theatrical shows, parties, movies, and concerts. As time went on, Father Irwin increasingly filled his letters with frustration and desperation: "I have been waiting for five years to begin a colored church here," he told Drexel, "and cannot put the matter off much longer or the colored people are beginning to get beyond my control. Some are slipping away. They need social life—music, altar boys, and things for themselves, and these advantages cannot be had in a white church. I am going to try this year to do something for them, as there have been two priests . . . here now for several years and we could attend two churches without much trouble."[56] He openly discussed using St. Benedict's Hall as a church and even began using the terms interchangeably. Parishioners who heard such talk in the midst of the ongoing threats from outsiders must have thought that some form of segregation of church services was coming.

The concerns of the Black congregation took on new weight on holidays, when parishioners would be bringing non-Catholic family members to Mass. Despite the country's growing nativist, anti-Catholic fervor, Irwin reported that "on this Easter Sunday 1925 we had 600 automobiles and between 2,000 and 3,000 people who spent the day at the church."[57] Black and white parishioners were still coming to Irwin's Easter Mass, even though white parishioners were likely to sit in the pew with their Protestant family members. It was also difficult for nervous parishioners to escape the Protestant outsiders' gazes after Mass, for these white families stayed to while away entire afternoons at the festival celebrations.

In the mid-1920s, Father Irwin's requests to Katharine Drexel became less desperately focused on a meeting hall; he had found other funders who did not share Mother Drexel's commitment to integration. But just as significantly, Father Irwin had also bent to the segregationists' demands. He now felt that building more shared spaces would not serve African American parishioners, and he began leaning on other financial partners who were more amenable than Drexel to helping build spaces reserved for African Americans only. Even with this shift, he still insisted that the existing spaces at St. Mark's remain biracial. In 1922 he successfully arranged a gift of $1,500 from the Catholic Board of Colored Missions and combined those funds with money from Bishop Hafey and the St. Mark's general fund to finish construction on the long-awaited St. Benedict's Hall.[58]

In 1926, he requested Katharine Drexel's help in paying off the remaining debt that had been incurred to build the hall. He assured her that the hall "will not disturb in any manner the seats reserved in the Parish Church for the colored people. Those seats will only accommodate about 60 people. But the hall will be used for missions—Spring Festivals, plays, etc. for the whole race—for any who wish to come up to 500."[59] Yet in describing the hall, he also noted its usefulness as a church: "It has a floor, colonial pillars in front, a fine portico, a good handsome tower, all painted without and decorated within. The finishing touches are now being done on the pews and windows and on Dec. 12 when the Bishop comes it will be formally opened for the colored people who can use it as a hall—and occasionally as a church, especially for protracted meetings (the altar and the altar platform are marble)."[60] Father Irwin concluded that fighting to maintain a strong community, offering African Americans moments of joy and togetherness, outweighed the larger concerns about mitigating segregation so long as the tradition of interracial, albeit internally segregated, Mass attendance remained.

Father Irwin's recognition of the destructive effects of the constant discrimination faced by Black Catholics both inside and outside the church mirrored some of the concerns that led Thomas Wyatt Turner, biology professor at Harvard University, to found the Federated Colored Catholics (FCC) in 1924 for Black laity to push for more Black priests and representation in the church. While there is no evidence that Father Irwin encountered the group, like Turner, he clearly found the current approach to race lacking as he struggled to lead an interracial parish within the post–World War I Catholic and American context.[61] While the FCC argued for racial solidarity and racial justice in Catholic institutions of higher education, Father Irwin sought to encourage African American community and commitment to Catholicism in order to avoid losing parishioners to African American Protestant Churches through the creation of occasional separate Masses and celebrations in this hall.

On April 23, 1927, Katharine Drexel agreed to advance Father Irwin's requested donation of $2,000. The contract between Katharine Drexel's Sisters of the Blessed Sacrament and Bishop Hafey stated that the money was to be used for "St. Benedict's combination church and hall for a building to be used as a church or school for the colored of Newton Grove."[62] Although Mother Drexel usually required interracial attendance at Masses, here she helped fund a separate complex of church, school, and hall for Black Catholics only.

While it was not the kind of fully segregated, separate parish that Drexel abhorred, the design was far from her ideal of a shared church with equal access to the sacrament. Perhaps her agreement to this contract—and her willingness to compromise on her principles—was an unstated nod to the Third Plenary Council of Baltimore's insistence on separate racial parishes. She might also have felt pushed to agree to Father Irwin's terms because the building was already under construction. Whatever the reason, this funding created the conditions necessary for the parish's eventual segregation. Now the wider culture, the Catholic Church, the parish's own benefactor, their priest, and, clearly, some of its parishioners were willing to compromise on the founding generation's vision of a racially unified church in which his whole family could worship under one roof.

In Father Irwin's correspondence about the contract, he described a parish procession to celebrate the new hall: "A procession of the children of both the white and the colored schools chanted in approved style the litany of the saints. The procession wound around the white school and then went five hundred feet to the end of the church property around the colored Hall and School."[63] Through the procession, Father Irwin integrated the sanctification of this new segregated space by including all children, both of their schools, and all the saints, from Saint Joseph to Saint Benedict the Moor in the effort. In that letter he also talked of Masses at St. Benedict's Hall, crowing to his donors about "our four colored altar boys." "One is very Black but intelligent," he wrote. "The other three are of lighter color, but the Black boy is so genuine a negro and so good and intelligent that all love him."[64] This statement reveals not only Father Irwin's pride in his successful mission to bring young Black men into visible leadership positions, but also his fixation on skin color, racial hierarchies, and stereotypes that have long existed in the United States as the most visible benchmarks for enforcing segregation. He refers to the darker skinned boy as "Black but intelligent" and not "Black and intelligent," suggesting that his norm for a Black person was one of lesser intelligence. The racial categories used by Father Irwin become even clearer as he struggled to elevate this altar boy above some assumed norm for a "genuine a negro" by characterizing him as "so good and intelligent that all love him." Obsessively preoccupied with the ways that his donors were assessing his charges, Father Irwin was proud of St. Benedict's and its parishioners. A month later he wrote about the new meeting space, "The Hall, which can also be used for a church, will seat 400 people, and was dedicated by Bishop Hafey on Dec. 12 in the presence of a large gathering of colored people."[65] Four hundred Catholics gathered in North Carolina was a huge number, but four hundred Black Catholics would have been unheard of. For Father Irwin, filling the hall was clearly aspirational. While he understood the new space to be a purpose-oriented infrastructure—a testament to spreading the faith and improving his Black parishioners' lives—the broader community likely saw it as an affirmation of the wider political and social system of segregation, a Black church for Black people.

BY 1927, FATHER IRWIN, now more than sixty years old, had been loudly hinting to the bishop that he was too tired for the kind of work necessary to keep the Newton Grove Catholic community thriving. In his inquiry about transferring the leadership of the parish, Father Irwin reminded the bishop of all the time and care he had put into the parish and its people. "As these people are genuine North Carolinians who have been on the soil hereabouts for 200 years, I trust that their welfare will be as dear to your Lordship as the apple of your eye."[66] With so few priests in North Carolina, Bishop Hafey answered these pleas for a successor by writing to missionary orders around the country. He reached out to groups of priests whose charism, or distinctive vocation, included working with African Americans. Even though they had experience working with Black Catholics, the arrival of a new group of priests from the Redemptorist Order posed a threat to the original vision of an integrated parish, since these outsiders were unfamiliar with the parish's unique religious identity and practice. As members of the parish's founding generation died, the next cohort of cradle Catholics faced the challenge of explaining this identity to their new clerical leadership, even as powerful social and economic changes continued to buffet the broader Newton Grove community.

CHAPTER FOUR

Maintaining Unity Through Segregation?
1926–1952

St. Benedict's, the new church for African Americans, held its first Mass as a stand-alone parish with its own priest in 1939, sixty-five years after John Carr Monk initially sought out a priest to start an interracial parish. The priest's notes in the annual report are brief: "September 19, 1939, Church for the colored reopened after many years. Father Thos. Gummer in charge. Colored school repaired and painted."[1] The parishioners could only guess what caused this division. Was it a push from a bishop who favored segregated parishes? Or was this separate parish a delayed response to Father Irwin's pleas for an African American worship space? Or the will of the Redemptorists? The archives, however, make it clear. In the chancery's parish history of St. Benedict's, it states, "In 1939 after the letter of Pope XXII [*Sertum Laetitiae*] to the US Bishops urging Catholics to greater interest in the colored and in the long-talked-of project of a separate church for the colored was realized."[2] The parish, like many other African American parishes across the country was created as a response to the US bishops: "We confess that We feel a special paternal affection, which is certainly inspired of Heaven, for the Negro people dwelling among you . . . We therefore invoke an abundance of heavenly blessings and pray fruitful success for those whose generous zeal is devoted to their welfare."[3] Unlike in 1870, when John Carr Monk, then a Protestant, cast his vote against segregation, this decision was made in the Catholic way, by bishops and perhaps priests. Being part of this global church offered parishioners distinctive economic and social opportunities, but it also meant having less local control. The parish's structure, leadership, and, most important, its mission were determined in Raleigh or Richmond. Many of the biggest decisions about parish life would be made by bishops in these distant cities, men who would never have to experience the consequences of their decrees in everyday life.

Decades earlier, Drexel's integrationist principles found a receptive audience in Newton Grove, even if the alliance sometimes produced misunderstandings. However, by 1939, segregation was now the American church's official missionary method. The parishioners, priests, and sisters who supported the Catholic Church in Newton Grove would have to adjust accordingly. With the changes in personnel and the aging of the founding generation, it's unclear how many parishioners would have been aware that segregation went against the original vision for the parish.

The notes Father Gummer, C.Ss.R., made in preparation for the first official Mass at St. Benedict's on September 10, 1939, make no mention of its history; they simply begin, "Congratulate." The next bullet point was "Encourage attendance." These short notes give little sense of the atmosphere at Mass or of the thoughts of the attendees. The creation of St. Benedict's stretched to the breaking point the parish's original vision of Catholic unity as racial inclusivity. Simultaneously, however, it offered new opportunities for Black lay leadership as well as a degree of safety to members of both parishes. When the diocese created St. Benedict's parish, just a short walk from the original church, it also renamed St. Mark's to Holy Redeemer to signify that the Redemptorists had charge of the parish. Father Gummer did not appear to mention the Mass at the now all-white Holy Redeemer that day. Yet simply by knowing its new segregated status, we cannot assume that the parishioners were now following the racial norms of the Catholic Church in America. In less visible ways, it maintained elements of its firm understanding that its form of interracial worship was truly Catholic and God's will, the belief that its founders had stood up to defend.

How did a parish founded on unity become segregated, or, perhaps, how did the parish withstand the pressures of segregation and continue to hold its interracial, if internally segregated, worship for sixty years? And what finally forced the community to comply with local norms? Since its founding, St. Mark's was not an impermeable, power-free, equal space, but it was a sacred alternative to what has been perceived as the monolithic (Protestant) South.[4] Unlike in other public spaces in North Carolina, white parishioners and Black parishioners in Newton Grove crossed paths, were explicit about their spiritual kinship, and often still acknowledged their biological one. By the late 1920s, however, the community's identity was changing, a process sped up by the departure of Father Irwin. The Redemptorist Fathers out of Baltimore, whose mission is to "serve the poor and most spiritually abandoned," took over care for the parish in 1928, inaugurating a new era for the parish. They knew little of the founding generation and even less about how Father Irwin had struggled to serve an interracial parish. As the generations changed, Newton Grove's Catholic community now had to wrestle with weakening internal bonds, which allowed the norms of the Catholic Church to hold greater sway in the parish. In many ways the dynamics in the parish mirrored those occurring within the Federated Colored Catholics (FCC) in the late 1920s and early 1930s where different factions had different ideas about how to support the Black Catholic community. These debates led to divisions between its lay founder, African American Thomas Wyatt Turner, who sought a strong Black Catholic community, and Fathers John LaFarge and William Markoe, white Jesuit priests, who sought Catholic interracialism and founded The Catholic Interracial Council in 1934.[5] While the goal of the FCC was for racial solidarity with equal access to Catholic education for African Americans, the goal of The Catholic Interracial Council was to end Black parishes, uniting the races in worship as they were (at least theoretically) in the Body of Christ, the Universal Church. While these issues were primarily academic for LaFarge and Markoe, the Catholics of St. Mark's knew all too well how difficult it was to attempt such unity in a church and in an America that both overtly and covertly pushed for racial segregation at every turn.

In Newton Grove in the late 1920s and early 1930s, the African American parishioners and Father Irwin were beginning to wonder if the parish's current form of interracialism was working for them the way that it had for their parents and grandparents. The results in the parish, however, would be toward segregation, not bolstering interracialism. Although it's unclear whether the Redemptorist Fathers in Newton Grove were aware of the debates going on in the FCC, the parish itself would become key in the Catholic Interracial Council's arguments against segregation by the 1940s when Vincent S. Waters became Bishop of Raleigh.

As the diocese debated how to best support this interracial parish during the rise of anti-Catholicism through the 1930s, the Redemptorists and their parishioners faced mounting external and internal demands to capitulate to the segregated norms of Southern society. The priests and parishioners took concrete steps to explore how to maintain some aspects of the parish's interracial mission preparing for and responding to the now inevitable segregation of the parish. This chapter will demonstrate how the schools served as sites within which the community could experiment with different ways of forming a cohesive Catholic identity across racial and religious divides in rural North Carolina.

Northern Leadership Navigating External Pressures of the Protestant South

During his brief visit to Newton Grove in 1927, Brooklyn-born Father James Barron, C.Ss.R., was bemused and appalled in equal measure. Newton Grove, he wrote to his superior general, is "next to nowhere, with territory about twenty miles in four directions." The buildings that Father Irwin worked so hard to build, the newcomer priests dismissed as crude, rickety shacks. "Kerosene lamps are used in the house. The nearest telephone, I believe, is twenty miles away. Telegraph and railroad are at least that far away." He summed up his situation with a snide, if accurate, quip: "The Bishop says that it's a rural parish; I add rural, superlative degree, for I have been to Newton Grove."[6]

A year later, the first Redemptorist priest stationed at the parish, Father McQuaid, C.Ss.R., dubbed himself "the pioneer." The parishioners were drawn to his sense of humor, and he became a popular priest, although it's unlikely that he shared with them his discomfort about being in the South. Instead, he complained to his superiors that he and his confreres were out of their depths there. "Well, we'll probably venture to do our bit, but I don't know how Fathers used to New York, Boston, and other large cities, are going to adapt themselves to acres of cotton and tobacco."[7] Father McQuaid went on to describe the sweltering heat of a North Carolina summer in words that ring true to anyone who has spent time in the Piedmont: "Our bread becomes very molding very soon. The swamps moisten this atmosphere. According to the papers you are having hot weather. Down here, we are living in an inferno."[8] These letters home to urban Catholic priests conjure images of a remote mission parish. However, the Redemptorists, in their shock, betray no knowledge that they were joining a well-established community with a rich history. Where Fathers Barron and McQuaid saw simply a technologically deprived outpost, this community, this "Catholic City," was intertwined with, and heavily influenced by, the mores and social norms of the South in general and North Carolina in particular.

Learning the subtle mores of relations between the races would prove challenging for the priests. Father McQuaid would frequently send letters to his superior filled with sardonic comments highlighting how distinctly different Newton Grove was from the Brooklyn community of his youth. His ministry seemed to come with its own internal hecklers. His mockery of the South might have helped him survive his posting; it also might have caused him to dismiss some of the real concerns of his congregation. On January 19, 1928, the day the church was first illuminated with electric lights, he remarked, "Yankees take notice! General Lee's Birthday is a legal holiday in the South."[9] While celebrating General Robert E. Lee was jokeworthy to Father McQuaid, the holiday's existence should have alerted him to how the Confederacy was being valorized and re-remembered throughout the white South to support white heroism and supremacy in the past and the present.[10]

Without this deep context, Father McQuaid had the difficult task of helping the parish survive in its hostile environment. To do so, he had to learn how to navigate Newton Grove's shifting racial and religious norms, employing the tools that brought to reality the founding generation's original vision for the parish: Catholic connections and Southern hospitality. He would have to learn the subtleties of rural white supremacy, if he hoped to sustain his parish.

The work of folklorist and Sampson County resident Celia M. Benton from this period exposes the usually hidden subtleties of the white supremacist regime in this area. She wrote an oral history of corn shuckings held between 1900 and 1930, noting specifics like where to sit during a corn shucking or other outdoor event. "At corn shuckings in general," Benton described, "whites and blacks shared alike in the work, though this equality would not be carried over into the social sphere. . . . While they worked, everyone did his share, and the seating was without regard to race. When mealtime came, if it was served outdoors, they sat anywhere they chose." "Anywhere they chose" meant on the ground, on barrels, or on other makeshift outdoor seating, to eat with a plate in their laps. "If the weather was rainy or too cold," she continued, "the meal was eaten indoors where two tables were served: all the white men ate first . . . then the black men took their places."[11] Despite how much interracial comradery might have been had during the shucking, which often included drinking and singing through the night as folks worked, the people of Sampson County knew the limits. Black and white community members could work together and lounge on the grass on a farmer's lawn but could not sit at tables together. They could go to Mass together, if they did not sit next to one another in the pews or enjoy entertainment together at a formal picnic. Unlike Father Irwin who learned these practices alongside the parish founders as the practices developed, the Redemptorists had to rely on the community's second generation to show the way, a generation that knew little about how the parish's interracial relationships grew from plantation family ties.

Internal Demands to Alter John Carr Monk's Vision

Being a part of the parish and being seen as a rightful inheritor in John Carr's lineage likely gave one credibility in the eyes of all the members of the parish. Yet as the second generation of parishioners came into their own, these roots of social authority seemed to be shifting, leading to a conflict that not only reached North Carolina's bishop but also revealed the crumbling communal foundations of their biracial experiment. Within six years of the

Redemptorists' arrival, at least one African American woman, Mrs. Cora Robinson, reached out to Father Irwin in his new position. She wrote to express distress about the changes in the parish. He clearly took her concerns seriously. Perhaps feeling that the fragile interracial experiment might be ready to implode, he took the rather extraordinary step of sharing these concerns with the bishop. Although Father Irwin mentioned that he was including Mrs. Robinson's letter in his correspondence, it has not survived. When I asked her descendants if they might have the letter, they replied, "No, but it sounds just like her to be the spokesperson for the community."[12] According to Father Irwin's own report, Mrs. Robinson "knows her rights and is rather warlike in setting them forth. She is 45 and not easily intimidated."[13] Having grown up in the parish and attended St. Francis's School, Mrs. Robinson knew well the rights and privileges the church offered her and the care the entire parish needed to take negotiating their interracial racial dynamics to maintain them.

Father Irwin recounted her complaint to the bishop that the larger white congregation had begun spilling over into the pews set aside for Black parishioners. They had also taken to using portions of St. Benedict's Hall during meeting times set aside for the Black community. African Americans like Mrs. Robinson, for whom the hall was built, were being ignored or dealt with ineffectively.[14] After all, according to the agreements made with Mother Katharine Drexel, the Hall was to be a space for African Americans to gather, not simply one more building on the Newton Grove campus for white parishioners. Father Irwin paraphrased Mrs. Robinson to say that these infringements represented "oppression." Such rude behavior, he claimed, "would not have [been] permitted in the church or on the grounds" during his tenure.[15] The white community, he argued on Mrs. Robinson's behalf, no longer respected, or perhaps even understood, the unspoken agreements of time and space that had allowed this parish to function smoothly for decades under his leadership.

Father Irwin would have understood the gravity of the crisis at Newton Grove, for he knew the unwritten rules that had come down from John Carr to govern everyday life in this community. Father Irwin's experience as the first long-serving priest in the parish meant that he had had daily encounters with the Catholics who had converted to be part of this experimental parish in the 1870s and 1880s. He understood the customs and norms that parishioners had developed to resolve disputes, practices that also protected the interests of the Black community against the parish's dominant white lay leadership. Now, in contrast, the Redemptorists were learning the parish norms from the children (probably mostly white children) of those converts. These cradle Catholics, born into the community, had not participated in the development of those norms or necessarily understood or appreciated their significance. Thus, the Redemptorists were at a deep disadvantage when it came to defending Black parishioners' informal rights. They had little guidance from the church, and perhaps the parishioners as well, to help them understand how to maintain the boundaries by sustaining the unspoken practices of etiquette and respect that used to bind Black and white parishioners together. Mrs. Robinson's letter reveals that by the 1930s, many African Americans in the parish were questioning whether the founders' vision was meant to last.

Father Irwin concluded his letter in support of Mrs. Robinson with a warning to the Redemptorists, mentioning that he knew of "colored congregations in North Carolina to come to nothing [to collapse] following a change in pastors."[16] He felt strongly that using St. Benedict's Hall as an African American church and gathering space was the only way to support his Black parishioners. Within the next five years, the Catholic hierarchy would require that St. Mark's parish follow the pattern of segregation set in the rest of the diocese. They took Father Irwin's advice to establish a separate parish for African Americans in Newton Grove. Although dividing the community betrayed the founding parishioners' sacrifices for unity, the choice relieved the parish's social and financial pressures. Their interracial experiment of having white and Black Catholics worshipping under the same roof lasted for more than seventy years, much longer than similar parishes across the South. The question now was in what form the founding vision of racial unity would continue, if any.

During the hard economic times from the Depression to the Second World War, the Newton Grove community got by however they could. These rural Southerners depended on the talents and gifts that everyone — regardless of race or confession — had to offer. The years of financial disaster and desperation led many sharecroppers and tenant farmers to leave the land that could not provide them with even a basic survival income. Landowners used subsistence farming to feed their families. Consequently, the membership of the parish, both Black and white, did not drop significantly during these difficult years, because these parishioners valued their landholdings and were able to provide enough for their families. The enrollments of both parish schools actually increased by approximately 23 percent during the 1930s.[17] Still, the parish population remained majority white with about 300 white and 60 African American parishioners. The community did not grow as it might have during a period of prosperity, an economic condition during which Catholic couples may have responded by having more children. Some families, particularly Black tenant farmers and their children who inherited little land, had been leaving the area, or at least the parish, in search of opportunities for better lives.

During the 1920s and 1930s, Catholics exchanged what manual labor or farm produce they could for the continued maintenance of their parish. The long depression that began in the South in the early 1920s with the coming of the crop-killing boll weevil meant there was increasingly less to take to market.[18] What they had to sell was worth less. Cotton, for instance, which sold for thirty cents a pound in 1919, had fallen to only six cents a pound in 1931. Tobacco prices faced similar declines as the cost of mechanizing production increased.[19] Under these circumstances, many parishioners were happy just to grow enough food for both trade in kind and subsistence. Farmers, like most of the parish's Black and white founding families, paid their debts by offering the nuns food and meat. The parishioners made these deep sacrifices out of gratitude that the sisters spent their days teaching their children, instead of raising food. These exchanges, then, were part of the unwritten rule of Southern hospitality, a way to demonstrate how much the parents valued the education their children received. As one pupil remembered, "Since money was scarce in those days, the sisters were paid very little, but . . . I remember Fridays being the day for taking food to the sisters such as butter, eggs, baked bread, dressed chickens, and special canned fruits that were prepared by my mother. This was the mind-set of the people, to keep them well fed."[20] The sisters, however, needed more than just food to thrive in their new home.

Before their arrival in Newton Grove, Father McQuaid pleaded with his vice provincial to raise the funds: "We have been waiting for the opening of the school, the sale of the crops, etc. before inaugurating any plan for increasing the contributions of the faithful. But yesterday we made an appeal to the parishioners to contribute to a fund to make the convent decent and comfortable for the Sisters. How they will cooperate remains to be demonstrated." With that request, he waited, hoped, and economized.

Things had gotten desperate for the priests. He noted that without the sisters to help them, the priests had been cooking their own meals: "We are sizzling in this heat, and to add to our troubles, we are cooking our own meals. God bless the man who invented canned goods and the can-opener. We would starve without them."[21] The vice provincial must have responded to this rather pitiful picture by helping Father McQuaid strategize, for soon after receiving the reply, Father McQuaid wrote the bishop to say that the parish and the Redemptorists had already contributed $4,000 to get ready for the sisters. Parents and children were eagerly awaiting their arrival, he insisted; one parishioner had even offered to repaint the convent. It was all he could do, McQuaid confessed, since the man had no cash to give. Knowing that the Redemptorists and the parishioners were contributing both money and labor, Bishop Hafey provided the remaining funds needed to ensure that the convent was ready for the arrival of three Sisters of Mercy on October 21, 1928.[22] The sisters would staff the parish's schools until the last one closed in 1954.

When the sisters arrived, Father McQuaid was working to dismantle the parish's boarding schools as part of his agreement to lessen their responsibilities.[23] The Sisters of Mercy had been in touch with the Dominican Sisters of Hope, newly returned from Newton Grove. They offered frightening tales about unrelenting work and meager pay while they had staffed the parish between 1907 and 1922. The priests hoped to decrease the incoming sisters' workload by shutting down the boarding program, thus relieving them of this burden. Now, the children would return home every afternoon while the sisters spent time in prayer, teaching music, and developing the curriculum. Further, though the parish had worked on getting electricity and indoor plumbing for the convent, the schools were another matter. Lauren, who attended St. Mark's School in the 1930s and 1940s, recounted running to the outhouse in the winter morning darkness and the latrine's stench in high summer. Her own house, she laughed, had had a flush toilet for years before the school got one.[24] Given his limited resources, Father McQuaid could not improve the schools, the convent, the rectory, and the sanctuary, all of which needed dire attention. He had to choose. He chose to focus on gaining the material resources and financial reserves to ensure the sisters' happiness. He knew that they were essential to the schools' success, and the schools' success was the parish's success. So, he worked hard to make the convent comfortable for the Sisters of Mercy. As his early letters reveal, he understood the hardships that came from moving to Newton Grove.

The Catholic Hierarchy's Shift to Segregated Parishes

Keeping the parish itself in working order was just one of the Redemptorists' tasks. They also had to maintain relationships with the wider Protestant community within which the parish sought to flourish. They could not turn their backs and pretend that these outsiders did not exist. The parishioners had to guide Father McQuaid in gaining a new understanding of interfaith marriages and Protestant attendees of Catholic schools. From the first days of the parish well into the 1960s, over two-thirds of the marriages in the parish were interfaith. Andrew, an eighty-two-year-old white parishioner, recalled telling the priest in the 1940s: "Of course my fiancée is Protestant; I'm *related* to all the Catholics here."[25] He, like his parents before him, was part of an interfaith marriage that eventually led to his wife's conversion. In the decades before she became Catholic, she, like most other non-Catholic spouses, attended parish events and occasional Masses with her Catholic husband and children. Although the priests warned against interfaith marriages, they also accepted them. Given the population of the area and the formation of the parish, there was simply no other choice. Reading the banns of marriage took on an intensity within this community it might not have had in other parishes. When the priest said, "If there is any kinship by blood or marriage — or other relationship or being godfather or godmother or sponsorship or any other irregularity or impediment known to any one he must make it known to the pastor at once under pain of mortal sin," surely many a bride and groom feared that they might indeed be unwitting kin.[26]

Through these marriages the Protestant spouses came to know the Catholic Church, softening anti-Catholic sentiment. In the same way, the schools' inclusion of Protestant students tamped down the town's fears about the pope. But the Redemptorists also needed to reach out to Protestants in the broader area. Protestants still feared that Catholics were undermining white American and white southern values of local control, segregation, and individual dedication to God with their dedication to the pope in Rome. The priests' need to educate the surrounding townspeople about Catholicism was so great that by 1941, they had developed their own version of the "mobile mission." They bought and renovated an Airstream trailer to serve as a chapel on wheels.[27]

The Redemptorists' "Perpetual Help Motor Chapel" made it possible to cover the vast distances between parishes and Catholic chapels in the rural South.[28] The refurbished Airstream, an iconic American choice, served as a means by which to teach their faith.[29] The priest wrote that approximately 500 people came to see this motor chapel on one outing in the summer of 1941 in an area that the priest felt was a "bigoted neighborhood," presumably anti-Catholic.[30] They dispelled mistaken preconceptions that Catholics worshipped Mary, were more devoted to the pope than to God or country, and did not read the Bible. Through personal interactions at the parish or during the mobile missions, the priests sought to challenge the anti-Catholic boilerplate that otherwise spread through public schools, Protestant churches, and the mainstream press. Through these efforts the parish hoped to lessen the threats felt by the parishioners. As they had in the parish's early years, the schools remained the most effect way for these Catholics to build lasting, positive relationships with each other and with the Protestants.

Schools, Buses, and Survival

The two parish schools did not need to be well appointed to be well loved. Former students, perhaps through a screen of nostalgic haze, laughed and remembered their school days with fondness: The nuns had high expectations for their students and were strict but nurturing. Many alumni from the 1940s and 1950s, both Black and white, remember doing homework by the light of kerosene lamps in houses without electricity after spending the afternoon in the fields. Some families did not get electricity to their homes until the late 1950s. But no one wanted to squander their opportunity for an education or to disappoint the sisters, who believed in them. Dorothy, an eighty-six-year-old white woman, recounted how much joy she found at school. Holy Redeemer school was where the nuns taught her the fine points of public speaking: how to emphasize key phrases, captivate an audience, and write a speech that listeners would remember. She and her cousins were also taught geography and went to Wednesday Mass where they prayed together in Latin. The nuns, she said, taught them with love, creating an environment where they could learn joyously.[31]

Richard, an eighty-nine-year-old African American man, remembered, for instance, an unexpected touch on the arm the nun gave him on his first day at St. Francis's School (later renamed St. Benedict's School in 1939): "The sister [Sister Mary Louise] was walking around and introducing one person to the other ones and whatnot. And she came to me, and she said, 'Richard.' . . . And I just ignored her because I had never been called my given name before. And she touched me and said, 'Richard, I'm talking to you.' And I said, 'Well, that's not my name.' She said, 'Well, what is your name?' 'Jumbo,' I replied. But she ended up calling me Richard."[32] School introduced Richard to white people who centered the teacher-student relationship over the demands of white supremacy. The sisters grabbed their arms, touched their shoulders, or rapped their knuckles when necessary. They did not keep a fearful distance. Moreover, the sisters expected their students to look them in the eye and speak formally and directly.

The school was small, but not as small as Richard remembers. There were fifty Black students enrolled that year, not twelve as he recalled. Although, perhaps, only twelve regularly attended. Still the intimate setting meant that he knew his teacher well, and she him. Like most people I spoke with, his math and history lessons have long since faded from memory. Nonetheless, these lessons were important to him and his family, so important that there are stories of students at St. Benedict's repeating the eighth grade just to prolong their education.[33]

In 1950s Sampson County, the average African American adult would have complete five years of schooling, whereas white folks typically completed two more years before shifting to full-time work. Two-thirds of both Black and white parishioners farmed, although African Americans earned 23 percent less on average than their white coreligionists.[34] In contrast, African American members of the Newton Grove parish probably reached educational parity. The support of the Catholic Church enabled Black parishioners to get a more academically focused education at St. Benedict's School than was available at the segregated public schools. The sisters taught reading, writing, arithmetic, public speaking, geography, and history, not trades. Moreover, the parish provided them with transportation, a schedule adjusted for the demands of the farm, and opportunities to continue their education postgraduation.

All these educational benefits led many Protestant families in the Newton Grove area to send their children to the parish schools even after a White Oak school opened for African American students in Sampson County in 1919.[35] White Oak was one of hundreds of schools built across the rural South by the Rosenwald Foundation, a public-private partnership between Booker T. Washington's Tuskegee Institute and Julius Rosenwald, the president of Sears, Roebuck and Company. Rosenwald Schools were designed to improve opportunities for African American children in rural Southern towns like Newton Grove, with a focus on the basics of academics, agriculture, and industrial skills.[36] While the addition of these school improved opportunity across the county, Rosenwald Schools did not have the academic focus or the stable funding of the parish schools, which led to inconsistent school years and frequent closings.[37] When they were open, they also offered a less extensive curriculum than the parish schools. More important, perhaps, schools like White Oak could not provide transportation. The parish school appealed to the counties' children because it solved families' practical problems and opened new avenues of inquiry for their children. Moreover, the parish had religious obligation to its children;

Saint Benedict's Church and School. Courtesy of Our Lady of Guadalupe Parish.

Saint Benedict's Church interior. Courtesy of Our Lady of Guadalupe Parish.

Black Catholic children were encouraged to attend the parochial school by their priests and by the dictates of the Catholic Church emanating from the Vatican in Rome.

Being in a firmly Catholic environment allowed the Catholic students to relax. Smiles and laughter seemed to fill former students' memories of the school day. When I asked Rachel how her parents remembered St. Benedict's school, formerly called St. Francis's School for African American Children, she burst into a grin. "I think if you get them past the laughing and telling the stories about pranks and things that they used to play . . . they are laughing and talking about the things that they used to do to upset the whole apple cart, if you will."[38] The school also offered structured recreation. Richard, a St. Francis alumnus, remembered that "we played baseball on the campus . . . on the side of the church but in front of the school. . . . It was a big yard out there, for us to play in."[39] Through play, the children established communal bonds with classmates from across the county. For Richard's brother, who later fell in love with a Protestant classmate from outside Newton Grove, these bonds led to marriage, while for other children, they led to important business connections in their adult lives.

That same bond-building play and mischief happened in the white school as well. Lauren, an eighty-nine-year-old white woman who attended St. Mark's school through eighth grade, remembered regularly sneaking out of class: "Mr. David Herring owned a grocery store [near] Saint Mark's property. This street had large ditches on each side that were lined with grown-up bushes that hid us as we slipped away from the grounds to spend a few pennies that were very scarce in those days to buy candy or a sweet bun."[40] This childish miscreantism built connections between the students, both Catholic and Protestant. According to the students, the sisters never discovered their charges' truancy, but the escapades clearly served to build bonds.

The children knew better than to joke or make mischief with young parishioners of another race; still, they also understood that they were related to each other. Lauren said that she was always aware that many of the students at the Black school were descendants of John Carr. Although it wasn't openly acknowledged in the white community at that time, in her words, "it was known."[41] There might have been a closeness in the knowing that could not be expressed directly. Other interviewees, particularly men, reported that the school yards were right next to each other, and that they would play marbles and other games across "the line," as Andrew called the division between the white and Black children.

The white school children knew, seemingly instinctively, they were not supposed to play with their Black neighbors during school even though they would "sit around and talk to them, and knew them, who they were."[42] Both white and Black children understood that close connections should only be expressed in private spaces, such as while picking and planting on family land. Few alumni (Black or white) mentioned taking part in official activities together. Nonetheless, the priests' daily notes record a fair amount of interaction at school and at Mass, but the priests also never escaped their nervousness about hosting interracial events, especially considering the pervasive segregation then imposed by community pressures. Father Timothy Sullivan, C.Ss.R., noted on February 13, 1953, that "white and colored children practice the contest speeches together in Holy Redeemer Hall. The colored children were applauded generously by white children. In the afternoon white children went to the colored school and gave their speeches."[43] The final recitations were a few days later, according to Sullivan's notes. "The program began with a half-hour lecture on Negro Achievement by Father Egan," he continued. "It commemorated Negro History Week."[44] As with earlier interracial, if segregated, parish events, priests decided to hold these gatherings inside. Such decisions marked one way the parish negotiated between their own mission for racial inclusiveness and the demands of their region and their church for racial segregation.

For parishioners in Newton Grove, Catholicism and limited interracialism went hand in hand. While the Catholic Church understood itself as universal, as in global, some parishioners still hoped they could be a model for sustaining a unified, racially inclusive community within a single parish. The adults I spoke with remember the parish as a uniquely Catholic place. Lauren, who grew up in the parish and later joined the Sisters of Mercy, said, "All my friends growing up were Protestant. My family wouldn't say the Rosary in the home when you had friends come over. It's not considerate." But, she continued, at the parish school she did not have to hide her Catholicism.[45] No one would question the Rosary, a feast day procession, or the use of holy water. Further, students were both Catholic and Protestant, and Protestants also learned the meanings of Catholic theology and practice. The instruction the children received at school, according to all the former students I interviewed, was challenging and fun.

Elizabeth, a Protestant who attended the St. Benedict's School, also learned to defend Catholicism against its critics. She recalled rebutting her non-Catholic friends' negative ideas: "I tell them, 'That's a lie straight from hell' that they worship statues. . . . I don't ever remember my teacher telling me, 'You worship a statue.' And I look at them and I ask them, 'Do you have a picture of your mother, your father, your sister, your brother, your children in your house?' 'Oh, yes. Oh, yeah.' I said, 'Are you worshiping those pictures?' So that is a reminder, that's memorabilia that you hold onto."[46] In the Catholic school where Catholic children could learn and feel comfortable in their faith, Protestant children learned how to explain the practices of their classmates and teachers in their non-Catholic circles. These children, who had a firm footing in both religious worlds, acted as translators and protectors of the sisters and friends they held dear. The parish hoped that this spirit of respect and empathy infused race relations as well. And all the students came to know that those children playing across the color line were engaged in learning from the sisters, studying Latin, math, and history subjects just like they were.

Many of these children knew each other even if they didn't see each other at Mass or laugh with each other on the playground. They often lived on neighboring farms; they waited at the same stop for buses to school; they shared a deep affection for their teachers and priests. Lauren, who had snuck out of class to buy candy, joined the Sisters of Mercy. Amelia, an eighty-three-year-old white woman who was part of a large family living on a farm adjacent to the parish, remembered staying after school to help the nuns. Her father, she said, struggled after returning from World War II and could be violent. She and her siblings would avoid a frightening home environment by taking piano lessons from the sisters.

Many children in Newton Grove, both Protestant and Catholic, went to the sisters to study piano. Mitchell, a lifetime Baptist, recalled his discovery that the nuns offered lessons. His parents let him work with Sister Mary Rose, RSM, because, in his words, "Membership in the Catholic church here, we held the people who went there in high esteem."[47] While his parents might have been suspect of the rituals they saw his piano teachers perform or the habits they wore, they felt certain about their character. After all, the Catholic Church was founded by some of the most important families in town and had long ago become the largest religious institution in the area.

Not only did the church have a large visible presence with a convent, two schools, and a rectory, but the parish also had a school bus, which was unique in the Newton Grove community when it first arrived. Just as John Carr and later parishioners had hit the road in his horse and buggy, Father McQuaid believed that St. Mark's should do the same to bring children to Sunday school. He imagined and eventually created bus routes that stretched between fifty and eighty miles each way.

In this cash-strapped parish, a bus seemed like an impossible purchase when first considered. Yet unlike their Protestant counterparts, whose resources were primarily local, the parish's far-flung donor base meant that the priests could appeal to the church's national hierarchy for financial help. Father McQuaid followed the chain of command by first appealing to the bishop for help raising $900, the cost of a used school bus he had his eye on. He listed the additional upfront costs like a driver, fuel, repairs, and insurance, but he trumpeted the benefits as immeasurable: "It carries 12 children. A large outlay for so small a number. Still, when a soul is at stake, no security can be too great."[48] Both men hoped that a bus would mean more children could attend school and get to know the Catholic Church. Father McQuaid knew well that many families of both races walked up to five miles each way to attend Mass on Sundays.[49] While such a trek might be possible on a Sunday, it was not feasible for young children to undertake such a journey every day.

Buses would become key instruments of nationwide school desegregation from the mid-1950s in New York City and through the mid-1970s in North Carolina. However, in the 1920s in Newton Grove, the parish bus was simply a resource to extend the mission of the parish: to educate its young Catholics and increase regional Protestant families' exposure to Catholicism.[50] Eventually there was one bus for each school to meet the South's demand that transportation be segregated. This also allowed the parish's schools to reach more children. The vehicles brought Catholic and Protestant children to the Black and white parochial schools where, despite this segregation, young people of both races would regularly encounter each other during Mass at the interracial, if internally segregated, church.

The bus also opened the school to impoverished students from the wider community. Working to shift the schools' organization from boarding to day students took on even greater importance during the economic depredations of the Great Depression. Moreover, in 1931 Newton Grove's local bank closed, putting the parish in an even more precarious financial position. On December 28, 1931, Father McQuaid wrote to his superior with the bad news: "Our balance in the savings account amounts to $2954.80 and in the check account about 1869.00. . . . The closing of the bank has simply stunned the whole town as it was so unexpected. —$60 cash on hand."[51] Out their entire savings, a desperate situation for Father McQuaid grew far worse. They had no money for the essentials. Thoughts of a rectory and a school bus faded.

Two years later, however, the situation had improved enough for the diocese to purchase a bus. It was up and running by 1933 with long routes from farm to farm. Former students remember walking as much as a mile to their bus stops and then waiting in the dark for the glow of the bus's headlights to appear on the lonely country road.[52] Even with the long travel times, the buses increased the schools' attendance. In fact, enrollment at the Black school more than doubled from nineteen students to fifty after the purchase of the bus. A less drastic but still meaningful increase occurred at the white school, with enrollment increasing from forty-four to seventy-nine students between 1930 and 1935.[53] As Richard remembers it, "they didn't even have public buses for the Protestant children back in those days when Father Gomer told St. Benedict's bus driver, 'Let's pick up everybody and bring them to school.' And so, with the promise of regular transportation, the [Black] school grew until they had to separate the grades."[54]

The bus proved to be life-changing for many families in the area, but especially for Black children since transportation was more often than not a tool of white supremacy used against them. "I was not born Catholic," Louise, an African American woman, told me. Yet, because she lived less than a half-mile from the church, she explained, "When I started school at six years of age, it was the only school in the area that I lived, and they had a little bus that would pick up kids."[55] While buses were becoming accessible for rural white children in North Carolina, they were still a rarity for African American students. Building schools but refusing to help Black children get there was one of segregation's most effective tactics, a way of making universal education exist on paper but not in reality, such that Black children were not able to school themselves out of economic and social subservience.[56] Insisting that the parish provide equal access to education for all students, against the then segregated regional norms, was another way this Catholic parish maintained its vision of racial unity, even as it began to further segregate its worship practices. On the one hand, former white students recounted switching from the parish school to public school a decade later when the buses stopped running during World War II. Gas rationing shut down the free transportation service from 1940 to 1945. On the other hand, African Americans didn't refer to the war when they thought about the bus's role in their education. They focused on the fact that their aunts, uncles, and parents had to stop going to school when St. Benedict's ended in the eighth grade. Without transportation to reach the African American public high school in Clinton, they had little choice but to replace learning mathematics with working in the fields. Until 1946, when a bus began running to the Black public high school for the first time, thanks to the insistence of alumni of St. Benedict's School that their children receive secondary education. Before that year, Black students' educational opportunities ended before high school, unless the parish helped them attend the normal school or Black Catholic institutions.[57]

The African American community understood how essential transportation was to their success and the success of their children. The parishioners of St. Benedict's used their bus on Sundays as well, while the white parish provided no comparable form of transportation. The Black families pooled money for gas and recruited Paul Robinson, a parishioner and alumnus of the school, to drive the bus to Mass. After farming all week, Robinson would rise before dawn on Sunday to walk the five miles to the church parking lot where the school bus sat idle. He climbed behind the wheel and headed out along the country roads, picking up every African American family who needed a ride to Mass. After more than an hour on the road, he would park the bus at the parish and head into the sanctuary with his family and his other passengers. After Mass, he would do the whole thing in reverse, ending with the five-mile walk home. This personal sacrifice and dedication to the parish, to his extended family, and to the Catholic Church ensured that St. Benedict's could thrive.[58]

Maintaining two separate buses became a time-consuming task for the Redemptorists as well as a major point of contention between the priests and the bishop, but the children who rode them were the ones left to imagine terrible things about what might happen when one of these buses broke down, which they did frequently. Parents warned their children not to get on the bus designated for children of the other race. They frightened their children into respecting racial norms with warnings about Ku Klux Klan vigilantes stalking the buses on isolated rural roads.[59] Corporal punishment was a possibility if Klan horror stories didn't work: Andrew, a white student who attended Holy Redeemer School in the 1940s, remembers his father informing him that if he ever rode on the Black bus, he would "get a whooping." The day finally came when the white bus broke down. The bus driver told the white children to board the school bus with their Black counterparts. Andrew recounted, "My [nine] brothers and sisters and I got off the white bus and refused to get on the Black bus. We listened to Daddy and walked the seven or eight miles home, taking turns carrying my five-year-old sister."[60] All the children were exhausted and relieved when they reached home. Fears that they would meet with a Klansman's wrath on their way had not come to pass. They could finally relax. Andrew and his father feared that the bus might cross paths with white

Procession of parishioners of St. Benedict's parish, 1943. Courtesy of Our Lady of Guadalupe Parish.

folks who would punish the children for pushing the parish's commitment to interracial worship beyond the accepted norms. Any of the young white children who did troop onto the other bus to sit with Black children from their Catholic parish, and the Black children who did not get off the now integrated bus, suddenly found themselves in the middle of the nightmare tales their parents had scared them with for years. For generations, the memory of this incident served as an example for generations that segregation meant safety.

Just as the buses helped expand the parish's reach, they also became a stand-in for broader conversations about segregation. Reading between the lines of the countless letters between the two offices concerning bus maintenance, one might imagine that freeing himself of the albatross of the buses, which often needed repair, was a motivating factor in the bishop's decision to merge the segregated St. Benedict's and Holy Redeemer parishes in 1953. Ending segregation would mean staffing only one school and paying for the maintenance of a single bus. Nonetheless, throughout the 1940s and into the 1950s, Father Sullivan persisted in his efforts to support the entire parish in ways he felt would allow it to thrive, whether as a unified community or as two racially segregated congregations.

Unity in Segregation?

Little has been recorded or remembered about weekly worship at St. Mark's, except the brief house notes with the date and name of the priest presiding over the Mass. When the Redemptorists took control of St. Mark's, it had one church, two schools, St. Benedict's Hall, a convent, and a makeshift rectory that housed the priest. A few wooden outbuildings completed the parish's physical plant. Mass was not yet being said regularly at St. Benedict's Hall, but the hall was being used to build community for the African American parishioners away from the social stigma and fears that came with worshipping with white people in a segregated society.

On November 14, 1927, for example, Father McQuaid recorded that, "Beginning next Saturday night and Sunday night at 7 o'clock—Father Irwin will open a song and hymn festival for the Colored people at St. Benedict's Hall—If the colored people will come with their wives and children, the pastor will take pleasure in teaching them for several nights, the beautiful songs and hymns of the church."[61] In the earliest days of St. Benedict's Hall, the parish used the hall primarily to house Catholic entertainment, like the hymn festival, for the African American community. Convention dictated that African Americans could not attend such events at St. Mark's, which had by then been renamed Holy Redeemer. Only Masses could be interracial, not other events. The presence of segregationist Protestants, who frequently attended the parish's social gatherings, would have struck fear into the Black congregants' hearts, causing them to avoid such events. In case someone might want to stay, making the interracial mission public, nonliturgical events like the clergy-led hymn-singing class were officially segregated. While a departure from the founding vision, the clergy hoped these gatherings provided the African American community with an opportunity to worship in a more carefree environment.

When the Sisters of Mercy arrived in 1928, African Americans had developed a schedule of events that allowed them regular access to St. Benedict's Hall. They used the space for social events as well as occasional Masses. African Americans, according to a tacit agreement, had first claim to this part of the parish's built infrastructure. Meanwhile, Masses at St. Mark's welcomed everyone, with the understanding that African Americans entered the church through the door on the left and sat in the corresponding pews, which the white folks left empty for them. In the early days, the priests ensured that African Americans could freely access these seats to guarantee they met Katharine Drexel's demands, but by the 1920s, these seating assignments had become unspoken norms. Self-policing by all adherents meant that Black Catholics could move through the parish without worrying about a confrontation over accidentally taking their white coreligionists' seats.

Such tacit agreements meant the parish avoided dealing directly with the power differential between its members. Any interaction, particularly with folks outside the community, could potentially lead to violence. The priests noted that special events and holidays always necessitated careful scheduling. Black parishioners needed space and time to worship, while the parish also had to welcome white Protestants from interfaith families. Father McQuaid, for example, was surprised at how fast African American attendees left his first Mass: "We celebrated the first Mass at 7:30ish to give our colored Catholics an opportunity of fulfilling their obligation. They all disappeared after the early Mass knowing it would not be well for them to attend the late Mass with so many Protestants present."[62] Since interfaith marriages were the norm for both Black and white Catholics, each spouse typically attended a different church.

After his first Easter in Newton Grove, Father McQuaid mused at the wonder on the Protestants' faces when they attended this Catholic Mass: "Our white folks remained on the grounds after the Mass. . . . The tourists entered the church and walked about gazing at the Stations of the Cross and the statues talking all the while in a low reverent voice. . . . Solemn High Mass was scheduled for 11:15. It was amusing to see the smiles and dodges of the Protestants, as we passed thru the aisles, sprinkling rather trying to give them a bath of Holy Water. The church was packed with a Mass of humanity."[63] Easter was one of the many moments when the broader Newton Grove community's segregationist demands became a sensitive concern at parish religious services. While white families were encouraged to gather, linger, and worship together at the parish church, Black families could attend Mass but could not socialize afterward. Even their presence at Easter Vigil Mass, sitting down the side aisle across from the white parishioners, made the priests worried about safety. These infractions of the social norms risked upsetting a visiting white Protestant enough that some sort of punishment might be meted out on the parish as a whole or on its African American members specifically, for acting outside the communal norms. The priests knew that they could not protect their parishioners after the Mass ended. By thinking of all the potential consequences of public actions and celebrations, the clergy and the parishioners, both Black and white, did their best to preempt any violence.

St. Mark's parish on Easter in the 1930s. Courtesy of Our Lady of Guadalupe Parish.

St. Mark's parish interior. Courtesy of Our Lady of Guadalupe Parish.

The wider white community only accepted the parish's efforts at racial unity when they were invisible to non-Catholics. The priests' daily notes make this plain. Further, while the intermingling of whites and Blacks at a church service could be considered transgressing the framework of segregation, by the late 1920s, African American parishioners were far more likely to be punished for it than white attendees. As Father Irwin had said in his letters about the building of St. Benedict's Hall, the African American parishioners were not able to experience the fullness of the faith under these circumstances. While earlier in the parish's history white parishioners felt the public backlash or a threat from Ku Klux Klan involvement—in 1872 Enoch Godwin hid in a barrel to avoid the Klan after he converted—as the years progressed the threats were directed more pointedly toward African Americans. However, the white Catholic community remained justifiably fearful.

Responding to newly established norms in the Catholic Church as well as internal and external pressures in Newton Grove, the Bishop facilitated the parish's formal separation. The same parish campus now featured Holy Redeemer Church, implicitly for whites, signaling what had been St. Mark's was now under the Redemptorists's care, and St. Benedict's Church for African Americans, but parishioners haven't preserved a unified narrative about how this division occurred. As we saw in chapter 3, Father Irwin used St. Benedict's for segregated Masses before the Redemptorists arrived. The hall was not designated as an African American parish, however, until well into the Redemptorist's tenure. The shift from holding occasional Masses for African Americans in St. Benedict's Hall to turning St. Benedict's into a separate African American church was supported by Bishop Eugene J. McGuinness, who became Bishop of Raleigh in December 1937.

McGuinness, an expert fundraiser who had also specialized in handling the administration for missionary orders, had long embraced prosegregation policies. Before coming to North Carolina, he had overseen the Society for the Propagation of the Faith, which coordinated assistance for priests and nuns assigned to distant and isolated missionary outposts. In this role, he developed a reputation as a strong supporter of religious orders that worked with African Americans and Native Americans. In his January 1940 pastoral letter to the Catholics of his diocese, McGuinness announced $4,500 in grant money that the diocese had received from the "Commission for the Catholic Missions among the Colored People and the Indians"; but the US bishops had formed this Commission to effect their new policy for "racial parishes."[64] Practically speaking, the decision to segregate also freed up diocesan funds since the Black parish used money from the Commission on African American Catholic institutions rather than from local Catholic coffers, which eventually formed the backbone of North Carolina's African American middle class. Spiritually speaking, the idea behind racial parishes, according to the bishops, was that African American Catholics could focus on the rites of the church rather than the racism they encountered in integrated Masses. Faith would be central to life in Black-only parishes, rather than the humiliation of waiting last in line for the Eucharist or being barred from serving at the altar.

Parts of the founding vision did survive, even as the decision to segregate allowed for greater African American attendance at Mass. The two parishes (both white and Black) held Mass at 8:30 a.m. On the first Sunday of the month, however, priests celebrated Mass at 10:30 a.m. Having Masses at the same time, Father Sullivan wrote in the house notes, "ensure[d] respective attendance of the whites in their church and the colored in theirs."[65] The two parishes were also able to meet all together. The availability of a bus to pick up African American families thus helped sustain elements of John Carr's vision for a racially inclusive, albeit segregated, Catholic community. Richard recalled that his father would go to the church to "get the bus, and then he would have a bus route. He would collect all the Black folks, take them to church and then bring them back home."[66] Attending St. Benedict's was easier than attending most of the neighboring Protestant churches, which did not provide transportation, and the children of St. Benedict's parish could attend the African American parish school as well.

Oral histories reveal that during this period of formal separation, Father Sullivan and the Redemptorists worked to reintegrate the parish in small but significant ways. As would be the case again and again, the school served as their main site of integration. Inside the school's main building, the priest could lead biracial celebrations without needing anyone's approval. When the weather warmed, he gathered both Black and white children on the back side of the parish property for the crowning of Mary each May. Photographs from 1940s show the white children proceeding over to St. Benedict's, the church for Black parishioners, to attend Mass. Other times white boys were altar servers at St. Benedict's, although no one ever spoke of the reverse happening. One former white altar server recounted, "I celebrated Mass in St. Benedict's during the May festivals, where we would have Mass at their church. And I would be a part of that as an acolyte."[67] He went on to highlight St. Benedict's marble altar along with its overall beauty. This former altar boy felt a sense of jealousy, mixed with trepidation, as he entered the church. Crossing into the Black parish, even

St. Mark's school bus under repair. Courtesy of Our Lady of Guadalupe Parish.

at the priests' insistence, felt transgressive. Looking back on the event, he avoided any discussion of race or segregation. These recollections demonstrate a way of being together as a biracial parish without recognizing the reality of African American life in the parish or in the wider community. However imperfectly, then, these gatherings kept alive the traditional connections between the Black and white sections of the original parish, even as each church community became formally segregated.

The boys from both Holy Redeemer and St. Benedict's enthusiastically took up the task, by no means easy, of learning how to be altar servers. White Catholics from other Southern communities were often incredulous that Black southerners could share their tradition. Richard recounted an incident when a white man came up to him after Mass with a surprising opinion: "I have never seen a Black boy serve Mass," he told Richard, "and I was really critical of you. I was an altar boy, too, when I was young. And I just waited for you to make some mistakes, but you never made a mistake."[68] Although the man had a surprisingly positive reaction, his statement was still a backhanded compliment at best. Newton Grove's interracial Catholic rituals were in fact unusual, especially for white Catholics. For most Northerners too, the sight of a Black Catholic serving at Mass would have been striking. What is more, the white man who felt entitled to address Richard, a young Black man, after Mass was also confessing that he had hoped for Richard's failure. He was testifying to the white Catholic community's hostility toward African American Catholics. But Richard was also recalling how rigorously Newton Grove's priests and nuns trained their acolytes. The Northern observer, who claimed to be a ritual expert himself, ended up admiring Richard's precision, albeit from a position of presumed superiority. Nonetheless, these two men shared the experience of performing an important role in the Mass. The kinship network of the Catholic faith stretched far beyond the Newton Grove parish and far beyond what Richard could imagine when he was a child.

In these days before Vatican II, the style of the Mass was determined centrally by the church hierarchy, administered by priests, and said in Latin. As a result, local character, which in rural North Carolina always involved agricultural production as well as negotiations over Southern segregationist norms, came through in festivals and other paraliturgical events. In 1949, for instance, Holy Redeemer began holding a "Harvest Day." It was originally a one-off fundraiser to pay for Holy Redeemer's new heating plant, but the gathering was so successful that the parish repeated it annually. For that first event, according to the house notes, the congregation had a "barbecue and chicken salad supper in the School Hall and an auction sale of donated articles." The event raised $640 for the heating plant through that auction.[69] However, there is no mention of African Americans attending that first Harvest Festival. Nor are St. Benedict's parishioners mentioned as attendees in the accounts of other social events held at Holy Redeemer during the 1940s. Perhaps, as was the case in earlier decades, African American Catholics were not welcome at social events held at Holy Redeemer. Any mixing of Black and white parishioners—be it children on their school's playground, adults picnicking on the lawn at Easter, or families enjoying Harvest Day—raised the ire of the white community, including some members of the parish, who felt that separation of the races in social situations, as part of God's design, needed to be enforced with threats and even violence.

To avoid this, St. Benedict's held its own social events at the parish and other designated places where African Americans were allowed to gather. The *North Carolina Catholic*, for example, notes an end-of-term picnic held on May 20, 1947. The event took place at Chavis Park, Raleigh's segregated downtown green space about forty-five miles from Newton Grove. Two days later, the same column recounts that the white students had their picnic at White Lake, also about forty-five miles from the parish.[70] In its commitment to represent the activities of Black and white Catholics equally, *North Carolina Catholic* presented a picture of the diocese as Bishop Waters, the Bishop of Raleigh from 1945 through 1974, hoped it would be. Bishop Waters was deeply invested in the church's effort to integrate. In 1941 while working in the office of the Bishop of Richmond, Waters helped ensure that the Catholic Church was included in the Virginia Commission on Interracial Cooperation. He then used the knowledge he gained to assist in creating the North Carolina Catholic Layman's Association (NCCLA) encouraging African American lay leaders to meet and exchange ideas with white lay Catholics.[71] By 1948, with Waters's support, the NCCLA elected their first Black officers.[72] Despite these interracial efforts outside of Mass, white and Black Catholics still operated in primarily in separate communities.

In the pages of *North Carolina Catholic*, which Bishop Waters published and personally edited, the segregation of North Carolina parishes meant that news about processions and parties of Black and white Catholics in North Carolina could not appear together in the same column of copy. For instance, one article stated that to begin the month, 200 people attended a parish picnic at Holy Redeemer. The report described "the spacious parochial grounds" and how the event took on "the proportions of a large family gathering" with food and games galore. The article described no similar event for St. Benedict's Parish.[73] Yet, former St. Benedict's parishioners showed me pictures of their mothers and aunts unloading their picnic baskets for church gatherings. The *North Carolina Catholic* didn't cover these events because they were run by the parishioners, not the priests. Covering only official parish events meant that the periodical missed much of what made St. Benedict's a place for social as well as spiritual sustenance. Focused as it was on the schools, however, the columns did highlight some of the ties among the Newton Grove Catholics in the separate racial parishes.

Father Sullivan, in fact, hoped that parishes could integrate, privately and quietly, as an arrangement among the parishioners. He began the experiment with the parish's children, according to his daily diary, in early 1951. He may have felt authorized by a new appeal, issued by Bishop Waters, to support "Negro and Indian Missions." Sullivan read the bishop's appeal aloud to the parish, reminding his listeners that "Christ's Church in this world is Catholic. This means that it is as broad as the human race itself. . . . Equal rights are accorded, therefore, to every race and every nationality in any Catholic Church, and within the Church building itself everyone is given the privilege to sit or kneel wherever he desires."[74] Of course, the priests in Newton Grove, along with Catholic clergy throughout North Carolina, knew that their ability to enact this directive would be difficult. Parishioners in this period had been justifiably fearful when they crossed the color line. Still, a week after the bishop's statement, on February 8, 1951, Father Sullivan wrote to his superior that "there is nothing that I would like better than to integrate the two parishes—whether I will or not, only time will tell. I have begun daily Mass as of last Wednesday . . . and the colored and white children are both coming to the one Church, naturally. This may possibly be a start to something."[75] Nowhere else in North Carolina in 1951 were white and Black school children sitting together for an hour a day.

Father Sullivan's letter about his plans to bring the parish under one roof contains no mention of the bishop's prointegration position. The parish would not push unity's boundaries further than it had in the past, since full integration would be met with a harsh negative reaction. Father Sullivan was only willing to make a private, internal arrangement to hold integrated Masses for the parish—and only at Holy Redeemer. Anything more would threaten the public's perception that the parish willingly complied with the South's customary segregation.

Working to end the practice of racially dividing parishes, including St. Benedict's and Holy Redeemer, advanced Waters's overall goal. However, the bishop knew nothing of the Redemptorists' efforts. As bishop during the 1950s, when the parish would face another turning point, Waters began a very public effort to desegregate North Carolina's Catholic Church. His convictions, like those of John Carr Monk, would reshape the identity of the Newton Grove parish in ways that put the parish once again at the vanguard of Southern and Catholic race relations.

CHAPTER FIVE

Can Two Become One?
Striving for Unity, 1953–1974

Patricia, an older white woman, remembers her family going to Holy Redeemer for Mass on that hot day of May 31, 1953, only to drive back home without ever getting out of the car. They turned around, she recalled, when they saw her uncle on the church lawn with a pitchfork. He was at the front of a group of angry white people, including parishioners, shouting at the Catholics walking toward the church doors.[1] As Father Joseph Driscoll recounted the event, many white parishioners he knew had transformed into a mob: "Catholic men and woman—young boys and girls with good honest and friendly faces—now their features distorted with a fierce determination and hatred."[2] They and their Protestant neighbors hurled ugly curses, while cars full of scared parishioners in their Sunday best, both white and Black, cautiously looked for a safe place to park. News vans from some of the most prominent global newspapers, some of which had been stationed at the parish for the prior week in anticipation of this momentous event, were parked there too. Reporters scurried about with their notebooks, pens scribbling. Seeing the chaos on the lawn, Patricia's father exclaimed, "We're not getting involved. We're getting out of here." Soon, she was watching the scene disappear out the back window of the car as they drove to nearby Clinton for Mass.

This was Trinity Sunday, 1953, at Holy Redeemer Parish in Newton Grove, North Carolina. Trinity Sunday celebrates the unity of one God in three divine persons: Father, Son, and Holy Spirit. It would make for a nice symbol of inclusion, Newton Grove's presiding bishop, Vincent Waters of Raleigh, had thought when he picked this holiday to merge Newton Grove's white parish of Holy Redeemer (formerly St. Mark's) with the Black parish of St. Benedict's to create the unified parish of Holy Redeemer.[3]

As a longtime champion of racial equality, he felt certain that segregation in the diocese had to end and that the Newton Grove congregation had to be forced to engage across racial lines to experience each other's humanity.[4] For the bishop, uniting the parish was a matter of conviction, a matter of conscience.[5] In the weeks before Trinity Sunday, when news media caught wind of the bishop's decision, he refused to share his doubts. He projected absolute confidence and predicted that the community would not offer any resistance. Privately, Bishop Waters worried that the priests at Holy Redeemer would be too afraid to carry out his order. So, he drove to the parish himself that Sunday to make sure his subordinates locked the doors to St. Benedict's as he had ordered. He would stand behind his words alongside the faithful parishioners, facing shouting, spitting, and whatever else might come from disgruntled white parishioners and the broader community alike. Many parish families turned their cars around, like Patricia's, then drove in silence to another parish for Mass. The parishioners knew that they could do little to stop whatever would happen next. Then the wider world, which had been held at bay by the constant, careful attention to the public demands of segregation, descended on the parish.

Nathaniel Cox, Beatrice Cox's brother, had no interest in risking his life for the bishop's decision for Catholic racial equality. He was the only African American to give an interview to the *Raleigh News and Observer* on May 27, 1953, saying, "I have built up my place here over the years and I would hate to see all of that go for nothing should I get in any sort of that kind of trouble—and especially in the church."[6] Some African American Catholics stayed away out of fear that neither the bishop nor the priests could protect Black parishioners. Nathaniel Cox wanted none of "that kind of trouble" that came from becoming a Black, Catholic symbol for racial equality in the white, Protestant-dominated and segregated South.

Yet many African American parishioners did attend Mass that day, forming, along with a few white Catholics, a small remnant of the congregation inside Holy Redeemer. Henry, then three or four years old, had attended the service with his father, aunts, and uncles, an event that was recorded by a newspaper photographer. He remembers walking into Mass that morning. "We were all terrified," he explained, "but my father was determined that they would attend Mass at our parish."[7] For Henry's father, John, who had grown up in the parish and met his spouse at the parish school, missing Mass in Newton Grove was out of the question. Francis, a white woman, recalled that her father had a similarly adamant attachment to the parish. "You know," he told her at the time, "y'all can go to church at Clinton, which weren't but twenty miles away, or Dunn, all these churches . . . I'm going to go right on to the church I've been going to."[8] Similarly, Dorothy remembers her father instructing the family that they would all go into Mass together. Nonetheless, her mother got separated from the family by the protestors. Her mother tried unsuccessfully to push her way to the sanctuary door and missed Mass that day. Until her death, Dorothy's mother worried about being

African American parishioners entering the first desegregated Mass, May 31, 1953. © Associated Press.

classified by the press as a protestor rather than the obedient Catholic she sought to be.⁹ Dorothy, herself, remember being happy at Mass because the church was where she felt "the most at home."¹⁰ No amount of protesting could change that.

Once inside the sanctuary, these parishioners were shocked by the presence of Bishop Waters. From their point of view, his presence served to increase the agitation among white onlookers. The bishop came to oversee the parish "merger," as he referred to the events that Sunday morning. However, such a bland word failed to describe what this "merger" fully meant. The parish would stand as one of the few publicly integrated institutions in the state of North Carolina at a time when schools, parks, swimming pools, hospitals, restaurants, and other gathering places were strictly segregated.¹¹ Three-year-old Henry, for instance, would graduate fifteen years later from the segregated Pleasant Grove Public School. With this interracial Mass, the bishop put the North Carolina Catholic Church at the vanguard of the American civil rights movement. For his bold action, he was a hero to many.

To some parishioners, however, no matter the boldness of the action, the order itself was ill conceived and unjust. After all, the bishop had decreed the merger from "on high," and he was set to leave town once Trinity Sunday was done. He did not live in the community that would have to bear the consequences of his order; he was not living out the impact of his pastoral calling. For while the Diocese of Raleigh made statements about integrating other schools and parishes in North Carolina, no such action had been taken. The rural community of Newton Grove alone bore the weight of this decree. Once again, the parish stood out for its stance to advance racial equity as it had in the 1870s, but this time not of its own accord as it had in its founding years with John Carr and Martha and Solomon Monk and without the careful attention to minimizing the impact of its actions on its Protestant neighbors that had been the hallmark of the parish since its inception.

The parish began as a local protest against the segregation of local Protestant churches in Newton Grove. By the 1950s, both the parish and the community had carefully negotiated boundaries around racial and religious encounters, which included not only two separate parish institutions but also a limited repertoire of highly concealed opportunities for informal interracial interaction. Having become comfortable with this arrangement over the past fourteen years, many parishioners did not want to risk participating in the change.

Patricia's family, like Nathaniel Cox, turned away from the parish, and the threats and menace kept them away. They didn't step foot in Holy Redeemer for the next decade. While parish attendance did suffer, Newton Grove's history during this period offers an important corrective to the stereotype of white Christians abandoning interracial churches en masse in the postdesegregation South. Within a few years, Holy Redeemer's membership numbers would near premerger levels.[12] Many white and Black Catholics chose to stay in or return to this Catholic community.

This chapter analyzes how the parish reimagined itself following the merger of 1953. Unlike its formative early years when support for, and nascent steps toward inclusion of, African Americans dominated the mission of the parish, the parish now wrestled with how to incorporate emerging mid–20th-century integration-era practices of racial equality within the framework of the Catholic Church. In the process, the parish renegotiated the meaning of Catholic unity alongside their African American coreligionists, a contentious and fraught effort the parish would now take up once again. Many of the ancestors of the parish families, both Black and white, had founded this parish. No outside upheaval, whether coming from the bishop, Protestant neighbors, or readers of the *New York Times* across the nation, would cause them to abandon it. As Father Irwin described his jubilee Mass at Holy Redeemer in 1950, "Any other parishes will be heartily welcome. It will do them good to see a firm Catholic congregation, but out of the people who settled the soil originally and who are as indigenous to North Carolina as tar pitch turpentine and fat lightwood."[13]

Follow the Bishop? Integration Sunday

The parishioners, like the reporters who took their pictures as they went into the church, learned of the merger through a pastoral letter from Bishop Waters. After Mass on April 19, 1953, Father Sullivan read Bishop Waters's letter to the white parishioners gathered in the pews of Holy Redeemer. Then he walked 200 yards, his long alb dragging over the parched and brown lawn, to read the letter again to the parishioners of the Newton Grove's Black parish, St. Benedict's.[14] At the time, Holy Redeemer had approximately 350 members, and St. Benedict's around 90.[15] Bishop Waters began, "The enemy of God and the church, and of mankind itself uses the 'spirit of division' to break, if possible, the unity of the Mystical Body of Christ. He uses traditional hatreds of nations, of races, of classes, of minorities . . . to foment his divisions among men." At the end of the letter, Bishop Waters declared his position—and that of the diocese—in capital letters: "THERE IS NO SEGREGATION OF RACES TO BE TOLERATED IN ANY CATHOLIC CHURCH IN THE DIOCESE OF RALEIGH."[16] News of this letter then spread fast.

Although the impending end of segregation might have taken the parishioners by surprise, Father Sullivan had already spent years trying to achieve this goal in a gradual way. In 1951, Father Sullivan had written his superior insisting that "I have begun daily Mass . . . and the colored and white children are both coming to the one church, naturally. This may be the start of something."[17] Further, in January 1953, Father Sullivan used the occasion of a broken wood stove in St. Benedict's to bring the two parishes together for Mass in Holy Redeemer. A mere four months before the merger in May, Father Sullivan noted the interracial gathering in the house diaries: "The Stovepipe at St. Benedict's was blocked filling the church with smoke at Mass time. Fr. Egan said Mass for the people at Holy Redeemer Church. This was the first time the colored had Mass in the 'white' church since we segregated them. . . . We could reduce expenses and avoid segregation by having both Masses in one church, Holy Redeemer, the 'white' one." Father Sullivan took this idea of remerging the churches to the parish. "Few seemed opposed," he wrote.[18] Perhaps the lack of opposition stemmed from the fact that a formal uniting of the parishes seemed so far-fetched to the many parishioners who had long since forgotten the original mission of the parish that it seemed unlikely to become a reality. Despite Father Sullivan's more participatory, gradualist strategy, which had not yet achieved its goal, the bishop's decree blindsided the parishioners. The intense parish debate sparked by the decree also may have been fueled by parishioners feeling that they had lost control of the matter when the bishop's plan was made public to their surprise. That feeling only grew in intensity when reporters began showing up in town to interview them.

Once it became clear that news of the impending merger had hit the papers, Father Sullivan sent a letter to Baltimore sharing his parishioners' worries. He speculated that an ugly incident was brewing. "Enough Non-Catholics will come to spread in front of the Church and that if the Colored insist on entering, there might be a scene, if not an unfortunate incident. . . . Since the actual date of the integration has been publicized, there is some danger that bad publicity to the Church could result by any incident however it might be created."[19] Sullivan clearly knew that locals were plotting a protest and that violence on the parish's hallowed ground was a distinct possibility. Yet he finished his letter reassuring the bishop that the merger "will go along very smoothly." In the short time that remained before the merger, Father Sullivan hoped to bring about this peaceful ending by facilitating conversations with prominent white and Black parishioners together to discuss how to support the community. Perhaps because of a lack of time or parishioner interest, such conversations never occurred. Neither the parish nor the diocese held formal conversations to assist the parishioners in handling their own fears, outside threats, and internal feelings of obligation to their faith and to other family members of another religion.

Since its formation, the parish had found modest ways of bringing its Black and white parishioners together. Father Sullivan's integrated daily Masses for school children did foster inclusion, but quietly, to avoid offense. What the parish had never done before was to make a public announcement about a biracial practice and attempt a complete and total institutional integration on the grounds of Newton Grove's Catholic parish. John Carr Monk, after all, had only envisioned a parish that would enable a small number of households, families, and neighbors, both Black and white and often bound by kinship, to worship together. He had not envisioned a public stand by the parish on racial integration, one that openly defied segregationist norms. He, like the later parish priests, understood that for the parish to flourish, it

Can Two Become One? 127

needed to keep a careful balance between its Catholic identity and the realities of racial life in Newton Grove.

In the house diaries, Father Sullivan noted "extreme resentment and dissatisfaction" at the announcement.[20] Parishioners were also resentful of the bishop's decision to integrate the parish's schools as part of his merger plan. White men would neither send their children to an integrated school nor allow their wives into an integrated church.[21] One white parishioner even taunted Father Sullivan that he need not "worry about the school buses anymore, since the school would soon be closed."[22] On May 10, 1953, a group of white parishioners met with his superior and left "unconvinced."[23] Others then traveled to Raleigh to meet with the bishop, but they were turned away.

Sixty out of the 350 parishioners at Holy Redeemer signed a petition opposing the decree. They tried in vain to explain the local customs they had always lived with. Though they had crossed racial lines in their own parish, they explained, their Protestant spouses would draw the line at full integration. "As you are aware, interracial gatherings are opposed in the South, social or religious. . . . What is more serious is the fact that we have so many mixed marriages in the parish, some who have gone through all kinds of trials in getting to church and having their children reared in the Faith, and now all these non-Catholics absolutely refuse to let their children attend services with unsegregated congregations, this partly due to the fact that other denominations do not allow mixed races."[24] The bishop's demand put their families in danger, and they predicted that this approach to integration might even tear their children from the Catholic faith.

They also wrote individual handwritten letters imploring the bishop to halt his plans. Many letters reflected the justification for segregation prevalent among white Southerners at the time. One such letter read, "I do truly believe in justice and equal rights for all human beings, but so far, I have not been able to bring myself to believe that the different races should intermingle. God, Himself, drew a line by the very fact of creating people with different colors. . . . This does not mean that I think the colored race is not loved by God as much as the white race."[25] The white female author of this letter, like many others, goes on to suggest that the African Americans in Newton Grove were being treated well and that she had heard no complaints from them about their second-class status. She writes, "I believe colored people should have their churches and schools and be able to use them unmolested. So far as I know the colored Catholics of Newton Grove were enjoying these privileges, and if there was any dissatisfaction among them, I have not heard about it."[26] The author's implied intimacy with Black

Catholics is dubious. Considering the white population's dominant social status, it would have been highly unlikely that parishioners from St. Benedict's would have confided to their white coreligionists their feelings about segregation, and certainly they would not have openly expressed dissatisfaction.[27]

Yet this woman was not merely an example of a condescending apologist for white privilege and Jim Crow racism. She felt drawn to the same vision of Catholic unity that motivated previous generations of integrationists in Newton Grove. She was caught between being a good Catholic, who does as her bishop asks, and a good southern Catholic who remains attentive to—even if she did not live perfectly within—segregation's racial boundaries. Yet, her allegiance to the separation of the races remained clear, despite her protestations about God's equal love and "justice and equal rights for all human beings." In the last analysis, she uses her faith to justify segregation by arguing that "God, Himself, drew a line by the very fact of creating people with different colors." Here she asked the bishop to affirm the very sentiment that had caused John Carr to turn to the Catholic Church in protest—that different skin colors were evidence of God's desire for segregation in worship.

In response, the bishop sent a strongly worded letter and attached his previous pastoral letters on racial justice. "Through the valiant leadership of Dr. Monk, they . . . came to know the True Church from a printed sermon on the Unity of the Church. . . . Has the Catholic Church any less Unity today? Your attitude on the Unity and Authority of the Church would make your dead parents and grandparents blush for shame. . . . The Catholic Church does not get its teaching from the laity but from Christ. . . . The Catholic Church does not obey the mandate of the laity but of the Pope, the Bishop, the Priest and the people obey the mandate of Christ through them."[28] The bishop, despite his harshly admonishing language, was right that John Carr as well as Solomon and Martha Monk would have objected to the parishioners' rationale for opposing segregation. However, the parish's founding families would have objected as well to the bishop's precipitous manner of achieving integration. The Monks, like the current parishioners, would have understood that integration was a "family affair," not to be broadcast to outsiders. Such broadcasts, like public thwarting of norms, would bring about the parish's certain destruction rather than help sustain it into the future. The bishop's very public rebuttal—the response also made its way to the press—simply fleshed out Newton Grove Catholics' impression that Bishop Waters had no interest in the parish's more nuanced approach to skirting segregationist norms. The bishop's lesson in Catholic authority had the opposite of its intended effect. Parishioners became angrier and more alienated from the church.[29]

Since the passing of the first generation of Newton Grove converts, parishioners seemed to have forgotten the parish was founded on a desire to embody God's wish for racial unity in worship. Remember, for instance, Cora Robinson's letter in 1934 in which she sought Father Irwin's help in reasserting the parish's ethos of interracial respect.[30] Robinson, an African American and lifelong parish member, did not invoke John Carr's mission in the way the bishop did when she asked for help in keeping her white coreligionist from encroaching on the space reserved for African Americans in the pews and St. Benedict's Hall, perhaps because she did not know the story. Similarly, newspaper articles from 1939 reference John Carr without any discussion of his stand for racial unity in worship.[31]

In centering John Carr Monk's role, Bishop Waters legitimized his demand for a contemporary unified church by rooting it in the parish's founding.[32] Unlike the unity that John Carr sought in 1870, which required Black and white parishioners to worship under the same roof, the 1953 version required equality rather than inclusion alone. The bishop mandated mixed seating in the pews and called on parish groups to welcome everyone. His mandate was a major change and guaranteed that the controversy continued after Trinity Sunday. In an interview in 2011, a lifelong member named Jean recalled vigorous arguments breaking out during parish meetings. "They'd get mad," she told a parish oral historian. "They'd say things and go back and forth."[33] Long into 1953, parishioners spoke, sometimes confrontationally, across racial lines. They would tell the priests and their fellow parishioners about their concerns and how they felt about the challenge of navigating everyday life in the newly integrated parish. The bishop ignored these conflicts. Perhaps he disdained people he considered to be retrograde segregationists for seeking further discord. Maybe he dismissed the disruptions as passing growing pains. In any case, from the parishioners' perspectives, the bishop did not seem to think much about life after his integration decree for the people of Newton Grove. His job was done once the parishioners were worshipping side-by-side, and he assumed they would gradually come to know each other as fellow Catholics, much as he had done in his own life.

The Bishop's Commitment to Interracial Catholicism

Born in 1904 in Roanoke, to a devoted Catholic family, Vincent Stanislaus Waters recalled beginning his life with "typical Southern values."[34] Like the

Catholic youth of Newton Grove, he attended parochial school.[35] As a sixteen year old, Bishop Waters moved to North Carolina to attend Belmont Abbey Seminary. His desire to become a priest then led him across the ocean to a place many Newton Grove parishioners would have had difficulty even imagining: the gilded, Romanesque 16th-century palazzo that housed the Pontifical North American College in Rome. He attended seminary alongside fifty or so other young ordinands from across North America and was eventually made a priest in 1931.[36] Besides his seminary colleagues from North America, he also met and befriended several African priests, some of the 500 priests who came to Rome during the 1930s to fill Vatican posts and study at other Catholic seminaries. Monsignor Lewis, who worked under Bishop Waters in the 1960s and 1970s, explained the powerful effect these relationships had on the bishop: "When he got to Rome and saw people from countries around the world in the different colleges, it made him understand that one group is not better than another. He gained this strong desire to help bring about an equal society in America and particularly in the church."[37]

Bishop Waters later admitted that during this period he felt tormented by his racist upbringing. He grappled with deep-seated bigotries as he worked with African priests. Eventually, the future bishop repudiated his childhood community's biases. "Prejudice is where the devil works, in the emotions," Waters wrote in 1935. "The only way we will ever be able to lose prejudice is to allow the right emotions according to logic and truth to influence our wills in the right way and to get rid of the wrong emotions."[38] Custom drove his fears until they were countered by logic and truth. With that realization, derived from his lived experience abroad, he embraced a more complete version of the unity of his church. On returning to the South, he dedicated himself to building a global faith that embraced peoples of different cultures and racial backgrounds.

Waters began his tenure as a bishop in North Carolina by keeping the US bishops call in 1942 to "acknowledge and respect" the rights of African Americans.[39] He created a task force of fifty-five priests working among African American Catholics to exchange ideas about how to best address the needs of these parishioners.[40] A year later, in 1946, he founded a diocesan newspaper, the *North Carolina Catholic*, with a goal that it cover both white and Black Catholic stories equally, as discussed in the previous chapter.[41] Although the Bishop made the diocese's commitment to racial justice explicit in a 1951 pastoral letter denouncing segregation, he did not mandate then that all church services and parishes had to be integrated. Instead, he focused on integrating Catholic life beyond the parish. He took the step of integrating

Catholic lay organizations and societies. Before then, in 1947, he had created a new volunteer organization, the North Carolina Catholic Layman's Association and required that it be open to Black Catholics. Although it was a radical move, the bishop also showed restraint. His mandate applied only to diocesan-wide groups, not to parish-based societies such as the Knights of Columbus or Ladies' Altar Societies. Bishop Waters worked where he could have immediate and lasting influence, believing that when white Catholics engaged in common purposes with Black Catholics, they would embrace a shared humanity.[42]

Bishop Waters decided to use Holy Redeemer to expand his desegregation plan to parishes for one reason: The two parishes, one Black and one white, were only two hundred yards apart. He would have been deeply troubled by the visually dramatic juxtaposition. African American parishes in the North's urban areas were situated in neighborhoods whose residents were predominantly Black. As geographically defined communities, the spatial separation of these neighborhoods provided its own justification for racial parishes. In this way, geographical and racial segregation combined to keep Black parishes out of sight and out of mind of the white Catholic population.[43] In contrast, the fact that these separate white and Black churches were located so close to each other could not be explained away by convenience; the sole reason for the parishes' separate existence was to separate the races. For a principled bishop who was also worried about his colleagues' perceptions, it was a potent reminder that, despite the church's theology of inclusion and his own personal abhorrence of racism, his diocese accepted the sin of segregation.

Bishop Waters called it "a scandal to the Church in other parts of the country" and set out to make an example of Newton Grove.[44] The hypocrisy he saw there encapsulated the hypocrisy he saw afflicting the whole of the American Catholic Church, a church that called itself universal while allowing—even encouraging—segregation. Once again, Bishop Waters believed the parish in Newton Grove should serve as a model for a truly Catholic parish for the Catholics of his diocese, the South, and the nation. The parishioners, as Bishop Waters would discover, were less eager to find themselves on this regional and national stage.

Although publicly he remained adamant in his efforts to dismantle segregation, privately, the bishop was surprised by the white parishioners' response. He thought they had the potential to be integrationists like him because he had witnessed their closeness with their Black neighbors. He admitted his frustration and confusion to a young nun a few months after

Trinity Sunday. Sister Dolly recalled the bishop saying, "You know, they sell their tobacco together. They go into the fields, you know, and they eat together. All that is okay, so he thought it was just a waste of personnel" to administer segregated parishes.[45] While the bishop focused on the power of experience, the parishioners centered the importance of maintaining the nuanced framework of segregation, which they had relied on to keep their interracial practices out of their neighbors' sight and minds. Whatever any particular person's interior state might have been, behaving in societally agreed-upon ways at work and at play was essential to sustaining the parishioners' relationship with the wider community, a relationship that the bishop's focus on emotion eclipsed.

White and Black parishioners in Newton Grove conformed to these norms to preserve both their safety as well as harmony with their neighbors due to white supremacist hate groups infiltrating their communities. The two Newton Grove parishes maintained long-standing informal understandings with the wider community about the kinds of public and private interactions they could engage in without risking outsiders' violent responses. Processions that included both Black and white school children, for instance, were secreted away in the church's backyard, not out front where anyone might see. Priests scheduled joint Masses at odd hours, even after segregation was the norm, so that Protestants would not attend. Mass seating was still segregated; African American parishioners even used the lefthand-side door while whites entered on the other side. The parish did not have painted signs for "Colored" and "White" like those in town, so without these marks of legally enforced explicit segregation, the bishop may have mistakenly thought that parishioners only begrudgingly took up the segregated practices that he had seen structuring everyday life in the parish.

While the bishop highlighted many reasons for the integration, the parishioners focused on one thing only: their parish. In their discussion with Bishop Waters's representative, for instance, they demanded, "Why doesn't the Bishop close all the churches for colored in North Carolina instead of picking on us?" They complained in letters to the auxiliary bishop, "Why didn't the Bishop do this in one of the larger towns instead of in a country place like this?" and "Why start this trouble now, when things have been going along peacefully all these years?"[46]

In fact, Bishop Waters made an example of their parish for a reason that he kept secret from them. He understood the parish as Father Irwin did, as made up of "people who settled the soil originally . . . [as] indigenous to North Carolina as tar pitch and turpentine."[47] Late in 1953, he confessed to the parish's priest that he would have desegregated the entire diocese, but he feared the rest of his flock's lukewarm loyalty. He worried over the more transient Catholic congregations found in North Carolina cities. Would they leave a newly integrated parish? Would he have to take the publicly embarrassing step of shutting down one of his small handful of churches?[48] The bishop also mentioned the Newton Grove parish's history of standing up to racial injustices after the Civil War, hoping these Catholics would find purpose in that cause. He felt that these native North Carolinians, who had remained Catholic for generations despite pressures from their Protestant neighbors, would stay loyal even if the merger resulted in upheaval. If the bishop had shared his esteem for the parish and its history publicly, the parishioners might have felt more common cause with him. At the very least, such disclosure might have assuaged the parishioners' feelings of being singled out and picked on for the sin of being segregated. Instead, both Black and white parishioners remember feeling scared, ignored, and misunderstood.

On that last Sunday of May in 1953, with articles about the merger appearing in newspapers throughout the world, many Americans who read these reports believed that social justice was finally arriving for a group of North Carolina African Americans. Famed Catholic interracialist Father John LaFarge, SJ, himself wrote to the bishop to applaud his decisive step toward interracialism in a long line of Catholic action, when in fact, few Catholic bishops had taken such steps toward goals of racial justice.[49] This justice, however, came on a white Catholic bishop's terms alone; its immediate positive impact on the Black parishioners was suspect.

Henry, who was there on Trinity Sunday, summed up the mixed results of Bishop Waters's action: "[Integration] really did not have an impact at that time. It was a bold step. But really, we lost our church that day. That said, I think that it may have helped tremendously as you got into the sixties, and you got into the civil rights era."[50] For many of the parishioners of St. Benedict's, the immediate sense of loss would slowly change as they adjusted to its reality. The press, in contrast, did not follow up their initial reports to tell their readers what the merger of the two parishes actually achieved. Within a few weeks, they were chasing the next story.

The Press and the Public

Newspapers across the United States and the world carried headlines announcing the forced desegregation of the Newton Grove parish and cheered Raleigh as the first diocese to make such a move. In western Michigan, the *Daily News* ran the headline "Segregated Church Won't Be Tolerated Says Raleigh Bishop," while the St. Louis *Post Gazette* reported, "Melee Marks Interracial Church Event." The bishop was transfixed by the coverage, even if he complained about the violence. He, or someone in his office, cut out and saved nearly thirty newspaper articles. They tracked down articles from newspapers in New York City, Cleveland, Minneapolis, and Chicago alongside a feature from a Dutch newspaper. Even *Le Monde* and *La Figaro* covered the story.[51] The *Chicago Defender*, an African American newspaper, stated, "Bishop Takes Bold Step." Whatever the bishop's reason for collecting these newspaper articles, the publicity was focused on parishioners' divisions, fears, and disappointments and highlighted the well-worn trope of southern white racism contrasted with Bishop Waters's enlightened views and courage.

One white parishioner told a reporter that she attended the integrated Mass because of her biblical beliefs. On her way to her car she said, "The order didn't come from the Bishop . . . It came from the Bible."[52] Many of her white coreligionists used interviews to disagree with the bishop's order, but they insisted it was a conflict of styles, not substance. John Carr's nephew, who was described as an "elderly man" in a 1953 *Raleigh News and Observer* story, insisted that "the time is not right for such a thing."[53] Other parishioners quoted in the piece took issue with the timing and were also skeptical about the bishop's focus on their parish alone. These were the main ways that white parishioners addressed the merger, strategies that allowed them to dodge the issue of race.

After the merger, many African American parishioners felt alienated and unwanted at the church rather than inspired by the possibilities of this merger. Henry, for example, was a young child when the merger occurred. However, he recalls feeling ill at ease at subsequent Masses: "The experience was actually much more strained and reserved than having our own church, to be honest. Have you ever attended something, and you didn't feel welcomed? That is how it felt."[54] Outsiders' strong approval of the bishop's action was tempered in Newton Grove by the reality of isolation and fear. The *News and Observer*, published in Raleigh, was likely the only newspaper to interview an African American parishioner. Very few reporters even sought out commentary from white parishioners. Readers at the time were left with the impression of white parishioners' deep anger. These one-dimensional depictions have also left an indelible mark on historical scholarship, such that few have tried to explain where this anger originated or how it affected Black and white parishioners' feelings about integration.

Only the *Carolinian*, an African American paper in Raleigh, criticized the diocese's move. The editors objected when it became clear later that year that the merger at Holy Redeemer was an anomaly rather than the initial sign of a new diocese-wide policy. Bishop Waters's pastoral, they wrote, "hailed by Negroes, as a kind of second Declaration of Human Rights, so far as Durham Negroes both Catholic and non-Catholic are concerned, turns out to be just so much sounding brass and tinkling cymbals. Bishop Waters may not have feet of clay but the big toe that sticks through his ragged Catholic sock into Durham is one of mud."[55] The author tempers the praise that the white mainstream media was heaping upon Bishop Waters by emphasizing that, practically speaking, little had changed for African Americans in his diocese. Given that the bishop's immediate efforts at integration did not extend beyond a single parish in a small country town, the desegregation of Holy Redeemer and St. Benedict's rang hollow.

Newspapers, both Black and white, referred to the events of Trinity Sunday as a "failed integration." In sum they reported that Newton Grove's racist white residents had rebelled; parishioners were unable to carry out the bishop's decree. While the decree was a courageous initiative to advance the cause of racial integration, from the bishop's perspective, it only required parishioners to follow their founders' original vision. However, the parish community had changed since John Carr's conversion. Parishioners no longer felt the bonds of kinship in the same way that Solomon, Martha, and John Carr's immediate family felt these bonds in the years after the Civil War.

On Trinity Sunday, when the parishioners walked into Mass at Holy Redeemer, they used the racially coded doors their parents and grandparents had used before the segregation of 1939. Fear permeated the air as onlookers gawked. Their worship had been transformed from an act to honor heavenly kinship to an earthly protest against an ungodly division. For all present, the parish harbingered the struggle toward an integrated norm for secular institutions in the United States. While the African Americans of St. Benedict's quietly applauded this move in ways that never received press coverage, they also knew that as forerunners to social change, they would find little support inside the Catholic Church and no protection outside it. Like their ancestors before them, they were embarking on a new path of uniting religion and race. This time, however, the choice to assume this public identity had been the bishop's.

Difficult Choices All Around

To Bishop Waters's chagrin, many parishioners refused to return to Holy Redeemer after the merger. In 1954, the bishop asked Baltimore's Sisters of the Mission Helpers of the Sacred Heart to take a Catholic census of Newton Grove. The sisters' task was not simply factual but also pastoral, according to Sister Dolores "Dolly" Glick, the young white nun Bishop Waters sent to Newton Grove. Sixty years later, when I interviewed the now frail but jubilant nun over the phone from her Baltimore convent, Sister Dolly spoke about going door-to-door, talking to the Catholic families with emotion and humor that offered a glimpse at the attitude that had convinced so many disgruntled parishioners to open their doors to her. She was appalled. "This bigotry," she recalled, thinking after an early interview. "It's just awful. And it's my responsibility to try to bring this into a oneness of unity."[56]

Mixed marriages made her work even harder. Many white Protestant fathers refused to convert, even though their wives and children were Catholic. These white Catholic women had once felt comfortable practicing Catholicism around their husbands. Now, Sister Dolly discovered, they waited until "their husbands went out to work in the fields" to teach their children the catechism. They even hid the catechism of the Catholic Church volume under the bed.[57] One white mother complained, "My husband will never go to church there ever, ever, ever, ever."[58] Others would claim to be taking their children shopping when, really, they were taking them to Mass at a nearby parish. Perhaps they also attended Mass where their neighbors would not see them and their husbands would be less likely to discover their alliance with a religion that rejected segregation.

According to the diocesan records, the number of Black families also dropped precipitously out of their anger and fear of retaliation at the merger that resulted in the loss of an overt acknowledgment of African American presence in the parish. Sixty members, Black and white, dropped themselves from the rolls. While the rolls tell us little about Mass attendance, they do record the number of parishioners who were angry enough to formally leave the parish. The official rolls continued to decline, reaching their lowest point in 1956.[59] By 1960, however, they recorded only ten fewer members than there were in 1953. Mass attendance by all accounts was considerably lower. Although the parish no longer counted parishioners by race, anecdotally the African American membership of the parish was noticeably smaller, perhaps in part because the parish bus service ended. In 1959, those parishioners who did come to Mass would have seen the first

African American priest in the Raleigh Diocese, Father Thomas Hadden, on the altar.

Some white folks, like Chris, regretted this outcome: "It were the Coxes, the Robinsons, the Carnegies, they stayed on, and the rest of them. . . . A good portion of the Black population, we lost them to other religions and the whites stayed."[60] Other interviewees confirmed that uncles and cousins who left the parish converted to Protestantism. African American parishioners mostly joined White Oak, a Black-led Disciples of Christ congregation next door to Holy Redeemer, as well as other African American churches. St. Benedict's, which had hosted vibrant Black Catholic worship for a generation, now stood shuttered, its paint peeling and its wooden porch stairs splintering, a reminder of both segregation and a period of strong Black leadership in the parish. By 1965 the parish was asking for permission to tear it down. The priest, Father Robert E. McMahon, wrote to Bishop Waters in November of that year, "When I asked you about the disposition of the old St. Benedict's Church and school you told me to repair it. Dear Bishop, this is physically impossible in my judgement. . . . The old Church is an eyesore both physically and morally (our segregation policy of the past)."[61] While this comment emphasizes the Bishop's desire to fix the parish, as well as the priest's perspective that St. Benedict's was primarily about separation, the parishioners' own feelings are lost. What did it mean to the Black parishioners to walk past this once proud and vibrant building—the place where they had celebrated weddings, baptized babies, and mourned losses together—each Sunday on the way to Mass?

Before the merger, many Black Catholic families had supplemented their Mass attendance with celebrations and socializing at White Oak. Now, White Oak would be their home church, where they participated in congregational leadership. As Henry and his family, who remained parish members, considered their choices in 1953, he speculated that "certainly if we had been a member of White Oak Church, my dad might have been a deacon, or he might have been whatever, et cetera. You never know."[62] In the end, they decided to stay at Holy Redeemer. They wanted to participate in Christ's real presence in the Eucharist, and equally important, they retained the family pew and their connection to their ancestors who had founded the parish.

Black parishioners often struggled just to get to Mass, even though these struggles were mostly invisible to Holy Redeemer's white Catholics. John Carr, with his horse-drawn cart bouncing around the county's rutted byways, had realized that transportation was key to his experiment's success. John Carr's effort to provide a Catholic education to both races relied on providing free transportation. On Sunday mornings, too, he picked up parishioners and brought them to worship at the church. Integration ended free bus service to Mass and school; bus service was not offered at the beginning of the short-lived school year in 1954, and the diocese transferred the bus to another school in the diocese. Of the transfer Father Henry Voss lamented that the bus "now has the inscription 'St. Mary's School, Charlotte, N.S.' . . . The words 'Newton Grove' were obliterated in order not to attract undue attention."[63] For parishioners, the bishop's efforts to distance the diocese from Newton Grove and the events of Trinity Sunday were more than cosmetic. It meant shifting resources and attention away from their parish when it needed it most.

In later decades when parishioners had their own cars, some used them to attend Holy Redeemer, but others could travel more easily to neighboring parishes, which held a certain appeal to Black Catholics still alienated by the merger. African Americans only had to drive forty minutes from Newton Grove to attend two different African American parishes—St. Ann's in Fayetteville and Sacred Heart in Goldsboro. These parishes, unaffected by Bishop Waters's 1953 decree, had African American lay leadership and Masses that reflected the traditions of worship in the Black church, even if they were still led by white priests.[64]

Desegregation had far-reaching practical consequences that influenced parishioners' behavior as much as their confessional allegiances. Certainly, a significant factor was the impact on the Black parishioners who lost their church home at St. Benedict's and now would have to join the formerly all-white Holy Redeemer Church. The effect on white parishioners was also significant and especially negative for those parishioners married to Protestants. The loss of busing likewise seriously impeded attendance and contributed to the immediate postmerger decline in the parish's membership. Bishop Waters, driven to ardent action by his personal abhorrence of segregation, did not appear to seriously consider these consequences when issuing his decree. While the press focused solely on the integration of the two churches, for many in Newton Grove, both Black and white, the fate of the parish schools was just as important, if not more so.

An Integrated School in Rural North Carolina?

The two parish schools had long provided a clear road map to success, a respite from anti-Catholicism, and a way to deepen ties to the church and to each other, non-Catholic pupils and their families alike. Even before the merger was complete, the Redemptorists took the dangerously disobedient step of warning Bishop Waters that the merger would undermine the parish's educational mission. Father Sullivan wrote an impassioned letter to the bishop: "All agree very definitely that the white school will be closed if integration is forced upon them in the church. They will withdraw their children from school and refuse their customary support."[65] Many white families did just that. While a few white students like Paul kept attending, taking their seats among rows of suddenly empty desks, other children rode buses to Protestant-dominated public schools in Newton Grove, Clinton, and Dunn. Some preferred to travel nearly fifty miles each way rather than sit in the parish's integrated classrooms. By June 3, 1953, however, it had all become too much. Father Sullivan wrote, "We closed the school today—Report cards were given out."[66] They even cancelled the "end of school year" picnic.

The bishop allowed the two parish schools to be segregated for one more year, but everyone knew that the institutions were soon destined for closure. In the fall of 1953, while the bishop was in the process of removing the Redemptorists for insubordination after their inability to ensure a harmonious merger, the Sisters of Mercy continued running the parish schools. Sister Mary Charles Cameron, who came to the parish after the desegregation, remembers teaching at the white school, while Sister Lily Rose, who was from the South, taught at the Black school.[67] Despite the sisters' effort to put a good face on the situation, Father Voss reported that "the opening of school was a sad affair. We sent the bus around and not one child came out to the route. Only a few children from the neighborhood came."[68] One can imagine that parents would have worried about putting their children on what seemed to be an integrated school bus to travel the rural roads in 1953, just as they worried as children decades earlier. In all twenty white children and twenty-two Black children were enrolled on opening day. That Sunday forty-three white parishioners and thirty-two African American parishioners attended Mass, and the community seemed to be failing. Now there were five nuns teaching forty students; trying to keep their spirits up with Halloween festivities and other events only seemed to highlight the dwindling population, especially of white students.[69] In final count, the African American school had sixteen students and the white school twenty-eight. With so few students, Sister Mary Charles spent as much time packing as teaching. She assembled the school's files into boxes and stacked them in the office, a visual acknowledgment to both students and staff that there was little real hope of continuing as an integrated school in Newton Grove.[70]

When the newly integrated parish school opened in September 1954, no Black students enrolled. Most likely the risk to personal safety was just too great.[71] Only a few white families from the neighborhood sent their children. Given that later integration initiatives in the 1960s were met with Ku Klux Klan rallies, arson, gunshots, and other terrorist violence, Newton Grove parents, even in the 1950s, recognized such threats and feared exposing their children to such violence. Yet the fact that a single school opened in the fall of 1954 with no public opposition is perhaps telling of the parish's remaining influence in the community. The school closed permanently after only a few days. Some white students now went to a new white parochial primary school in nearby Clinton. Other white children attended the local public school, where they reported being more than a year ahead of their classmates.[72] There was no evidence that Black students had enrolled in other Catholic schools, all a long drive from Newton Grove.[73] These children now went to the segregated public primary school where much of the day was spent on vocational training.

Looking back at this time, many parishioners, both Black and white, felt strongly that Newton Grove suffered no violence because residents had gotten used to the local Catholic parish. With its schools, the parish had provided a mutual benefit to the wider community. So did its effect on farm labor, where Black and white Catholics met to plant and bring in the harvest. Further, many parishioners were related by blood and by baptism. Talking to those who lived in more rural areas; however, the picture becomes less rosy. "This was a big KKK country," Linda, a white woman in her seventies, told me. "Even as a teenager [in the 1970s], when I was driving a school bus, there was a place between here and South Johnson [County] that, about two or three times a year, they burnt this huge cross with cloth wrapped all around it. When I got there in the mornings . . . you could still see the smoke from where they had burned it the night before."[74] Still, she had little fear of integration, she insisted, because for her entire life she had attended an integrated church and Sunday school. But she felt deeply for the Black children on the bus who had to endure the stench left behind by the Klan.

Others remember the price paid by the African Americans who, in the 1970s, chose to send their children to integrated (white) public schools. Richard, an elderly African American man, described how white townspeople "would come by my brother John's and sister-in-law's house at night, on the truck or whatever, and shoot towards, shoot up the windows and whatnot in John's house. They did that until my brother started shooting back."[75] John, like Richard, called the Newton Grove parish home and remembered fondly walking with his young son up the church stairs as a crowd gathered on the lawn and jeered at them on Trinity Sunday. Perhaps those earlier experiences in an integrated environment gave him the courage to insist that his children had a place in those integrated schools, no matter the white response. Tempers, he knew, would eventually calm, as they had at the Newton Grove parish, where Black and white families had slowly learned to come together well before the town and the public school system were willing to do so.

An Integrated Parish Bubble in a Segregated Land

In the first decade after the merger, integration in the parish church did not extend beyond attending Mass in the same building.[76] Henry emphasized how the parish's atmosphere had changed from years immediately following 1953 when he felt distinctly unwelcome as an African American child in his formerly white parish. In the late 1950s, however, the whole parish came together for the November Harvest Festival where Henry's fathers and uncles took charge of cooking hundreds of pounds of barbecued chicken and pork through the night, while his mother joined the other women of the parish, both Black and white, the following morning plating up meals to be sold to benefit the parish. Families came from across three counties to buy meals, bid on auction items, picnic, and enjoy a Sunday afternoon away from the farm. Annual festivals were augmented by weekly youth activities by the early 1960s. The parish organized an all-inclusive youth group. "When you'd have the parish picnic and whatever," Henry told me, "we would all participate in preparing the food and doing all the other things. If they took the altar boys, once a year the priests would take us to the beach or something. We would go." He smiled thinking about having fun on the bus with the other kids. They spent hours roughhousing on the beach, and he remembered his friends' joyful closeness. His memories were gauzy and pleasant, dramatically different from the way many parents remembered the parish-wide events of the 1930s, or even the early 1950s, when white parents insisted that their children walk home from school instead of riding the bus with Black children. Henry, in contrast, did not recall his parents worrying about the potential for racist violence if people saw him laughing next to a white friend through the windows of the church bus.

Even though by 1958 the US Catholic bishops had issued strong statements about racial discrimination and the civil rights movement was in full swing, that interracial comradery was in the "parish bubble," a social enclave that recalled earlier decades when certain biracial encounters were kept from public eyes.[77] Henry told me about precautions the group took on the return trip from the beach. The bus stopped at a McDonald's restaurant to let the white boys off, while the Black altar boys stayed, Henry said. "Our food was brought out to us, right. Because again, you're in the late fifties and early sixties. And you couldn't go to do those kinds of things."[78] For Henry and his brothers, as well as all the white children who attended the youth group with them, being a part of the parish allowed for interactions between white and Black children that were forbidden in public spaces, but even in the confines of the parish they sat in separated pews at Mass.[79] There were still limits to parish integration.

But the resistance to the parish's practice of publicly visible segregation was gradually growing, often spreading from seeds of desegregation planted outside the parish. One such seed was the executive order signed by President Harry Truman on July 26, 1948, which mandated the desegregation of the US military. This integration had a profound impact on service members. One day in the early 1960s, Heavyweight, an outspoken African American man, decided to attend Mass on his first Sunday back to Newton Grove from a stint in the Army. In the middle of the service, he got up from his seat on the left Black side of the church. He crossed over and took an open seat on the right side reserved for whites. He took the seat of a white man, Ephraim, who had risen to collect the offering. It was a potentially controversial act since Ephraim had also helped start the "stay away campaign" to protest Bishop Waters's integration decree.

The congregation's response was not anger but amusement. Rachel, an African American woman, remembered that her grandmother laughed at the sight: "I sure hope Heavyweight makes it to the county line." Her granddaughter recalled her short prayer that this young man get himself safely out of Ephraim's reach. Rachel then explained, "That was a big moment during the church. But we all knew that that was different. Heavyweight was sitting over there where he shouldn't sit next to Ephraim's wife. That must've been a sight for Ephraim that moment to turn around and see that."[80] Ephraim took the provocation in stride. He sat in Heavyweight's seat and laughed. Meanwhile, the priest continued with the Mass as if the brief disruption had not occurred. Times were changing.

Black and white parishioners who attended Mass in the 1960s mingled their memories of integration with reconciliation among the parish's factions. White parishioners fondly reminisced about choir rehearsals led by Black directors. By the end of the decade, they also had Black Sunday school teachers. But Black parishioners' memories of bonhomie — such as the altar boys' beach trips—are shadowed by the reality of the "parish bubble." Henry, for example, recounted that those same friends he enjoyed on parish bus trips sometimes averted their eyes when they ran into each other in town. They were liable to walk away without acknowledgment. "It was a paradox as kid that I just did not understand," he shrugged. As an adult, he said, "[I understood that it] was part of the protective system for them [the white parishioners] because they didn't want to be seen as, I'll say a 'negro lover.'" White people who publicly displayed intimate friendship with African Americans were vulnerable. They were subject to, in his words, "the powers of the town who had the ability to cause pain in your life." It was likely to be vicarious pain, like the indignation caused by a smashed mailbox or the refusal to provide help. But bodily violence was always a possibility. This realization made Henry see his Sunday school friends differently. He began to see the pressure that both white and Black parishioners felt to perform the roles given to them by the surrounding segregationist society, especially when they weren't in the safety of the church or the farm.

They did find some safety at the parish. Father John Wall, who came to the parish in 1971, worked with Bennie Robinson, a popular young African American parishioner who had almost been voted president of his newly integrated high school, to expand the youth group. Together, they began developing weekend events for young people across the diocese. These gatherings created a space for Black and white Catholic youth to get to know each other and to see Bennie in a leadership position.[81] Similarly, Bennie's mother and other Black women became prominent members of the Ladies' Altar Society. They led meetings and parish projects alongside other African American and white matriarchs.[82] Twenty years after the merger, the parish was moving closer to equity in some ways. However, other important innovations, like "Carolina Cu-Pepper," a parish-organized cooperative distribution center for parish farms, maintained an all-white membership.[83] Thinking back on its formation, Father Wall, who had had meaningful relationships with the Black parishioners through his nurturing of the youth group, felt the segregation happened because the co-op did not explicitly invite Black farmers to join. This slight offered white farmers a business advantage, while it also highlighted that for integration to work it took constant communication and care, not just proximity. In business as in worship, unity necessitated intention.

Unlike their Protestant peers, by the 1960s, white Catholic parishioners in Newton Grove were comfortable with "mixed seating" and other gestures that conveyed respect for Black elders. It took time, but the message of Catholic unity, conveyed in the Newton Grove priests', nuns', and parishioners' practices, gradually supplanted the broader community's hostility toward integration, at least for these white Catholic congregants. They, too, remember the day in the 1970s when Bishop Waters unexpectedly stopped into a couple's anniversary party. The husband had made frequent trips to Raleigh in 1953 to oppose the merger. At that time, he was a belligerent ringleader against integration. At that anniversary party many years later, however, he offered the bishop a seat at the table among the party guests. Bishop Waters even led grace before dinner.

Leaving the Parish: Protest or Possibility

The parishioners who left in 1953, like the reporters and journalists who quit town after Trinity Sunday, could not imagine the parish would adapt and survive by fostering biracial practices. Those who stayed, however, watched and participated in the church's step-by-step adjustments. Within a few years, some Catholics approved of what they saw happening at Newton Grove and rejoined.[84] Others never did come back. It's possible that race did not play an explicit role in everyone's decision to cut these formal ties. "All of my brothers and sisters left Newton Grove after high school," Henry told me, "for various destinations and careers." Henry himself pursued job opportunities that also took him away; he spent three years in the US Army stationed in Okinawa during the Vietnam War. Although he returned home to attend community college, work once again took him away. Upon graduation, he moved to Raleigh where Father Wall helped him work for a major tech company and where he stayed for thirty-one years.[85] Henry's older relatives remained members of the parish even though they occupied pews that began to look rather empty with just the grandmother and grandfather sitting in a row that once held ten.

The loss of land ownership made the urge to leave Newton Grove much stronger for Black parishioners than for white Catholics. Structural differences also made it harder for Black Americans to keep their farms than for their white counterparts. Farming became more mechanized after the Great Depression. In the 1960s, young white Catholics on graduating from high school often found themselves returning to their family farms.[86] Newton Grove had always been a rural farming community, and even as highways and car ownership made leaving Newton Grove more of a possibility, they were disinclined to leave the land so long as they saw a way to make a living from it. In contrast, the African American parishioners I interviewed often attributed their family's land loss to "individuals not being good stewards" or to "predicaments." African American farmers could not get loans necessary to purchase increasingly expensive farm equipment. Regulatory obstacles prevented them from benefitting from state and federal programs designed to help farmers with financing and other support. Further, many family farms became smaller as inheritance divided the land among the next generation. This trend toward smaller farms took place just as farmers began to need more productive acreage to keep their farms profitable.[87] The farmers who survived did so by investing in moneymaking side ventures like crop processing plants and storage facilities. To diversify their operations, these predominantly white farmers relied on business loans that were difficult for Black farms to procure.

Farming was becoming increasingly expensive as it demanded new machinery and increasing amounts of labor and land. Farmers had long depended on family members to perform daily agricultural tasks. The adults I talked with spoke of childhoods in which they missed school to plow the fields behind mules, picked cotton alongside their fathers, planted sweet potato slips with their siblings, and spent Saturdays cropping tobacco with their cousins. Few of these folks, Black or white, remained in Newton Grove, and fewer still had large families like their parents. This labor pool was dwindling as corporate farming was displacing small farmers, and land dispossession grew apace. Neighbors could no longer help a farmer perform the labor necessary to make the land profitable. Planting and harvesting community work parties gradually disappeared. By 1990, along with expensive plows, farmers also needed costly machines to weigh, sort, and sticker each sweet potato, cantaloupe, or watermelon before it could be sold in local supermarkets. These changes in farming affected each family farm differently, so when the farm finally failed, these Black families understood, as many white folks did not, that the failure was caused by circumstances beyond their control. Both Black and white farmers faced this ever-changing, increasingly industrialized form of farming. White farmers, however, often had more resources on which to rely. In the end, governmental efforts to feed the nation and uplift some types of agriculture did less to benefit smaller family farmers and did next to nothing to support the needs of the African American farming community.[88]

Although during much of the year the bishop's integrated mission might have looked like a failure since those coming for Mass were overwhelmingly white, summertime revealed something very different. The death of the smallholder family farm did not result in the dissolution of practices that tied

Black Catholics to the Newton Grove parish. By the late 1960s, the African American families who left the parish to move to the North or to larger southern cities were bringing their children back to Newton Grove in the summer. Unlike their parishes in the North which might have adopted elements of African American culture into the Mass, Mass at Newton Grove remained culturally white, even though post–Vatican II the Masses were now in English.[89] During those summers, Black Catholic children received the sacraments at the parish and connected to their ancestors by working whatever remained of the land owned by their relatives in Newton Grove. The children would meet the year-round parishioners for Sunday school in integrated classrooms. Despite the expense and unease brought by travelling south, many Black families made a yearly pilgrimage to Newton Grove to visit grandparents and to preserve their ties to the parish.

While many children sat in segregated classrooms during the school year until 1970, attending an interracial church helped prepare them for the shift in race relations that would come thereafter. Rachel, an African American woman who returned to Newton Grove each summer, said that her public schoolteacher had once told her that "white children were very smart and prepared. They read the whole newspaper every morning with breakfast."[90] At the parish as a child, Rachel had often answered catechism questions that the white children could not. She realized those white children were no different than her Black friends, and she shared this knowledge with her fellow Black students. The inclusive relationships that the Newton Grove parish allowed between African American and white children gave them insights and confidence during the movement toward integration that other children (and adults) simply did not have.

During these decades, many members had left the parish to pursue educational and employment opportunities elsewhere. Henry, for example, left Newton Grove to attend seminary in Ohio. Without the parochial school to socialize him into the faith, the priests at Holy Redeemer inspired Henry and at least five other boys from the Sunday school to consider serving the church. Both Black and white Newton Grove Catholics sought seminary or preseminary training as Father Koch, Father Wall, and other priests and nuns nurtured the young people in a parish that maintained integrated space despite threats and pressures. Through the parish these young people continued to connect to Catholic institutions throughout the country to receive secondary educations that could not be found in Newton Grove. This network of Catholic institutions meant that sometimes it was much more feasible for the parish's young people to travel to a seminary in Ohio or to Belmont

Abbey in Charlotte, North Carolina, than it was for them to embark on their daily journey to the local public high school. By launching themselves on trajectories that led beyond their natal community, these boys then emulated the integrity of Newton Grove's white priests who had lived out their commitment to the church.

Like Henry, the vast majority of the parish's children learned skills to help them chart their futures elsewhere. By the late 1960s, many of the parish's youth, both Black and white, went to North Carolina State University. Although NC State was historically the agricultural branch of the state's higher education system, it was expanding the curriculum to teach engineering, computer science, and business. Newton Grove's best and brightest used it to forge careers in cities like Raleigh, Durham, Atlanta, or New York City. Still emotionally tied to their family land, these transplants returned to Newton Grove for visits, spending as little as a few weekend days or as much as a week or two of their vacation in their ancestral homes. In keeping with national trends, according the 2022 survey of Black Catholics, the regular African American attendees at the parish are the minority—in this case, an extreme minority—when compared to fifty years earlier.[91] In 2022, African American attendance at the parish had dwindled to two elderly men and one woman who sings in the choir. Parishioners seek out these three elders each Sunday, making a special point to offer them the kiss of peace at Mass and check in on them when they miss a service.

The social forces at play both inside and outside the parish had kept it from fully achieving the first generation's vision of racial inclusion embodying Catholic unity. They are still working toward that true church. Yet the history of this small Catholic parish demonstrates that, over time, much can be achieved with the persistence and vision of key individuals: determined priests like Fathers Irwin and Sullivan, dedicated nuns like Sister Josita, and a soon-to-be-saint like Mother Katharine Drexel. Most important was the germinating vision and commitment of John Carr Monk and the brave families who joined him in embodying his vision of Christianity that supported and sacralized his entire family, both Black and white. Had it not been for the support he received from this extended family the parish would likely have dispersed after its founder's death just three years after the building of St. Mark's. But the founding vision was a common one, held by John Carr, Solomon and Martha Monk, Enoch Godwin, J. T. Gregory, and their families throughout the generations, including my interviewees, who vigilantly maintained the relationships that allowed it to survive. They lived an imperfect version of racial inclusion that consecrated kinships between Black and white families that were quickly becoming taboo in the post–Civil War era after Reconstruction. In doing so, they made these connections legible—and to some degree acceptable—for the wider community.

The parish's successes and failures were landmarks along the road to a more racially inclusive Catholic Church and nation, however fragile. Newton Grove's parishioners struggled mightily—and not always successfully—with the surrounding community's norms and commonly shared understandings of Christian discipleship. While the parish did not build a fully inclusive and integrated community, over time it achieved much in promoting this inclusive Christian vision. The children in its parish schools were enriched by the opportunities and experiences that Catholicism provided. Parish teachers sought to be supportive neighbors to the entire Newton Grove community, welcoming all children, both Protestant and Catholic, both Black and white. Over time, respect and perhaps even friendship developed between the leaders of the parish and the white residents in Newton Grove who sometimes had harshly opposed integration. So often in history books we recount the lives and achievements of the rich, the privileged, and the powerful; the story of the parish in Newton Grove is not this narrative. It is a testament to the significant changes that can come about through daily efforts made by ordinary people.

Afterword

St. Benedict's School has been moved from the parish campus. A flatbed came and drove it a half mile down the road and turned into a freestanding family home. The young family whose children's tricycles litter the yard probably have no idea about their home's historic provenance. Not far away, John Carr Monk's house is rotting in the woods on farmland still owned by the Gregory family. I'm told that if you search for it in the winter, you might be able to see some windows or pieces of the cupola through all the kudzu vines. Time has a way of covering over the past, even more effectively than the paint that erased "Newton Grove" from the side of the buses that once drove children to the parochial schools via the rural roads of North Carolina, knitting the parish to the community before the bishop's "merger."

For many years, the bishop tried to help time along, or so it seemed. Decades later, in a retrospective of his career, the *North Carolina Catholic* said two things about 1953: "The Mission Helpers of the Sacred Heart arrive in the Diocese. Bishop Waters published a Pastoral Letter June 12 on Christian Concerns of Race."[1] Nothing about desegregation or the "merger." Already in the months following Trinity Sunday, Bishop Waters was distancing himself from the controversy. First, he renamed the parish Our Lady of Guadalupe. He even printed new letterhead for the priests: "Our Lady of the Americas' Church, Newton Grove, North Carolina."[2] He chose this name because it honored Mary, in a year the Catholic Church had dedicated to the mother of Jesus. He hoped to "obtain her powerful protection and assistance" for the parish.[3] Waters, still eager to burnish his racial justice bona fides, also hoped the name would impress Native Americans in the area.[4] Although the bishop might have known about Juan Diego, the indigenous Mexican man to whom the Virgin appeared, few Catholics in the area knew the story of the Virgin of Guadalupe for whom their parish was named. Despite these many efforts to help the name resonate with the population, often the parish was simply called "the Catholic Church in Newton Grove."

Within the next twenty-five years, however, the new name would indeed begin to resonate with Latinx Catholics who were moving into the area. The arrival of these newcomers gave the descendants of the parish's founding families an opportunity to peel back the paint and tear down the vines that had been hiding their community's history.[5] Learning how their grandparents lived out the parish's mission of racial unity reconnected the parishioners to community memories while providing them with a way to reach out to these more recent arrivals. Far from a parish standing stubbornly against the past, Newton Grove's Catholics are resolutely moving into the future in all its messiness.

In the 1980s, as family farms were giving way to large commercial agricultural operations throughout the state, the latter desperately needed new sources of low-cost labor. North Carolina agribusinesses went to Mexico and South America to find workers willing to accept the meager wages these big conglomerates were offering. Mexican migrants began attending Mass at Our Lady of Guadalupe during harvest seasons. They came to Newton Grove because the parish was the only one in North Carolina dedicated to Mexico's patron saint, the Virgin of Guadalupe. With a new group of Catholics in its territory, the diocese now turned to the parish to do another kind of missionary work: The diocese created The Migrant Ministry, an outreach program for migrant farm workers, and housed its headquarters in the parish. Spanish-speaking white priests celebrated Mass in the evening, when workers were done in the fields and after the year-round members had gone home.[6] No other parish in the diocese had such a ministry, and the parishioners themselves were never consulted about its formation. While the ministry was a boon to the migrants, it made many white and Black parishioners feel as if they were once again "the bishop's guinea pigs," according to eighty-three-year-old Amelia.[7]

Initially, migrant workers came to Newton Grove for short periods. By the 1990s, after movement across the US–Mexico border was restricted, entire families began making Newton Grove and other towns in North Carolina their permanent home.[8] And, they began making Our Lady of Guadalupe their parish home. Moving from Migrant Ministry to pastor of the parish, Father James Garneau carefully began highlighting stories from Mexican Catholicism in his sermons. For instance, he told the Anglo parishioners the story of the indigenous farmer, Juan Diego, to whom Our Lady of Guadalupe first appeared on the hill of Tepeyac in Mexico in 1531. Father Garneau recounted how the bishop ignored Juan Diego's pleas to listen to what the Virgin had told him; the bishop had assumed he was ignorant and backward. One Anglo parishioner called out, "We know all about that, Father!" From the days in 1953 when Bishop Waters refused their input on the merger to today's Migrant Ministry, they were used to imperious treatment from ecclesiastical authorities.

Throughout the sermon Garneau encouraged the parishioners to see themselves in this story. Afterward, he hoped the Anglo congregation would begin to understand that they had much in common with the seeming foreigners who came for Spanish Mass each weekend.[9] Father Garneau understood himself as a bridge—finding and strengthening connections between these two ethnic communities so that the parish could build a new collaborative self-understanding. He would not make dictates like Bishop Waters, nor would he wait for one courageous parishioner, like John Carr Monk, to stand up for racial unity in the church based on inclusion and equality.

The Migrant Ministry led some parishioners to feel that the parish had chosen the recent migrants over the longstanding members who ran the farms. Divisions between "us and them" that were expressed by many white parishioners grew out of differences in culture, language, and tensions around farming and labor. Priests attempted to offer support to all their parishioners, new and old. Still, many who traced their roots back to the days of Saint Mark's felt just as overlooked as they had at the time of "the merger" in 1953.[10] Once again, they were losing control of their parish.

Within a few years, Father Garneau arranged a pilgrimage to Mexico for thirty-five Anglo parishioners. He recounted how, in Mexico, they first experienced a thoroughly Catholic culture, noting the significance of "all the things that Mexicans would do in public that *they* [as Catholics in the Protestant South] wouldn't dare do in public—from making the sign of the cross to traveling on their knees before the shrine of Our Lady of Guadalupe." The parishioners came back feeling more comfortable being openly Catholic in the community. Further, some of the Anglo members now envied the Mexicans' intense devotion to the Virgin Mary. He recalled Anglo parishioners' apprehensions about saying the Rosary in their kitchens decades earlier. They had worried about being discovered by a Protestant neighbor. Now, it seemed almost impossible, but these coreligionists were standing in public chanting, "Hail Mary, full of grace."[11] Slowly, perhaps, the fears of the past would disappear as they learned from these newcomers how to be publicly Catholic.

As the Migrant Ministry expanded, so did an effort to refurbish the sanctuary. Rebuilding meant taking time to explore their own genealogies as well as parish history to ensure that it was properly highlighted in the renovation. As one white parishioner recounted, "The project has allowed us to get back in touch with the history of our parish, to pass it on to our younger people. . . . This is the best thing that has happened in this parish since the conversion of Dr. John Carr Monk."[12] By tracing their family backgrounds together, the parishioners, both Black and white, could excavate the stories that remained in the community, demonstrating that despite the efforts of their parents and the Catholic hierarchy to dissociate themselves from this painful moment in their past, much of the moral framework of that original southern Catholic identity remained. As a historian himself, Father Garneau could help the community contextualize the parish's founding mission alongside its past successes and injustices. Eventually, the parish created a historical society. Together, they interviewed parish elders and learned about the role of now-canonized Saint Katharine Drexel and reminded the parish that their remodeled church building came about because of her devotion to the Black parishioners of their parish. This collective remembering offered an opportunity to acknowledge the spiritual kinship and concrete contributions made by both the Black and white founding families in those early years. In so doing, they helped to foreground that sustaining this interracial, no longer internally segregated community took the careful collective effort of the parishioners as well as the individual initiatives of the Monk brothers, Drexel, and Fathers Irwin, Wall, and Garneau. Although some parishioners continued to feel overlooked and underappreciated, the parish's momentum had returned to fulfilling the founding generation's desire for a unified church in the segregated South. For many, the current, conscious effort to publicly join the African American, white, and Latinx parishioners in sermons, festivals, and personal interactions was a welcome counterpoint to memories of the merger as a public relations debacle.

In 2024, struggles remained between and among the Latinx and Anglo communities within the parish, though the acknowledgment that farms rely on immigrant labor and the familiarity that Anglo parishioners have with these workers helped to lessen the tensions. Simultaneously, these connections have started to nurture a new kind of ethnically inclusive unity in the parish. The Spanish, almost entirely Latinx, weekend Mass recently grew so large that a second one was added to the Sunday schedule. In contrast, there are plenty of open pews in the two English-language Masses, where the average age of attendees continues to rise. There are exceptions, of course. Just as it did throughout the parish's history, youth activities have brought young Anglo and Latinx children together, creating opportunities to fall in love. As these parish couples marry and have families, they join second-generation Latinx families who move comfortably between the English and Spanish Masses and act as cultural intermediaries working to unite the two communities.

Many Anglo parishioners praise this shift, but not all. As Father Garneau highlighted in an interview, "There's a cost; there's a price; there's a strain at times."[13] In recognizing this price and attending to their history, Father Garneau and many of the priests and lay leaders who followed him did something that many wished Bishop Waters had done—they listened to the communities' concerns and helped them tie their local knowledge to the Roman Catholic Church's global mission. Together the parish continues to highlight the founders' quest for a truly unified church as a north star by which to navigate the path toward inclusiveness in their parish life, now an inclusion that attempts to bring together Anglos, Latinx and African Americans connected to the congregation. This effort at inclusion has been much more difficult for the African American families that remain in the area. After all, the parish in the 1990s could include Latino culture in the Mass in ways that it could not for the African American community in the 1950s and 1960s, when the Vatican would not allow such additions.

The parish's hopes for the future and connections to its past were on clear display, for example, on Friday, March 8, 2019, as the children from the post-desegregation era sought to do integration right, if only for one night. On that Lenten Friday, parishioners made their way to Saint Katharine Drexel Hall, the space where the African American parish of St. Benedict's once stood, to enjoy a traditional Lenten fish fry. The Anglo and Latino men of the Knights of Columbus who hosted the community-wide fundraiser were intentional in their choice of side dishes: Southern hush puppies and slaw sat nicely next to the Mexican verde sauce. They served fish as a main course that, upholding church doctrine that members over fourteen avoid meat on Fridays, was a public statement about their commitment to the global Catholic Church. Here was a gastronomic display of an ideal: Catholicism with cultural accompaniments, an inclusive parish where individual traditions were easily recognizable even as they mixed seamlessly.

Into the 1990s the priest guided these integration efforts with frequent reminders in his homilies of the first generation's vision of the universal church. These references to the parish's history are aspirational, a thoughtful departure from 1953 when Bishop Waters used a reprimand to remind the parish of their ties to John Carr Monk. Since the 1990s, the community, led in large part by the parish historian, has worked hard to embed the first generation's vision in Our Lady of Guadalupe's own self-understanding. The process required drawing a direct line from the parish's current actions back to the original one, John Carr Monk's post–Civil War conversion. In a parallel story to the parish's founding, when Catholicism served to reinvent pre–Civil War kinship as spiritual relatedness, by the 2000s, Catholicism was tying Latinx Catholics to the Monk lineage. In the parish's preaching and ministries to migrant workers, Latinx parishioners are becoming godchildren as well as sons- and daughters-in-law of the founding families. Like John Carr Monk before them, many of Our Lady of Guadalupe Parish's elders now stand, when called to the altar for weddings and baptisms, as witnesses for Latinx families taking part in the church's most fundamental sacramental rituals. While Anglo parishioners today have diverse views on immigration, from fearing that immigration threatens jobs to supporting citizenship pathways, the parish has created discussion forums and community events to help lessen those fears.

These efforts, always imperfect, continued as the community prepared for its 150th anniversary. This event, like the remodel, served as a moment to apply the founding story to the present. Vacation Bible School in the summer of 2024, called Jubilee Station: Celebrating 150 Years, taught young white and Latino attendees along with their parents about their parish's vision of unity over the decades with displays on parish families and culture, education, and historical events that included contributions from white, Black, and Latinx parishioners and former parishioners. While the unity presented to the children remains aspirational in many ways, it also represents a community truth—these parishioners were and are part of a single parish, with a mission to replace the "us versus them" of secular divisions with a spiritual kinship of brothers and sisters in Christ.

Just as the parish seeks to learn from the mistakes of its past as it reaches out to Latinx Catholics, its Anglo members have long sought to rebuild relationships with the African Americans who left the community. In many ways, the parish has passively rekindled these relationships by maintaining the open sense of family that it has fostered since its founding. When Richard's mother, a lifelong Baptist, died in 1991, he went to the priest to ask if she could be buried in the cemetery with the rest of her (Catholic) family. He felt an immense amount of trepidation as he asked Father Garneau, since he realized that it was customary to restrict burial in parish cemeteries to Catholics only. He was both relieved and exhilarated when Father Garneau replied, "You know that I love your mother and father. . . . Yes, you can bury your mother there right next to your father."[14]

Richard remembered the kindness, love, and belonging he had felt as a child when he attended school and Mass. After the funeral, he told me through tears that "they had a women's auxiliary there cooking; they had plenty of food ready for everybody that came to the burial."[15] For Richard, his mother's funeral doubled as homecoming. It brought together his schoolmates from both St. Benedict's and Holy Redeemer along with their children as well as their shared ancestors, amongst whose graves they stood. Now, there were no rules of segregation to observe. The guests could pray, cry, and eat together however they wanted. In fact, the Anglo women of the parish cooked and served everyone. The freedom and abundance Richard experienced at the funeral stood in stark contrast to the fear and restrictions of his childhood. Despite the daily distance between Richard and the parish, the kinship between them remained, revealed by the way his voice cracked when he recounted this story.

At every moment in its history, the Catholic parish in Newton Grove has highlighted the concerted and sustained effort it takes to maintain any type of integrated religious community in North Carolina's overwhelmingly Protestant hinterlands and America more broadly. John Carr Monk, for instance, did so much more than call a priest to Newton Grove; he himself started a Sunday school for African Americans. With both acts, he set an example of standing up for his principles without turning his back on his family or his community. Although he stood alone against seceding just before North Carolina entered the war, he still hosted his brother's regiment before it headed into battle. He demonstrated how to be true to the entirety of his conscience, even if with today's eyes it looks hypocritical to us.

Just as the arrival of the Latinx population offered the community an opportunity to rediscover its past, in 2016, the Redemptorist Fathers also returned to oversee the parish. As soon as they arrived, the priests reached out to former parishioners, Protestants, and new migrants. They sought to demonstrate that the parish is open to all and that they are, as Father Moley explained in 2018, "everybody's priests."[16] Denominational lines matter less here, where land dispossession and the younger generation's urban migration have left many older people alone and in need of pastoral care.

Still, for many African Americans, these efforts do not go far enough. For instance, Marilyn, a sixty-year-old African American woman who had recently returned to the parish after thirty years in a southern city, described her homecoming with tears in her eyes: "The first time I came back to Mass here, I walked in the door, and this older white woman came over to me, took my face in her hands and said, 'I'm so glad you're here. You look just like your mother.' She continued, 'You see . . . I am mad that there are no African Americans here anymore, but these are my people. They know me, even if I don't know them.'"[17] These commingled feelings of unity and division, kinship and alienation, remain in a parish where power was never thoroughly shared through formal channels of parish leadership or informal pathways of lay influence.

Today, unlike when Marilyn and her cousins attended the parish in the 1950s and 1960s, white and Black Mass-goers, including Marilyn, speak openly about their common ancestors and recognize that the aging white population must find its place with young Latinx parishioners. Where once white children outnumbered Black children five to one, now the same is true of the proportion of Latinx to white children. Without land to tie them to place, young white people are now leaving town after graduation, while those African Americans who left in the 1960s and 1970s are returning to the family land after they retire.

New symbolism has replaced segregation, particularly in the parish cemetery. The "color line" that once governed burial is hard to see. Upon his death in 1974, Bishop Vincent Waters was buried in the priest's cemetery in Raleigh, although he had requested to be laid to rest in Newton Grove. In the mid-1980s, however, the diocese established a priests' section of the cemetery and relocated the bishop's remains. The diocese honored his request by placing his grave in a way that bridges and blurs the previously segregated land.[18] This last act emphasizes his commitment to the integration at Newton Grove and the diocese as a whole. Although in the 1960s and 1970s it seemed like the bishop had forgotten them, it's more likely that he was trying not to make that era's fight for integrated public schools more difficult. Perhaps he sensed that dictating from afar was no longer acceptable. Nonetheless, by the mid-1980s, when Bishop Waters's headstone was installed, he posthumously made it clear that he stood behind "the merger" and all the consequences it had for the parish, the diocese, the state, and the American Catholic Church.

Neither the bishop's symbolic act nor the community's continued efforts at inclusion have erased the residue of Jim Crow. Segregation is still embedded in the cemetery's layout. John Carr Monk will forever lie across the color line from his brother, Solomon, and the Black parishioners of St. Benedict's. Living with this past, parishioners have been trying to shape a future that reaches toward an ever-expanding mission of inclusion for over 150 years. Here, firmly planted in the American South, Newton Grove's generations of rural Catholics search their local southern and global Roman Catholic traditions to unite a parish family and speak directly to the contemporary moment, a moment when many in the church are seeking authentic Catholic paths to social justice. Building the racially unified church that John Carr Monk was inspired to imagine way back in 1871 remains an ongoing process.

Notes

Introduction

1. Stories of Solomon and John Carr Monk building the church together came through oral histories with Solomon's descendants done in the late 1990s and were relayed to me by Erich D. Jarvis in a phone conversation, September 28, 2023.

2. Donald G. Mathews, *Religion in the Old South* (Chicago: University of Chicago Press, 1977). The "Old South" excludes former French colonies, like Louisiana, which have a deep Catholic heritage.

3. For more on how Catholicism shaped race religions in the urban North after the Great Migration, see John T. McGreevy, *Parish Boundaries: The Catholic Encounter with Race in the Twentieth-Century Urban North* (Chicago: University of Chicago Press, 1996).

4. Section 15 of the 1868 North Carolina State Constitution mandated that all children must attend school until the age of eighteen. In 1875, legislators amended the Constitution to require racial segregation in education: "And the children of the white race and the children of the colored race shall be taught in separate public schools; but there shall be no discrimination in favor of, or to the prejudice of either race" (North Carolina Constitution, article 9, section 2).

5. Two extended pieces have been written on this topic: Cecilia A. Moore, "Dealing with Desegregation: Black and White Responses to the Desegregation of the Diocese of Raleigh, North Carolina, 1953," in *Uncommon Faithfulness: The Black Catholic Experience*, ed. M. Shawn Copeland (Maryknoll, NY: Orbis Books, 2009) and Blake Slonecker, "A Church Apart: Catholic Desegregation in Newton Grove, North Carolina," *North Carolina Historical Review* 83, no. 3 (July 2006): 322–54.

6. All my interviewees have been given pseudonyms to protect their identities, except for the priests, who spoke to me in their capacity as parish leadership.

7. Fifty-eight-year-old white woman, interviewed by the author in person, Newton Grove, North Carolina, June 29, 2017.

8. Similarly, in Catholic circles, the Georgetown Slavery Archive has united descendants of enslaved people who built and sustained Georgetown University. For more information on these descendants, see the Georgetown Slavery Archive online at http://slaveryarchive.georgetown.edu/descendants. This work, which includes reparations in the form of scholarships for descendants, has been a model for many other American colleges and universities.

9. Sixty-four-year-old African American man, interviewed by the author, telephone, February 13, 2021.

10. On African American Catholicism, see Danny Duncan Collum, *Black and Catholic in the Jim Crow South: The Stuff That Makes Community* (Mahwah, NJ: Paulist Press, 2006); M. Shawn Copeland, ed., *Uncommon Faithfulness: The Black Catholic Experience*

(Maryknoll, NY: Orbis Books, 2009); and Matthew J. Cressler, *Authentically Black and Truly Catholic: The Rise of Black Catholicism in the Great Migration* (New York: New York University Press, 2017). For some examples of scholarship on American Catholic history, see Jay P. Dolan, *The American Catholic Experience: A History from Colonial Times to the Present* (Notre Dame, IN: University of Notre Dame Press, 1992); McGreevy, *Parish Boundaries*; and Leslie Woodcock Tentler, *American Catholics: A History* (New Haven, CT: Yale University Press, 2020).

11. For explorations of religion in the American South, see Mathews, *Religion in the Old South*; Beth Barton Schweiger and Donald G. Mathews, eds., *Religion in the American South: Protestants and Others in History and Culture* (Chapel Hill: University of North Carolina Press, 2004); Christine Leigh Heyrman, *Southern Cross: The Beginnings of the Bible Belt* (New York: Alfred A. Knopf, 1997); and Charles Reagan Wilson, *Baptized in Blood: The Religion of the Lost Cause, 1865–1920* (Athens: University of Georgia Press, 1980).

12. Judith Weisenfeld, *New World A-Coming: Black Religion and Racial Identity during the Great Migration* (New York: New York University Press, 2016).

13. For more on the creation of communes and other religious communities to confront white supremacy, see Victoria W. Wolcott, *Living in the Future: Utopianism and the Long Civil Rights Movement* (Chicago: University of Chicago Press, 2022) and Weisenfeld, *New World A-Coming*.

14. McGreevy, *Parish Boundaries*. See also John T. McGreevy, "Racial Justice and the People of God: The Second Vatican Council, the Civil Rights Movement, and American Catholics," *Religion and American Culture: A Journal of Interpretation* 4, no. 2 (1994): 221–54.

15. I borrow this concept of racial formation through exchange, particularly in the context of North Carolina, from Kirsten Fischer, *Suspect Relations: Sex, Race, and Resistance in Colonial North Carolina* (Ithaca, NY: Cornell University Press, 2002).

16. Oral history, Sisters of Mercy, Catholic Schools at Newton Grove 1928–54. Sisters of Mercy Archives, Belmont, NC.

17. Cass R. Sunstein, "The Idea of a Useable Past," *Columbia Law Review* 99 (1995): 603.

18. David S. Cecelski, telephone conversation with the author, January 24, 2021.

19. Sixty-six-year-old white man, interviewed by the author, in person, June 2, 2021.

20. Sixty-six-year-old African American woman, interviewed by the author, Zoom, September 12, 2019.

21. Sixty-eight-year-old African American man, email to the author, July 15, 2019.

22. Sixty-two-year-old African American woman, phone conversation with author, July 22, 2019.

23. Sixty-two-year-old African American woman, interviewed by the author, in person, North Carolina, July 24, 2019. For more on the importance of storytelling as a means to visibility, see Barbara Meyerhoff, *Stories as Equipment for Living: Last Talks and Tales of Barbara Meyerhoff*, ed. Marc Kaminsky and Mark Weiss in collaboration with Deena Metzger (Ann Arbor: University of Michigan Press, 2007).

24. Sister Mary Charles, eighty-three-year-old white woman, interviewed by the author, in person, Charlotte, North Carolina, July 23, 2018.

25. Sixty-two-year-old African American woman, interviewed by the author, in person, North Carolina, July 24, 2019.

26. Seventy-year-old African American woman, interviewed by the author, in person, North Carolina, July 22, 2019.

Chapter One

1. Ninety-year-old white woman, interviewed by the author, in person, North Carolina, July 18, 2019.

2. Sixty-year-old white man, interviewed by the author, in person, North Carolina, August 5, 2018.

3. For more on the Catholic Church and slavery in the United States, see David J. Endres, ed., *Slavery and the Catholic Church in the United States: Historical Studies* (Washington, DC: Catholic University of America Press, 2023); Rachel L. Swarns, *The 272: The Families Who Were Enslaved and Sold to Build the American Catholic Church* (New York: Random House, 2023); and Kenneth J. Zanca, ed., *American Catholics and Slavery: 1789–1866: An Anthology of Primary Documents* (Lanham, MD: University Press of America, 1994).

4. Sixty-two-year-old African American woman, interviewed by the author, in person, North Carolina, July 24, 2019.

5. Eighty-nine-year-old African American man, interviewed by the author, by telephone, July 17, 2021.

6. Steven Hahn, *A Nation under Our Feet: Black Political Struggles in the Rural South from Emancipation to the Great Migration* (Cambridge, MA: Harvard University Press, 2003), 17.

7. Charles H. Bowman Jr., "Archibald Monk: Public Servant of Sampson County," *North Carolina Historical Review* 47, no. 4 (October 1970): 339, http://www.jstor.org/stable/23518201.

8. Bowman, "Archibald Monk."

9. R. H. Taylor, "Slave Conspiracies in North Carolina," *North Carolina Historical Review* 5, no. 1 (January 1928): 20–34, http://www.jstor.org/stable/23516312.

10. John Spencer Bassett, *Slavery in the State of North Carolina* (Baltimore: Johns Hopkins Press, 1899), 96–97. Fear surrounding these suspected revolts spread across Sampson and Duplin Counties.

11. Bowman, "Archibald Monk."

12. 1830; Census Place: *Sampson, North Carolina*; Series: M19; Roll: 125; Page: 171; Family History Library Film: 0018091. Accessed through Ancestry.com. The best we can do with this early census data is some careful conjecture. Censuses from the time list each enslaver as "head of household" with sections beneath his name to mark the age, race, and bondage status of each person who lived on his land. Except for the head of household, the census record does not identify anyone by name. Archibald's wife, for instance, is listed as a tick mark in the column "Free White Women" within her particular age division, while his sons are marked under "Free

White." The lists then continue with "Slave Males" and "Slave Females," also divided into age cohorts.

13. Many African Americans learned through oral tradition that Solomon had a twin brother, Kaplan Monk. While no written records confirm Kaplan's existence, this would not be unusual for an enslaved person. Those folks who understand Kaplan to be part of their family explain that he disappeared from the historical record because of his skin color: "No one knows what had become of Kaplan who later passed for white as an adult" (sixty-two-year-old African American woman, interviewed by the author, in person, North Carolina, July 24, 2019). Kaplan very well could have disappeared into white society even as a child. However, it does seem strange that these stories highlight Kaplan's actions as an adult, since he is already missing from Monk's household as of the 1830 census. It is also possible that his existence was originally symbolic: Family storytellers might have used him to talk about the gains and losses of having mixed ancestry. Through Kaplan's memory, they commented on how "passing" required individuals to turn their backs on family and break ties with their community. For Solomon's descendants and the descendants of other biracial enslaved peoples, Kaplan, whether actual or not, represented the mixed blessing of a life not lived. For more on Kaplan, see Pamela Monk Kelley, *All Roads Lead to Newton Grove: The History of the Monk Family* (self-pub., CreateSpace Independent Publishing Platform, 2010).

14. As we will see, most of the "first families" of the parish are interracial and interconnected. Although enslavers having children with the women they enslaved was not uncommon, what might have set this group apart was their desire to preserve the familial connection after emancipation and the enforcement of contemporary forms of segregation. Researchers continue to discover that there was more to the connection between the families beyond what we see in their shared efforts to run their farms, their recognized interracial families, and their desire to find an alternative to Protestant segregation.

15. Archibald Monk's African American descendants are working tirelessly to give names to each mark on the census. I rely on their work here to name and give life to as many people as possible. Kent Wrench, *The Sampson County Historical Society Huckleberry Historian: Issues 2004–2014* (self-pub., CreateSpace Independent Publishing Platform, 2014), 427.

16. "Slavery in Bentonville" Battle of Bentonville Lesson, accessed July 31, 2025, https://historicsites.nc.gov/lesson-plan-slavery/open. Of course, as Daniel L. Fountain argues, such statistics, which count only heads of slaveholding households, greatly undercount the number of white people who directly benefited from having enslaved people in their homes or working their land; see Daniel L. Fountain, "A Broader Footprint: Slavery and Slaveholding Households in Antebellum Piedmont North Carolina," *North Carolina Historical Review* 91, no. 4 (October 2014): 407–44.

17. US Department of Commerce, Bureau of the Census, "1850: North Carolina," US Department of Agriculture, Census of Agriculture Historical Archive, accessed March 3, 2023, https://agcensus.library.cornell.edu/wp-content/uploads/1850a-13.pdf.

Cotton and tobacco, the crops most associated with antebellum plantation agriculture, did not come to Sampson County until later; even then, in 1860, the region produced only 100 pounds of tobacco and 313 bales of cotton. See "United States Department of the Interior, National Park Service, National Register of Historic Places, Inventory Nomination Form," accessed March 3, 2023, https://npgallery.nps.gov/NRHP/GetAsset/NRHP/64000465_text.

18. Edward W. Phifer, "Slavery in Microcosm: Burke County, North Carolina," *Journal of Southern History* 28, no. 2 (May 1962): 138, https://doi.org/10.2307/2205185.

19. Guion Griffis Johnson, *Ante-Bellum North Carolina: A Social History* (Chapel Hill: University of North Carolina Press, 1937), 492.

20. Phifer, "Slavery in Microcosm," 148.

21. Mark Schultz, *The Rural Face of White Supremacy: Beyond Jim Crow* (Champaign: University of Illinois Press, 2007), 79.

22. John Spencer Bassett, *Slavery in the State of North Carolina*, Johns Hopkins University Studies in Historical and Political Science (Baltimore, MD: Johns Hopkins Press, 1899), 83.

23. Bassett, *Slavery in the State of North Carolina*, 85.

24. Charles H. Bowman Jr., "Dr. John Carr Monk: Sampson County's Latter Day 'Cornelius,'" *North Carolina Historical Review* 50, no. 1 (January 1973): 53. It's possible Archibald's commitment to education extended beyond his white children. Stories passed down by Solomon's children include tantalizing details that speak to Archibald's quest to educate his enslaved laborers, too. One African American woman, a descendant of Solomon's daughter, insisted that the enslaved people knew Gaelic so they could read the Bible. "It was illegal for them to learn to read and write, so that way if someone showed the slaves something in English and said, 'Can you read this?' the slave says no, but they could read and write in Gaelic" (sixty-two-year-old African American woman, interviewed by the author, in person, North Carolina, July 24, 2019). Besides educating the children on his plantation, Archibald Monk was County Superintendent of Public Instruction, practiced medicine, and operated a store and post office known as "Monk's Store." Rachel commented on this contradiction between Archibald Monk's educating enslaved people while refusing to free the enslaved. She spoke in Archibald's voice: "I'm a great person fighting for education, fighting for this, fighting for that, but I own other people . . . I'm Christian, I'm deeply devout in my faith and believe in God. And I got slaves." She concluded with the thought so common in working through this history: "That's always been a conundrum in my life" (sixty-two-year-old African American woman, interviewed by the author, in person, North Carolina, July 24, 2019). C. H. Hamlin, *Ninety Bits of North Carolina Biography* (New Bern, NC: Owen G. Dunn Company, 1946), 101, https://archive.org/details/ninetybitsncbio/page/101/mode/1up, accessed February 4, 2022.

25. Multifamily interview, interviewed by the author, Zoom, September 12, 2021.

26. Alexis Wells-Oghoghomeh, *The Souls of Womenfolk: The Religious Cultures of Enslaved Women in the Lower South* (Chapel Hill: University of North Carolina Press, 2021).

27. For an in-depth discussion about how birth and reproduction shape the lives of enslaved women, see Wells-Oghoghomeh, *The Souls of Womenfolk*, 51–94.

28. Eighty-nine-year-old African American man, interviewed by the author, telephone, July 17, 2021.

29. "Monk Heritage" given to the author by sixty-eight-year-old African American man after interview by the author (self-published, July 17, 2019).

30. Sixty-six-year-old African American woman, interviewed by the author, Zoom, September 19, 2021; sixty-two-year-old African American woman, interviewed by the author, in person, North Carolina, July 24, 2019.

31. Kelley, *All Roads Lead to Newton Grove*, 163.

32. Sixty-two-year-old African American woman, interviewed by the author, in person, North Carolina, July 24, 2019.

33. Anne Herring, "First Families: Cole—Colored Families" (undated manuscript), Newton Grove, NC: Our Lady of Guadalupe Archives.

34. Year: 1870; Census Place: Westbrooks, Sampson, North Carolina; Roll: M593_1159; Page: 396A; Image: 796; Family History Library Film: 552658. Accessed through Ancestry.com, March 15, 2023. "Martha Cole Monk" baptismal certificate, Our Lady of Guadalupe Archives, Newton Grove, NC.

35. For more on the Tuscarora, see David La Vere, *The Tuscarora War: Indians, Settlers, and the Fight for the Carolina Colonies* (Chapel Hill: University of North Carolina Press, 2013) and Gerald Sider, *Living Indian Histories: Lumbee and Tuscarora People in North Carolina* (Chapel Hill: University of North Carolina Press, 2003). For the Tuscarora's own account of their history in North Carolina, see the Tuscarora Nation of North Carolina website http://tuscaroranationnc.com (accessed October 26, 2023).

36. Steven Hahn, *A Nation under Our Feet: Black Political Struggles in the Rural South from Emancipation to the Great Migration* (Cambridge, MA: Harvard University Press, 2003), 17.

37. Hinton Cole Monk and Sarah Williams had ten children including Bertha (b. 1888), the grandfather of famous Washington Redskins football player Art Monk, and Thelonious (b. 1889), whose son Thelonious Monk Jr. became a world-renowned jazz musician. For more on the Hinton Monk lineage, especially Thelonious Monk Jr., see Robin D. G. Kelley, *Thelonious Monk: The Life and Times of an American Original* (New York: Free Press, 2009) and Sam Stephenson, "Is This Home? Thelonious Monk's Southern Homecoming," *Oxford American* 58 (Fall 2007), https://oxfordamerican.org/magazine/issue-58-fall-2007/is-this-home.

38. Sixty-six-year-old African American woman, interviewed by the author, Zoom, September 19, 2021.

39. Daniel Kilbride, "Southern Medical Students in Philadelphia, 1800–1861: Science and Sociability in the 'Republic of Medicine,'" *Journal of Southern History* 65, no. 4 (November 1999): 705.

40. Christopher D. E. Willoughby, *Masters of Health: Racial Science and Slavery in US Medical Schools* (Chapel Hill: University of North Carolina Press, 2022), 95.

41. John R. Logan and Benjamin Bellman, "Before *The Philadelphia Negro*: Residential Segregation in a Nineteenth-Century Northern City," *Social Science History* 40, no. 4 (Winter 2016): 683–706, https://doi.org/10.1017/ssh.2016.27.

42. Kilbride, "Southern Medical Students in Philadelphia," 699.

43. Bowman, "Dr. John Carr Monk," 54.

44. The National Archive in Washington DC; NARA Microform Publication: M432; Title: *Seventh Census of the United States, 1850*; Record Group: *Records of the Bureau of the Census*; Record Group Number: 29, accessed through Ancestry.com.

45. "Whig Meeting in Sampson County," *Fayetteville Observer*, February 20, 1854, 1.

46. Early genealogical efforts suggest that Euphemia may have grown up much like John Carr Monk with Betsey House as a near same-age playmate. Although she is listed as a white household member by name in the 1830 census, many believe Betsey is the same person as Betsey Thornton, who is listed as Black in later census material. More research is being done.

47. The National Archives in Washington DC; Record Group: *Records of the Bureau of the Census*; Record Group Number: 29; Series Number: M653; Residence Date: 1860; Home in 1860: Neuse River, Johnston, North Carolina; Roll: M653_903; Page: 406; Family History Library Film: 803903, accessed through Ancestry.com.

48. John Carr's farm produced crops and livestock, which the family sold for cash. His farm raised 40 swine, 625 bushels of Indian corn, 100 bushels of oats, 400 bales of cotton, 100 bushels of peas and beans, 50 bushels of Irish potatoes, and 400 bushels of sweet potatoes. Bowman, "Dr. John Carr Monk," 56. Archibald Monk's plantation grew the same mix of agriculture and livestock at about three times the size. Bowman, "Archibald Monk," 343.

49. Bowman, "Dr. John Carr Monk," 57.

50. Bowman, "Dr. John Carr Monk," 61. The record of what happened to these now freed men and women disappeared, if it ever existed. Unlike Solomon, who was held in bondage until the end of the war, they left Newton Grove, and perhaps the South, to make the most of their freedom. No one in the current Newton Grove church community that I interviewed traces their lineage through those folks who had been enslaved and later freed by John Carr. His influence is most keenly felt in the parish through direct connections to him as an uncle or to his half brother Solomon.

51. E. J. Hale and Sons, "For the Observer," *Fayetteville Observer*, June 10, 1861, 2.

52. John W. Moore, *Roster of North Carolina Troops in the War between the States [State of North Carolina]*, 2: 166.

53. Derrick Brown and Debra Westbrook, "Bentonville Battlefield Resting Place," *The Sampson County Historical Society Huckleberry Historian* 33, no. 11 (April 1, 2011): 5.

54. Bowman, "Archibald Monk," 58–59.

55. Mary Langston, "The Life and Times of My Grandfather, Enoch Godwin" (unpublished manuscript, 1977). Shared with the author in personal correspondence.

56. Philip Gerard, *The Last Battleground: The Civil War Comes to North Carolina* (Chapel Hill: University of North Carolina Press, 2019), 311–12.

57. Private letter shared with the author written by Enoch Godwin's granddaughter, Margaret Langston, August 15, 1977.

58. Hamlin, *Ninety Bits of North Carolina Biography*, 101, accessed April 5, 2024, https://archive.org/details/ninetybitsncbio/page/101/mode/1up. While North Carolina was not a solidly Democratic state immediately following the war, Sampson County voted for Democrat Horatio Seymour in the 1868 presidential election and had

consistent Democratic representation in the state house. Among those men in the minority who voted for Republican candidates, few of them were white and even fewer of them joined the party itself. For a county-by-county breakdown of the 1868 election, see *The Eagle* (Fayetteville, North Carolina), November 5, 1868, 2. For more on the makeup of the state at this time, see Jonathan Thomas Young Houghton, "The North Carolina Republican Party: From Reconstruction to the Radical Right," PhD diss. (University of North Carolina at Chapel Hill, 1993).

59. Rev. William E. Cox, *Southern Sidelights: A Record of Personal Experience*, quoted in David Cecelski, "The Scalawag's Tale," *David Cecelski* (blog), March 8, 2019, https://davidcecelski.com/2019/03/08/the-scalawags-tale/.

60. Cox, *Southern Sidelights*.

61. Cox, *Southern Sidelights*.

62. John Thomas Warlick IV, "'What's Past Is Prologue': North Carolina's Forgotten Black Code" (master's thesis, University of North Carolina at Charlotte, 2020), 12; Milton Ready, *The Tar Heel State: A New History of North Carolina*, rev. ed. (Columbia: University of South Carolina Press, 2020), 180–81.

63. Eric Foner, *The Second Founding: How the Civil War and Reconstruction Remade the Constitution* (New York: W. W. Norton, 2019).

64. Year: 1870; Census Place: Westbrooks, Sampson, North Carolina; Roll: M593_1159; Page: 396A; Image: 796; Family History Library Film: 552658, accessed through Ancestry.com, March 15, 2023.

65. 1880; Census Place: Westbrook, Sampson, North Carolina; Roll: 981; Family History Film: 1254981; Page: 150B; Enumeration District: 196; Image: 0765, accessed through Ancestry.com, March 15, 2023.

66. Kelley, *All Roads Lead to Newton Grove*.

67. Sixty-four-year-old African American man, interviewed by the author, telephone, February 13, 2021.

Chapter Two

1. Charles H. Bowman Jr., "Dr. John Carr Monk: Sampson County's Latter Day 'Cornelius,'" *North Carolina Historical Review* 50, no. 1 (January 1973): 60, 63.

2. John McCloskey, "Church Unity and Churchmen's Duty," *New York Herald*, January 2, 1871, 6.

3. McCloskey, "Church Unity."

4. McCloskey, "Church Unity."

5. Luretha Blackman letter to Bishop Waters, 1970, box 1, Our Lady of Guadalupe Catholic Church archives, Roman Catholic Diocese of Raleigh, North Carolina.

6. R. Bentley Anderson, *Black, White, and Catholic: New Orleans Interracialism, 1947–1956* (Nashville: Vanderbilt University Press, 2008), 3. For more see James B. Bennett, "The Decline of Interracial Catholicism," in *Religion and the Rise of Jim Crow in New Orleans* (Princeton, NJ: Princeton University Press, 2005), 162–92.

7. Leslie Woodcock Tentler, *American Catholics: A History* (New Haven, CT: Yale University Press, 2020), 137.

8. Luretha Blackman letter to Bishop Waters, 1970.

9. "Cardinal Gibbons in This State," *News and Observer* (Raleigh, NC), May 5, 1912, 4.

10. Cardinal Gibbons recounted the scene later, writing, "Father Gross received a letter, which was one of the inquiries about the doctrines of the Catholic Church, and from Dr. J. C. Monk. A correspondence was open between us after my return from Rome." "Cardinal Gibbons in This State," 4.

11. Dania V. Francis et al., "Black Land Loss: 1920–1997," *AEA Papers and Proceedings* 112 (May 2022): 38, https://doi.org/10.1257/pandp.20221015.

12. Seventy-year-old African American woman, interviewed by the author, in person, North Carolina, July 22, 2019.

13. For more on this phenomenon, see Mark Schultz, *The Rural Face of White Supremacy: Beyond Jim Crow* (Champaign: University of Illinois Press, 2010).

14. William A. Link, *North Carolina: Change and Tradition in a Southern State*, 2nd ed. (Newark, NJ: John Wiley & Sons, 2018), 249–50.

15. Bradley David Proctor, "The Reconstruction of White Supremacy: The Ku Klux Klan in Piedmont North Carolina, 1868 to 1872" (master's thesis, University of North Carolina, 2009), 10, https://doi.org/10.17615/esp3-kp96/.

16. "The Ku Klux Klan," *Wilmington Morning Star* (Wilmington, NC), March 22, 1868, 1.

17. Scott Reynolds Nelson, *Iron Confederacies: Southern Railways, Klan Violence, and Reconstruction* (Chapel Hill: University of North Carolina Press, 2005), 97.

18. Proctor, "The Reconstruction of White Supremacy," 5.

19. Donald G. Mathews, "Lynching Is Part of the Religion of Our People: Faith in the Christian South," in *Religion in the American South: Protestants and Others in History and Culture*, ed. Beth Barton Schweiger and Donald G. Mathews (Chapel Hill: University of North Carolina Press, 2004), 155.

20. Proctor, "The Reconstruction of White Supremacy," 13.

21. W. E. B. Du Bois, *Black Reconstruction in America: Toward a History of the Part Which Black Folk Played in the Attempt to Reconstruct Democracy in America, 1860-1880* (New Brunswick, NJ: Transaction Publishers, 2012), 534.

22. "Ku-Klux Trials and Oaths," *The Weekly Citizen* (Asheville, NC), January 6, 1872, 1; Mark L. Bradley, *Bluecoats and Tar Heels: Soldiers and Civilians in Reconstruction North Carolina* (Lexington: University Press of Kentucky, 2009), 248–50.

23. Bradley, *Bluecoats and Tar Heels*, 248–50.

24. Although the governorship did not change parties, the North Carolina legislature remained reliably Democratic and white supremacist in 1870s. Douglass C. Dailey, "The Elections of 1872 in North Carolina," *North Carolina Historical Review* 40, no. 3 (July 1963): 338–60.

25. Elsewhere in North Carolina opposing segregation was considered treasonous and heretical; perpetrators were lynched. As Governor Holden wrote, defending his decision to impose martial law, "during the last twelve months, not less than one hundred persons, 'in the peace of God and the State,' have been taken from their homes and scourged, mainly if not entirely on account of their political opinions." William Woods Holden, Letter from William Woods Holden to Honor. R. M. Pearson, July 26, 1870, *Civil War Era NC*, accessed July 31, 2025, https://cwnc.omeka.chass.ncsu.edu/items/show/994.

26. Ninety-year-old white woman, interviewed by the author, in person, North Carolina, July 18, 2019.

27. One would expect that similar encounters might have happened, particularly with Black parishioners. If they did, these stories were not passed down.

28. Frenise A. Logan, "The Movement of Negroes from North Carolina, 1876–1894," *North Carolina History Review* 33, no. 1 (January 1956): 45–65.

29. "Our History," Catholic Diocese of Raleigh, About, accessed October 30, 2023, https://dioceseofraleigh.org/about/our-history. Twenty years later, nearly 300,000 Irish immigrants had joined northern parishes, while North Carolina still claimed just five Catholic churches. Jay P. Dolan, *The American Catholic Experience: A History from Colonial Times to the Present* (Notre Dame, IN: University of Notre Dame Press, 1992), 128.

30. Dolan, "Schools," in *The American Catholic Experience*, 262–93; James M. Woods, *A History of the Catholic Church in the American South, 1513–1900* (Gainesville: University Press of Florida, 2011), 267.

31. *Sampson County Deed Book 5*, 35, accessed June 21, 2004, https://www.sampsonrod.org.

32. Kelley, *All Roads Lead to Newton Grove*, 248–308.

33. Michael A. Irwin, "A Thousand Catholics from One Man's Faith," *Columbian* 8 (Nashville, TN), June 1926, 7.

34. Sixty-eight-year-old African American man, interviewed by the author, in person, North Carolina, July 16, 2019.

35. John Tracy Ellis, *The Life of James Cardinal Gibbons, Archbishop of Baltimore, 1834–1921*, 2 vols. (Milwaukee: Bruce Publishing Company, 1952).

36. "Cardinal Gibbons in This State," 4. Cardinal Gibbons wrote *The Faith of Our Fathers: Being a Plain Exposition and Vindication of the Church Founded by Our Lord Jesus Christ* just four years after baptizing John Carr Monk. Here Gibbons demonstrates that he is well schooled in presenting Catholic tenets to anti-Catholic Protestants and potential Protestant converts like the Monks.

37. "Cardinal Gibbons in This State," 4.

38. "A Month in North Carolina: A Letter from Father O'Rourke," *The Woodstock Letters: A Record of Current Events and Historical Notes Connected with the Colleges and Missions of the Society of Jesus*, vol. 34 (Woodstock, MD: Woodstock College, 1905), 368–69, https://jesuitarchives.omeka.net/items/show/901.

39. "Woodstock Letters," 368–69.

40. "Cardinal Gibbons in This State," 4.

41. Ellis, *The Life of James Cardinal Gibbons*, vol. 1, 108.

42. Letter from daughter of Margaret Robinson Cox, Our Lady of Guadalupe Catholic Church archives, Roman Catholic Diocese of Raleigh, North Carolina. By 1873, *Sadliers' Catholic Directory*, which lists all the Catholic institutions in the United States each year, stated, "Newton Grove, Sampson Co. contains about thirty Catholics, all newly baptized." It concludes, "a new church is to be erected here." Rural Newton Grove would soon have a visible symbol of Catholic stability and universality. *Sadliers' Catholic Directory, Almanac and Ordo: For the Year of Our Lord 1873* (New York: D. & J. Sadlier & Co., 1873), 375.

43. Despite the existence of a few pictures, deciphering the construction of the earliest sanctuary was extremely difficult. Angela Page, the parish historian, spent many hours helping me understand the evolution of the church building and the sanctuary.

44. Bowman, "Dr. John Carr Monk: Sampson County's Latter Day 'Cornelius,'" 67.

45. Father Garneau, sixty-seven-year-old white man, interviewed by the author, in person, North Carolina, July 25, 2018.

46. Eighty-nine-year-old African American man, interviewed by the author, phone, December 17, 2021. John Robinson received his land from Pharaoh Lee, whose land he worked before the Civil War, as a free person. Lee enslaved five people in 1860. In his will he described the people he enslaved as "my faithful servants, whom I raised from children and who have stood by me under every circumstance so closely." To express his gratitude and affection, he bequeathed each person more than 200 acres of land. One of these five people was John's future wife, Betsy. When Betsy married John, they received some of this land and used it to start a farm for their family.

47. Sixty-eight-year-old African American man, interviewed by the author, in person, North Carolina, July 16, 2019.

48. For more on the effect of country roads (or the lack thereof) in North Carolina and the American South, see Isaiah Ellis, "Infrastructure between Anthropology, Geography, and Religious Studies," in *The Routledge Handbook of Religion and Cities*, ed. Katie Day and Elise M. Edwards (London: Routledge, 2020); Tammy Ingram, *Dixie Highway: Road Building and the Making of the Modern South, 1900–1930* (Chapel Hill: University of North Carolina Press, 2014); Martin T. Olliff, *Getting Out of the Mud: The Alabama Good Roads Movement and Highway Administration, 1898–1928* (Tuscaloosa: University of Alabama Press, 2017); and Howard Lawrence Preston, *Dirt Roads to Dixie: Accessibility and Modernization in the South, 1885–1935* (Knoxville: University of Tennessee Press, 1991).

49. Seventy-seven-year-old white woman, interviewed by the author, phone, May 12, 2022.

50. *Goldsboro Messenger* (Goldsboro, NC), April 29, 1889, 1. At this time the Catholic church did not have an organ. The younger Monk must have played the organ in her home and at other public events.

51. *Goldsboro Messenger*.

52. *Salisbury Evening Sun* (Salisbury, NC), November 20, 1899, 3.

53. *Raleigh Christian Advocate* (Raleigh, NC), February 5, 1879, 2.

54. Cindy A. Adams and Angela Godwin Page, *Road to the Cross: A History of the Catholic Church in Newton Grove, 1871–2019* (self-published, 2019).

55. Father Lewis's remarks for Mary Elizabeth Cox Monk's 100th birthday. Rev. C. Ralph Monk, "The Monk Family of Newton Grove," *North Carolina Catholic* (Nazareth, NC), January 21, 1973.

56. Letter from daughter of Margaret Robinson Cox.

57. Mark Newman, "'Racial Discrimination Can in No Way Be Justified': The Vatican and Desegregation in the South, 1946–1968," *Journal of American Studies* 56, no. 5 (December 2022): 672, https://doi.org/10.1017/S0021875822000135.

58. For more on Katharine Drexel's work within the church and her path to sainthood, see chapters 5 and 6 in Kathleen Sprows Cummings, *A Saint of Our Own: How the Quest for a Holy Hero Helped Catholics Become American* (Chapel Hill: University of North Carolina Press, 2019).

59. James F. Garneau, "Saint Katharine Drexel in Light of the New Evangelization," *Josephinum Journal of Theology* 10 (2003): 127. For more on Katharine Drexel, see Margaret M. McGuinness, *Katharine Drexel and the Sisters Who Shared Her Vision* (Mahwah, NJ: Paulist Press, 2023); Ellen Tarry, *Saint Katharine Drexel: Friend of the Oppressed* (Boston: Pauline Books & Media, 2000); Cheryl C. D. Hughes, *Katharine Drexel: The Riches-to-Rags Story of an American Catholic Saint* (Grand Rapids, MI: William B. Eerdmans, 2014); and Cordelia Frances Biddle, *Saint Katharine: The Life of Katharine Drexel* (Yardley, PA: Westholme Publishing, 2014).

60. Amanda Bresie, *Veiled Leadership: Katharine Drexel, the Sisters of the Blessed Sacrament, and Race Relations* (Washington, DC: Catholic University of America Press, 2023).

61. Garneau, "Saint Katharine Drexel in Light of the New Evangelization," 127.

62. Sixty-two-year-old African American woman, interviewed by the author, in person, North Carolina, July 24, 2019.

Chapter Three

1. Father James Garneau told me these stories that parishioners told him when he began doing the oral history of Our Lady of Guadalupe in the mid-1980s. The conversation occurred in person in Raleigh, North Carolina, on July 18, 2018.

2. Quoted in Cyprian Davis, *The History of Black Catholics in the United States* (New York: Crossroads, 1990), 217.

3. This idea of transgressing white supremacy while upholding it comes through strongly in Mark Schultz's fine work *The Rural Face of White Supremacy: Beyond Jim Crow* (Champaign: University of Illinois Press, 2007).

4. Fr. Edward, OSB, letter to Rev. M. M. Mother Katharine Drexel, 1899, Catholic Historical Research Center, Philadelphia, Pennsylvania: Sisters of the Blessed Sacrament; H10B incoming Mary Mother Katharine Correspondence (hereafter MMK Correspondence).

5. J. H. O'Rourke, "A Month in North Carolina: A Letter from Father O'Rourke," *Woodstock Letters: A Record of Current Events and Historical Notes Connected with the Colleges and Missions of the Society of Jesus*, vol. 34 (Woodstock College, 1905), 370.

6. Father Edward Meyer letter to Katharine Drexel, March 19, 1900, Catholic Historical Research Center, Philadelphia, Pennsylvania: Sisters of the Blessed Sacrament.

7. Sampson County had two African American schools in the 1880s, but neither lasted more than a few years. "North Carolina Education—Sampson County," Almost Everything You Ever Wanted to Know About North Carolina—Its History and Its People, Education, Education History by County, accessed November 9, 2023, https://www.carolana.com/NC/Education/nc_education_sampson_county.html.

8. "History of Sampson High School, Est. 1924," Sampson High School Alumni Association, About SHSAA, accessed November 9, 2023, https://www.sampsonalumni.org/history-of-sampson-high-school/.

9. The Oblate Sisters of Providence, a segregated Black order founded in 1829, began teaching Black children in 1831, but there is no evidence that Father Edward reached out to these sisters to teach the African American children. The parish never had an African American sister. Mark Newman, "Toward 'Blessings of Liberty and Justice': The Catholic Church in North Carolina and Desegregation, 1945–1974," *North Carolina Historical Review* 85, no. 3 (July 2008): 3. For more on the Oblate Sisters, see Diane Batts Morrow, *Persons of Color and Religious at the Same Time: The Oblate Sisters of Providence, 1828–1860* (Chapel Hill: University of North Carolina Press, 2002) and Shannen Dee Williams, *Subversive Habits: Black Catholic Nuns in the Long African American Freedom Struggle* (Durham, NC: Duke University Press, 2022).

10. Thomas A. Tweed, *Our Lady of the Exile: Diasporic Religion at a Cuban Catholic Shrine in Miami* (New York: Oxford University Press, 1997), 26.

11. Rt. Rev. Michael A. Irwin, VF, "Story of Fifty Golden Years Written by Msgr. Michael A. Irwin for His Jubilee Fete," *North Carolina Catholic* (Raleigh, NC), November 15, 1950, 3.

12. Michael A. Irwin, "Down in Sampson County—A Type of Country Parish," *Missionary* 17 (October 1911), 89.

13. Jay P. Dolan, *The American Catholic Experience: A History from Colonial Times to the Present* (Notre Dame, IN: University of Notre Dame Press, 1992), 262–93; James M. Woods, *A History of the Catholic Church in the American South, 1513–1900* (Gainesville: University Press of Florida, 2011), 267.

14. Section 15 of the 1868 North Carolina State Constitution mandated that all children must attend school until the age of eighteen. In 1875, legislators amended the constitution to require racial segregation in education: "And the children of the white race and the children of the colored race shall be taught in separate public schools; but there shall be no discrimination in favor of, or to the prejudice of either race" (North Carolina Constitution, article 9, section 2).

15. Sister Josita Cavagnaro, OP, letter to her family, 1914, in Parish Historical Society Notes, Our Lady of Guadalupe Catholic Church archives, Newton Grove, North Carolina.

16. "One Hundredth Anniversary of the Conversion and Baptism of Dr. John Carr Monk," 1970, Our Lady of Guadalupe Catholic Church archives, Newton Grove, North Carolina.

17. Redemptorist Archives of the Baltimore Province, 1908, Newton Grove, NC, House Annals.

18. Father Michael Irwin letter to Mother Katharine Drexel, 1911, collection H10B Incoming MMK Correspondence, box 30, Irwin Fr. MA 1908–1911, Catholic Historical Research Center, Philadelphia, Pennsylvania: Sisters of the Blessed Sacrament.

19. Father Michael Irwin letter to Mother Katharine Drexel, 1911.

20. Father Michael Irwin letter to Mother Katharine Drexel, 1911.

21. It was presented as a cautionary tale in the *North Carolina Catholic* during the 1968 race riots, which occurred in over 110 cities in the United States after the assassination of Rev. Dr. Martin Luther King Jr. "We deplore the frightening effects of 'night riders' who, years ago, rode up to the parish boarding school at Newton Grove and scared the wits out of the children and nuns who lived there."

22. "Dominican Experiment in the South," *Dominican Yearbook, 1909* (Newburgh, NY), 99.

23. Sister Josita Cavagnaro, OP, letter to Mother Katharine Drexel, January 10, 1915, correspondence, box 31, Catholic Historical Research Center, Philadelphia, Pennsylvania: Sisters of the Blessed Sacrament.

24. Bob Etheridge, *The History of Education in North Carolina* (Raleigh: North Carolina Department of Public Instruction, 1993), accessed November 12, 2023, https://files.eric.ed.gov/fulltext/ED369713.pdf.

25. *Thirtieth Census of the United States Taken in the Year 1910: Statistics for North Carolina*, https://www2.census.gov/library/publications/decennial/1910/abstract/1910-abstract-1-population.pdf.

26. Rev. Michael A. Irwin, "Down in Sampson County: A Type of Country Parish," *Missionary* (October 1911), 90.

27. Father Michael Irwin letter to Bishop Dunn, 1922–23, ARCDR, box 1, Newton Grove—Our Lady of Guadalupe History.

28. Bishop William J. Hafey, DD, letter to Father Irwin, ARCDR, box 3, Newton Grove—Our Lady of Guadalupe—Newton Grove/St. Benedict.

29. Eighty-three-year-old white woman, interviewed by the author, telephone, July 19, 2019.

30. Charles Craven, "Parish Discusses Merger Plans," *News and Observer* (Raleigh, NC), May 27, 1953, 5.

31. Sister M. Juliana letter to Rt. Rev. Wm. J. Hafey, DD, September 5, 1927, Rock Castle, VA, ARCDR, box 3, Newton Grove—Our Lady of Guadalupe History—Newton Grove/St. Benedict.

32. Bishop William Hafey letter to Sister of the Blessed Sacrament about Beatrice Cox, August 30, 1928, ARCDR, box 3, Newton Grove—Our Lady of Guadalupe History—Newton Grove/St. Benedict.

33. Beatrice Cox letter to Rt. Rev. William J. Hafey, September 12, 1930, ARCDR, box 3, Newton Grove—Our Lady of Guadalupe History—Newton Grove/St. Benedict.

34. Beatrice Cox letter to Rt. Rev. William J. Hafey, August 20, 1931, ARCDR, box 3, Newton Grove—Our Lady of Guadalupe History—Newton Grove/St. Benedict.

35. Beatrice Cox letter to Rt. Rev. William J. Hafey, August 14, 1933, ARCDR, box 3, Newton Grove—Our Lady of Guadalupe History—Newton Grove/St. Benedict.

36. "Beatrice Watkins," *Fayetteville Observer*, January 16, 2002.

37. Mary Cecilia Murray, *Other Waters: A History of the Dominican Sisters of Newburgh, New York* (Old Brooksville, NY: Brookville Books, 1993); Carlinthia Cox, email message to author, May 15, 2023.

38. Dolores Jackson, OP, "The Story of My Life, Sr. Dolores Jackson, OP" (unpublished, handwritten autobiography, n.d.), Dominican Sisters of Hope Archive.

39. Father Irwin letter to Rev. Mother M. Blanche, OJD, February 18, 1926, DSOHA N500, box 177, folder 74.

40. Williams, *Subversive Habits*, 59.

41. Father Irwin to Rev. Mother M. Blanche, O.J.D.," February 18, 1926. For more on racial passing within segregated orders of women religious, see Williams, *Subversive Habits*, 42–45, 56–60.

42. Sister Jeanette Redmond, OP, "Homily for Sister Dolores Jackson, OP," July 25, 1985, Newburgh, New York, Dominican Sisters of Hope Archive.

43. Father Irwin letter to Mother Katharine Drexel, January 26, 1914, CHRC, SBS Collection: H10B Incoming MMK Correspondence, box 30 folder 6, Irwin Fr. MA 1913–27.

44. Michael A. Irwin, "A Thousand Catholics from One Man's Faith," *Columbian* (Nashville, TN), June 8, 1926: 25–26.

45. Father Irwin letter to Bishop Leo Haid, OSB, September 21, 1910, ARCDR, box 2, Newton Grove—Our Lady of Guadalupe.

46. "Newton Grove, NC house annals, 1926," RABP, Newton Grove.

47. "The Boll Weevil vs. the Bale Weevil," *Progressive Farmer*, July 23, 1921, 14; "Boll Weevil Will Destroy Crop Lloyd, Farm Expert Says," *Asheville Times*, April 2, 1922, 13.

48. R. C. Jurney, *Soil Survey: Sampson County, North Carolina* (Washington, DC: Government Printing Office, 1926), 61, accessed June 6, 2023, https://digital.lib.ecu.edu/17085.

49. John M. Coggeshall, *Carolina Piedmont Country* (Jackson: University Press of Mississippi, 1996), 42.

50. Mary Cecilia Murray, *Other Waters: A History of the Dominican Sisters of Newburgh, New York* (Old Brookville, NY: Brookville Books, 1993), 155–56.

51. Father Irwin letter to Archbishop Curley of Baltimore, April 16, 1925, ARCDR, box 2, Newton Grove—Our Lady of Guadalupe.

52. Father Michael Irwin letter to the Bishop Leo Haid of Raleigh, September 22, 1922, ARCDR, box 2, Newton Grove—Our Lady of Guadalupe.

53. Michael A. Irwin, "Rev. Irwin Sets Forth His Views," *Sampson County Independent* (Clinton, NC), October 29, 1925, 6–9.

54. Rev. J. E. W. Cooke, "Foreign Hordes Are Threatening American Ideals," *Sampson County Independent* (Clinton, NC), September 29, 1925; Irwin, "Rev. Irwin Sets Forth His Views."

55. Father Irwin letter to Bishop Haid, 1925, ARCDR, box 2, Newton Grove—Our Lady of Guadalupe.

56. Father Irwin letter to Katharine Drexel, November 14, 1922, CHRC SBS collection: H10B Incoming MMK Correspondence, box 30, folder 6, Irwin Fr. MA 1913–27.

57. Father Irwin letter to Archbishop Curley of Baltimore, April 16, 1925, ARCDR, box 2, Newton Grove—Our Lady of Guadalupe.

58. This gift was made to Father Irwin under the auspices of the Archbishops of New York, Philadelphia, and Baltimore.

59. Father Irwin letter to Katharine Drexel, November 18, 1926, CHRC SBS collection: H10B Incoming MMK Correspondence, box 30, folder 6, Irwin Fr. MA 1913–27.

60. Father Irwin to Katharine Drexel, November 18, 1926.

61. Justin D. Poché, "Race and Catholicism in American History," *Oxford Research Encyclopedia of Religion*, February 26, 2018, accessed January 6, 2025, https://doi.org/10.1093/acrefore/9780199340378.013.496.

62. M.M. Mercedes letter to Father Irwin, April 23, 1927, ARCDR, box 3, Newton Grove—Our Lady of Guadalupe History—Newton Grove/St. Benedict.

63. Father Irwin letter to Rev. Mother M. Mercede, April 27, 1927, CHRC SBS collection: H10B, Incoming MMK Correspondence, box 30, folder 6, Irwin Fr. MA 1913–27.

64. Father Irwin letter to Rev. Mother M. Mercede, April 27, 1927.

65. Father Irwin letter to Rev. Mother M. Mercede, May 10, 1927, CHRC SBS collection: H10B, Incoming MMK Correspondence, box 30, folder 6, Irwin Fr. MA 1913–27.

66. Michael Irwin letter to Bishop Hafey about possible Redemptorist takeover, November 10, 1927, ARCDR, box 3, Newton Grove—Our Lady of Guadalupe History—Newton Grove/St. Benedict.

Chapter Four

1. Redemptorist Archives of the Baltimore Province (hereafter RABP), September 10, 1939, Newton Grove, North Carolina, house annals.

2. Excerpt from the Chancery Parish History file for St. Benedict's, Newton Grove, Our Lady of Guadalupe Parish archives.

3. Reverend John A. Risacher, SJ, "The Beginnings of the Jesuit Mission for the Negroes in Durham North Carolina, December 1939–December 1943" (unpublished manuscript), 1.

4. For more on the "solid South," see Donald G. Mathews, *Religion in the Old South* (Chicago: University of Chicago Press, 1977); Beth Barton Schweiger and Donald G. Mathews, eds., *Religion in the American South: Protestants and Others in History and Culture* (Chapel Hill: University of North Carolina Press, 2004); and Dewey W. Grantham, *The Life and Death of the Solid South: A Political History* (Lexington: University Press of Kentucky, 1992).

5. By 1934 the group of interracialists led by Father LaFarge had broken from FCC to form the first Catholic Interracial Council to seek racial and social justice within the church. Karen J. Johnson, "Beyond Parish Boundaries: Black Catholics and the Quest for Racial Justice," *Religion and American Culture: A Journal of Interpretation* 25, no. 2 (2015): 266–67. For more, see also Matthew J. Cressler, "On the Power and Limits of Parish Boundaries for Understanding White Catholic Racism," *American Catholic Studies* 132, no. 3 (2021): 3–7; Cyprian Davis, "Black Catholics in the Civil Rights Movement in the Southern United States: A. P. Tureaud, Thomas Wyatt Turner, and Earl Johnson," *US Catholic Historian* 24, no. 4 (2006): 74–78; Martin A. Zielinski, "Working for Interracial Justice: The Catholic Interracial Council of New York, 1934–1964," *US Catholic Historian* 7, no. 2/3 (1988): 233–62; and David W. Southern, *John Lafarge and the Limits of Catholic Interracialism: 1911–1963* (Baton Rouge: Louisiana State University Press, 1996).

6. Unsigned letter to Rt. Rev. John Dunn, DD., September 26, 1927, Newton Grove, North Carolina, RABP, Vice Province of Richmond File—New Grove, North Carolina: St. Mark's.

7. Unsigned letter to Rt. Rev. John Dunn.

8. Unsigned letter to Rt. Rev. John Dunn.

9. RABP, January 26, 1928, Newton Grove, North Carolina, house annals.

10. For more on the functions of Civil War remembrance from 1890 to the present, see, for example, W. Fitzhugh Brundage, *The Southern Past: A Clash of Race and Memory* (Cambridge, MA: Belknap Press, 2005); Gaines M. Foster, *Ghosts of the Confederacy: Defeat, the Lost Cause, and the Emergence of the New South: 1865 to 1913* (New York: Oxford University Press, 1987); Caroline E. Janney, *Burying the Dead but Not the Past: Ladies' Memorial Associations and the Lost Cause* (Chapel Hill: University of North Carolina Press, 2012); Charles Reagan Wilson, *Baptized in Blood: The Religion of the Lost Cause: 1865–1920* (Athens: University of Georgia Press, 1980).

11. Ceila M. Benton, "Corn Shuckings in Sampson County," *North Carolina Folklore Journal* 22, no. 4 (1974): 132.

12. Sixty-eight-year-old African American man discussing family history, email, March 16, 2023.

13. Father Irwin letter to Bishop Hafey, January 27, 1934, Archives of the Roman Catholic Diocese of Raleigh, Raleigh, North Carolina (hereafter ARCDR), box 3, Newton Grove—Our Lady of Guadalupe.

14. RABP, January 11, 1931, Newton Grove, North Carolina, house annals.

15. RABP, January 11, 1931.

16. RABP, January 11, 1931.

17. In 1925 St. Mark's (the white school) enrolled sixty white students and St. Benedict's (the Black school) taught twenty-two Black students; ten years later there were seventy-nine white students and thirty Black students. The parish statistics were compiled using the Status Animarum Reports that St. Benedict's and St. Mark's/Holy Redeemer filed with the Diocese of Raleigh each year. Parish Status Animarum Reports 1925–35, RDA.

18. Mark Schultz, *The Rural Face of White Supremacy: Beyond Jim Crow* (Champaign: University of Illinois Press, 2010), 21.

19. "The Depression for Farmers," *Anchor: North Carolina Quarterly Research*, accessed July 31, 2025, https://www.ncpedia.org/anchor/depression-farmers.

20. Sister Julia, "Catholic Schools in Newton Grove 1928–1954" (unpublished manuscript, undated), Sisters of Mercy Archives.

21. Father McQuaid letter to Very Reverend James Barron, Provincial, July 23, 1928, Newton Grove, North Carolina, RABP, Vice Province of Richmond File—New Grove, North Carolina: St. Mark's.

22. Bishop Hafey letter to Father McQuaid, August 30, 1928, RABP, Vice Province of Richmond File—New Grove, North Carolina: St. Mark's.

23. Father Provincial letter to Father McQuaid, December 29, 1927, Brooklyn, New York, RABP, Vice Province of Richmond File—New Grove, North Carolina: St. Mark's.

24. Eighty-two-year-old white man, interviewed by the author, in person, August 5, 2018.

25. Eighty-two-year-old white man interview.

26. RABP, 1908, Newton Grove. References to the marriage banns can be found throughout the priests' notes.

27. For more on the mobile mission, see "The Paulists," *Liturgical Arts* 6, no. 2 (1937); and Jeffrey Marlett, *Saving the Heartland: Catholic Missionaries in Rural America* (Dekalb: Northern Illinois University Press, 2002), 133–61.

28. Rev. John Renahan, C.Ss.R., letter to Vice-Provincial about Our Lady of Perpetual Help Motor Chapel, June 13, 1942, RABP.

29. "Motor Trailer Church Dedication to be held at OLPH on Sunday," *Bay Ridge Record*, May 22, 1941, n.p.

30. RABP, Summer 1941, Newton Grove, North Carolina, house annals.

31. Eighty-six-year-old white woman, interviewed by the author, in person, June 2, 2021.

32. Eighty-nine-year-old African American man, interviewed by the author, telephone, December 17, 2021.

33. Sixty-eight-year-old African American man, interviewed by the author, in person, North Carolina, July 16, 2019.

34. US Census Bureau, "Characteristics of the Population, Part 33: North Carolina, vol. 2 of US Census of Population: 1950" (Washington, DC: Government Printing Office, 1952), 130, 134, 154, 160.

35. Thomas W. Hanchett, "The Rosenwald Schools and Black Education in North Carolina," *North Carolina Historical Review* 65, no. 4 (October 1988): 441.

36. Hanchett, "The Rosenwald Schools and Black Education in North Carolina," 389.

37. Hanchett, "The Rosenwald Schools and Black Education in North Carolina," 389. Records for White Oaks school are scarce. There is little evidence of anything like a consistent school year during the time its existence is noted. Moreover, there is no evidence that the school existed very long. The Disciples of Christ Church that shared its land says nothing about the school in its history.

38. Sixty-two-year-old African American woman, interviewed by the author, in person, North Carolina, July 24, 2019.

39. Eighty-nine-year-old African American man, interviewed by the author, telephone, December 17, 2021.

40. Ninety-two-year-old white woman, interviewed by the author, in person, North Carolina, July 17, 2019.

41. Ninety-two-year-old white woman, interview, July 17, 2019.

42. Eighty-two-year-old white man, interviewed by the author, in person, August 5, 2018.

43. RABP, February 15, 1953, Newton Grove, North Carolina, house annals.

44. RABP, February 15, 1953.

45. Ninety-two-year-old white woman, interviewed by the author, in person, North Carolina, July 18, 2019.

46. Seventy-four-year-old African American woman, interviewed by the author, telephone, January 9, 2021.

47. Forty-three-year-old white man, interviewed by the author, Zoom, January 8, 2021.

48. Father McQuaid letter to Bishop Hafey, undated, RABP, Vice Province of Richmond File—New Grove, North Carolina: St. Mark's.

49. Eighty-six-year-old white woman, phone conversation with the author, June 24, 2024.

50. For more on this history of busing and desegregation in the United States, see Matthew F. Delmont, *Why Busing Failed: Race, Media, and the National Resistance*

to *School Desegregation* (Oakland: University of California Press, 2016) and Nikole Hannah-Jones, "It Was Never About Busing," *New York Times*, July 12, 2019, https://www.nytimes.com/2019/07/12/opinion/sunday/it-was-never-about-busing.html.

51. Rev. Joseph J. McQuaid, C.Ss.R., letter to Father Barron, December 28, 1931, RABP, Vice Province of Richmond File—New Grove, North Carolina: St. Mark's.

52. RABP, 1933, Newton Grove, North Carolina, house annals.

53. Status Animarum reports that St. Benedict's and St. Mark's/Holy Redeemer filed with the Diocese of Raleigh each year. RDA.

54. Status Animarum reports.

55. Seventy-four-year-old African American woman, interviewed by the author, telephone, January 9, 2019.

56. As historian Sarah Caroline Theusen finds, "In 1936–37, the state provided more than 4,000 buses to transport rural children to school, yet only 361 of those buses carried Black children." Sarah Caroline Thuesen, *Greater than Equal: African American Struggles for Schools and Citizenship in North Carolina, 1919–1965* (Chapel Hill: University of North Carolina Press, 2013), 161.

57. Eighty-nine-year-old African American man, interviewed by the author, telephone, December 17, 2021.

58. Ninety-three-year-old African American man, via email to the author from his cousin, June 25, 2024.

59. Although the Klan was not active as an organization in the 1940s, North Carolinians passed on stories to cautioned children about what might happen if they transgressed this community norm.

60. Eighty-two-year-old white man, interviewed by the author, in person, August 5, 2018.

61. RABP, 1927, Newton Grove, North Carolina, house annals.

62. RABP, April 8, 1928, Newton Grove, North Carolina, house annals.

63. RABP, April 8, 1928.

64. In 1939, the diocese established several parochial schools and created three new Black Catholic parishes in North Carolina, including St. Benedict's in Newton Grove. At McGuinness's request, the Jesuits founded Holy Cross Catholic Church in Durham, North Carolina, on the campus of the North Carolina College of Negros (now North Carolina Central). The bishop was also instrumental in founding St. Ann's Parish in Fayetteville, North Carolina, the home of the Fort Bragg military base. Like many of these parishes, St. Ann's formed because of the initiative of African American Catholics who had grown weary of the discriminatory practices of the American Catholic Church. Sixty-two-year-old African American woman, interviewed by the author, in person, North Carolina, July 24, 2019. McGuiness pastoral letter, January 30, 1940, ARCDR, box 3, Newton Grove—Our Lady of Guadalupe.

65. RABP, 1940, Newton Grove, North Carolina, house annals.

66. Fifty-nine-year-old African American man, interviewed by the author, telephone, January 22, 2020.

67. Eighty-two-year-old white man, interviewed by the author, in person, August 5, 2018.

68. Eighty-nine-year-old African American man, interviewed by the author, telephone, December 17, 2021.

69. "Newton Grove Parish Has Many Activities during the Month of May," *North Carolina Catholic* (Nazareth, NC), June 8, 1947, 7. Today, Harvest Day serves as a local Catholic counter to the homecoming events held at Protestant churches that welcome back members who have moved away.

70. "Newton Grove Parish Has Many Activities during the Month of May."

71. "Bishop Vincent Waters," Catholic Diocese of Raleigh, accessed March 13, 2025, https://dioceseofraleigh.org/african-ancestry/bishop-vincent-waters.

72. Mark Newman, "Toward 'Blessings of Liberty and Justice': The Catholic Church in North Carolina and Desegregation, 1945–1974," *North Carolina Historical Review* 85, no. 3 (July 2008): 312.

73. "Newton Grove Parish Has Many Activities during the Month of May."

74. Bishop's Fundraising Appeal to Negro and Indian Missions," 1951, ARCDR, box 3, Newton Grove—Our Lady of Guadalupe.

75. Father Timothy Sullivan letter to Very Rev. Father Vice-Provincial Joseph Driscoll, February 8, 1951, RAPB, Newton Grove.

Chapter Five

1. Eighty-three-year-old white woman, interviewed by the author, in person, North Carolina, July 16, 2019.

2. Joseph H. Driscoll, C.Ss.R., Vice-Provincial, "Integration at Newton Grove North Carolina," June 7, 1953, Redemptorist Archives of the Baltimore Province (here after RABP), Newton Grove, North Carolina.

3. Although Bishop Waters was in the vanguard of racial issues, he was not a progressive bishop in other ways. In 1970, one-fifth of the priests in the diocese asked for his resignation after he denied their request to create a priests' senate. Further, in early 1971, he insisted that religious women in the diocese wear their full habit and priests wear black suits and conventional clerical collars whenever they appear in public. A year later, he dismissed five sisters in Providence from the diocese for failure to comply with this order. "Bishop Waters Dies at Age 70," *News and Observer* (Raleigh, NC), December 4, 1974, 2; "Bishop Waters Led Diocese of Raleigh," *New York Times*, December 5, 1974; Bishop Waters Correspondence, 1971–73, CCPC 5/49, Consortium Perfectae Caritatis Records, CPC. University of Notre Dame Archives. Sister Mary Joseph Kennedy, OP, St. Rose of Lima Provincial House letter to Bishop Waters, West Palm Beach Florida. Enclosed was the Bishop's Pastoral Letter on Habits from July 27, 1971.

4. Although the bishop did not record his feelings about the desegregation of the parish, those close to him strongly believed that once he became Bishop of the Raleigh Diocese he "felt responsible" for the racist practices there.

5. Monsignor Gerald Lewis, eighty-six-year-old white man, interviewed by the author, in person, North Carolina, July 25, 2019.

6. Charles Craven, "Parish Discusses Merger Plans," *News and Observer* (Raleigh, NC), May 27, 1953, 5.

7. Sixty-eight-year-old African American man, interviewed by the author, in person, North Carolina, July 16, 2019.

8. Eighty-three-year-old white woman, interviewed by the author, in person, North Carolina, July 16, 2019.

9. Eighty-six-year-old white woman, author's group conversation with parishioners, North Carolina, June 1, 2024.

10. Eighty-six-year-old white woman, interviewed by the author, telephone, June 24, 2024.

11. For more on segregation in North Carolina hospitals, see Phoebe Ann Pollitt, *African American Hospitals in North Carolina: 39 Institutional Histories, 1880–1967* (Jefferson, NC: McFarland & Company, 2017); E. H. Beardsley, "Good-Bye to Jim Crow: The Desegregation of Southern Hospitals, 1945–70," *Bulletin of the History of Medicine* 60, no. 3 (1986): 367–86, http://www.jstor.org/stable/44442287. For more on parks, see William E. O'Brien, *Landscapes of Exclusion: State Parks and Jim Crow in the American South* (Boston: University of Massachusetts Press, 2016). For more on segregated swimming in North Carolina's pools, lakes, and oceans, see David Cecelski's ten-part series, "The Color of Water," June 2018, https://davidcecelski.com/tag/the-color-of-water/.

12. Status Animarum Reports that the St. Benedict's and St. Mark's/Holy Redeemer filed with the Diocese of Raleigh each year. Archives of the Roman Catholic Diocese of Raleigh, Raleigh, North Carolina (hereafter ARCDR).

13. Father Irwin letter to Father Fred, August 4, 1950, Newton Grove, North Carolina, parish archives, Our Lady of Guadalupe, Newton Grove, North Carolina.

14. RABP, 1953, Newton Grove, North Carolina, house annals.

15. Together the membership nearly matched the town's population.

16. Vincent S. Waters pastoral letters, May 23, 1953, Archives of the Archdiocese of Raleigh.

17. Father Timothy Sullivan letter to Vice Provincial Joe, February 8, 1951, RABP, Vice Province of Richmond File—New Grove, North Carolina: St. Mark's.

18. RABP, 1953, Newton Grove, North Carolina, house annals.

19. Father Timothy Sullivan letter to Bishop Waters," May 24, 1953, ARCDR, box 3, Newton Grove—Our Lady of Guadalupe.

20. RABP, 1953, Newton Grove, North Carolina, house annals.

21. Sister Dolly Glick, interviewed by the author, telephone, January 23, 2023.

22. RABP, 1953, Newton Grove, North Carolina, house annals.

23. RABP, 1953, Newton Grove, North Carolina, house annals.

24. Undated petition, office of Bishop Waters, ARCDR.

25. Undated anti-integration letter, ARCDR, office of Bishop Waters.

26. White parishioner's letter to Bishop Waters, May 25, 1953, ARCDR, office of Bishop Waters.

27. It is also revealing that the letter writer uses the word "privileges" when describing the access of Blacks to churches and schools, not that these African Americans had a right to such access. Again, the tone of this letter suggests that the author has superior status and is seeking to justify that superiority by the privileges that they have granted to the underclass.

28. Bishop Waters letter to parishioners of Holy Redeemer Parish, May 23, 1953, ARCDR, office of Bishop Waters.

29. Bishop Waters letter to parishioners, May 23, 1953.

30. Father Irwin letter to Bishop Hafey, January 27, 1934, Newton Grove, North Carolina, ARCDR, box 3, Newton Grove—Our Lady of Guadalupe.

31. Hoover Adams, "Religious Community Has Romantic History," *Charlotte Observer* (Charlotte, NC), November 30, 1939, 147.

32. The first time a discussion of the church's founding reappears in print is in 1952, when John Tracy Ellis published *Life of James Cardinal Gibbons*. Ellis highlighted John Carr's conversion and the original sermon that drew the patriarch to Catholicism. The Catholic press and likely the bishop learned of this story of Carr's conversion from Ellis's biography. "Sermon Was on Unity and True Faith," *Catholic Advance* (Wichita, KS), May 15, 1953, 7.

33. Lindsey Ruebens, "Black and Catholic in North Carolina," *Endeavors Magazine*, June 2, 2011, https://endeavors.unc.edu/black_and_catholic_in_north_carolina_0.

34. Monsignor Gerald Lewis, eighty-six-year-old white man, interviewed by the author, in person, North Carolina, July 25, 2019.

35. John Wiley, "The Soul of Magic City: Religion in Roanoke, Virginia, 1882–1914" (master's thesis, Morgan State University, 2017).

36. "Bishop Vincent Waters," Catholic Diocese of Raleigh, accessed October 10, 2023, https://dioceseofraleigh.org/african-ancestry/bishop-vincent-waters.

37. Monsignor Gerald Lewis, eighty-six-year-old white man, interviewed by the author, in person, North Carolina, July 25, 2019.

38. "Bishop Vincent S. Waters—The Man and the Prelate," *North Carolina Catholic*, November 1, 1970, 5.

39. Mark Newman, "'Racial Discrimination Can in No Way Be Justified': The Vatican and Desegregation in the South, 1946–1968," *Journal of American Studies* 56, no. 5 (December 2022): 676.

40. "Map Expansion of Work among Negro People," *Catholic Standard and Times*, September 7, 1945, 11.

41. Mark Newman, "Toward 'Blessings of Liberty and Justice': The Catholic Church in North Carolina and Desegregation, 1945–1974," *North Carolina Historical Review* 85, no. 3 (July 2008): 321.

42. Simultaneously, he asked that whites treat African American Catholics who came to their Masses as they would any other Catholic. Waters was not alone. In that same year, the Archbishop of New Orleans, Joseph Rummel, issued a letter that stated, "The lines of segregation must disappear in our churches, not only physically but in the true spirit of Christian brotherhood, in the seating accommodations, at the confessional, at the communion rail and in general in the reception of the sacraments and sacramentals of the Church." Like Waters, Rummel failed to back his letter with any action requiring the integration of the Catholic institutions for which he was responsible, from schools to hospitals to parishes. These statements from both the archbishop and the bishop were in effect aspirational. They simply announced the diocesan principles with respect to race relations, perhaps with the hope that, using this encouragement, the priests in the various parishes would take steps to eliminate what Bishop Waters

called the "heresy" of racism. "'Segregation Must Disappear,' says Bishop Rummell," *Carolina Times* (Durham, NC), March 3, 1951, 3.

43. Bishop Vincent S. Waters letter to Most Rev. Amleto G. Cicognani, DD, Apostolic Delegate to the United States, July 21, 1953, Newton Grove, North Carolina, ARCDR, Newton Grove, Our Lady of Guadalupe–St. Benedict.

44. Vincent S. Waters letter to Most Rev. Amleto G. Cicognani. RABP, 1953, Newton Grove, North Carolina, house annals.

45. Sister Dolly Glick, Mission Helpers of the Sacred Heart, ninety-year-old white woman, interviewed by the author, telephone, January 23, 2023.

46. Auxiliary Bishop George Lynch, "Some Questions at N.G.," May 31, 1953, ARCDR, Newton Grove/Our Lady of Guadalupe–St. Benedict, Auxiliary Bishop George Lynch papers, DRA.

47. Father Irwin letter to Father Fred, August 4, 1950, parish archives, Our Lady of Guadalupe, Newton Grove, North Carolina.

48. Father James Garneau, interviewed by the author, in person, North Carolina, July 24, 2018.

49. John LaFarge, SJ, letter to Bishop Waters, July 8, 1953, ARCDR, office of Bishop Waters. For a more detailed discussion of this exchange, see Blake Slonecker, "A Church Apart: Catholic Desegregation in Newton Grove, North Carolina," *North Carolina Historical Review* 83, no. 3 (July 2006): 347–48.

50. Sixty-eight-year-old African American man, interviewed by the author, in person, North Carolina, July 16, 2019.

51. Newspaper clippings, Newton Grove Merger, ARCDR, office of Bishop Waters.

52. "Merger Seems Permanent," *Carolina Times* (Durham, NC), June 6, 1953, 8.

53. Charles Craven, "Parishioners Discuss Merger Plan," *Raleigh News and Observer* (Raleigh, NC), May 27, 1953, 5.

54. Sixty-eight-year-old African American man, email to author, July 15, 2019.

55. "Catholic Church Segregation in Durham," *Carolina Times* (Durham, NC), September 11, 1954, 2.

56. Sister Dolly Glick, ninety-year-old white woman, interviewed by the author, telephone, January 23, 2023.

57. Sister Dolly Glick interview.

58. Sister Dolly Glick interview.

59. Status Animarum Reports that Our Lady of Guadalupe filed with the Diocese of Raleigh each year. RDA. Since the parish was no longer segregated, the race of the parishioners who left the parish was not recorded.

60. Sixty-year-old white man, interviewed by the author, in person, North Carolina, August 5, 2018.

61. Rev. Robert E. McMahon letter to Bishop Vincent S. Waters, November 29, 1965, ARCDR, Office of Bishop Waters.

62. Sixty-eight-year-old African American man, interviewed by the author, in person, North Carolina, July 16, 2019.

63. Father George Lynch letter to Bishop Waters, November 15, 1953, ARCDR, office of Bishop Waters.

64. Although official papal invitations to include Black culture in the Mass would not come until 1969, and then again in 1987, it seems likely that shifting the liturgy to embrace the vernacular would have had a marked effect on the form if not the substance of the Mass. For more on this issue, see Matthew J. Cressler, "Black Power, Vatican II, and the Emergence of Black Catholic Liturgies," *US Catholic Historian* 32, no. 4 (2014): 99–119; Mary E. McGann and Eva Marie Lumas, "The Emergence of African American Catholic Worship," *US Catholic Historian* 19, no. 2 (2001): 27–65, http://www.jstor.org/stable/25154767; and National Conference of Black Catholic Bishops, *Plenty Good Room: The Spirit and Truth of African American Catholic Worship* (Washington, DC: United States Catholic Conference Inc., 1990).

65. J. H. Driscoll letter to Bishop Waters, May 14, 1953, RABP, Vice Province of Richmond File—New Grove, North Carolina: St. Mark's.

66. RABP, 1953, Newton Grove, North Carolina, house annals.

67. Eighty-three-year-old white woman, interviewed by the author, in person, North Carolina, July 23, 2018.

68. Father Henry S. Voss, C.Ss.R., letter to Bishop Waters, September 3, 1953, ARCDR, office of Bishop Waters.

69. On Friday, October 30, the sisters held the Halloween party for the white students. Fifteen children attended, a big drop from the eighty the sisters claimed attended from the previous year. No mention was made of numbers for the African American Halloween party held the previous afternoon. Father Voss only noted, "They thoroughly enjoyed the party." Father Henry S. Voss, C.Ss.R., letter to Bishop Waters, October 30, 1953, ARCDR, office of Bishop Waters.

70. In September, six white students attended the first day of class. The local paper reported that "their training has been reduced to tutoring." In that same article, Father J. F. Rouche said that transportation woes led to the decline. The parish had no money for gasoline, but, he said, "Any student is welcome if he can pay for his own transportation." The school closed because white parishioners followed the majority in Newton Grove in opposing integration. By blaming the lack of transportation, Father Rouche saved face by tamping down the public's awareness of racial strife in the diocese. It wasn't until 1959 that Havelock Elementary School, which served Cherry Point Airforce Base and the surrounding area, became the first integrated school in North Carolina.

71. "Priest Says Newton Grove School Now Nonsegregated," *Asheville Citizen-Times*, September 4, 1954, 12.

72. Eighty-two-year-old white man, interviewed by the author, in person, August 5, 2018, and eighty-six-year-old white woman, interviewed by the author, in person, June 2, 2021.

73. "Priest Says Newton Grove School Now Nonsegregated."

74. Eighty-six-year-old white woman, interviewed by the author, in person, June 2, 2021.

75. Eighty-nine-year-old African American man, interviewed by the author, telephone, July 17, 2021.

76. Henry explained, "We were in the 1950s deep in the Jim Crow South. We didn't go to school together. Blacks couldn't go to local restaurants and sit for a meal. The

parks and everything else were segregated. You didn't go out of that church property and do things together. Unless you worked together." Public support and public spaces for developing interracial relationships were absent. Sixty-eight-old African American man, interviewed by the author, in person, North Carolina, July 16, 2019. Henry reiterated these ideas in an email to the author, June 29, 2023.

77. "Discrimination and Christian Conscience: A Statement Issued by the Catholic Bishops of the United States, November 14, 1958," *Pastoral Letters of the United States Catholic Bishops, Volume II, 1941-1961*, https://www.usccb.org/resources/Discrimination-Christian-Conscience-Nov-14-1958.pdf.

78. Sixty-eight-year-old African American man, interviewed by the author, in person, North Carolina, July 16, 2019.

79. Similarly, other African American parishioners remember going to the Harvest Day festival where both Black and white women prepared food and items to auction. Rachel remembers returning to Newton Grove from Raleigh every year with her mother and siblings.

80. Sixty-two-year-old African American woman, interviewed by the author, in person, North Carolina, July 24, 2019.

81. Father Wall, "How I Remember My Days at Newton Grove," notes from a public talk given to the author, May 4, 2021.

82. Ladies' Altar Society minutes, Parish Archives, Newton Grove, North Carolina.

83. Eighty-five-year-old white man, interviewed by the author, in person, North Carolina, July 18, 2019.

84. Their decisions are reflected in the growing church membership registry.

85. Sixty-eight-year-old African American man, interviewed by the author, in person, North Carolina, July 16, 2019.

86. The parishioners' life paths can be seen through the many obituaries collected by the Parish Historical Society. See Parish Archives, Newton Grove, North Carolina.

87. For more on how inheritance law affected America's Black farmers, see Thomas W. Mitchell, "From Reconstruction to Deconstruction: Undermining Black Landownership, Political Independence, and Community through Partition Sales of Tenancies in Common," *Northwestern University Law Review* 95, no. 2 (2001), and Thomas W. Mitchell, "Destabilizing the Normalization of Rural Black Land Loss: A Critical Role for Legal Empiricism," *Wisconsin Law Review* 557 (2005).

88. Valerie Grim, "The Impact of Mechanized Farming on Black Farm Families in the Rural South: A Study of Farm Life in the Brooks Farm Community, 1940-1970," *Agricultural History* 68, no. 2 (1994): 170, http://www.jstor.org/stable/3744410. See also Neil Fligstein, "The Transformation of Southern Agriculture and the Migration of Blacks and Whites, 1930-1940," *International Migration Review* 17, no. 2 (1983): 268-90, and Dania V. Francis, Darrick Hamilton, Thomas W. Mitchell, Nathan A. Rosenberg, and Bryce Wilson Stucki, "Black Land Loss: 1920-1997," *AEA Papers and Proceedings* 112 (2022): 38-42.

89. For more on the inclusion of African American culture in Mass, see National Conference of Black Catholic Bishops, *Plenty Good Room* and "A Statement of the Black Catholic Clergy Caucus, 1968," in *"Stamped with the Image of God": African Americans as*

God's Image in Black, ed. Cyprian Davis, OSB, and Jamie Phelps, OP (Maryknoll, NY: Orbis, 2003), 11.

90. Sixty-two-year-old African American woman, interviewed by the author, in person, North Carolina, July 24, 2019.

91. According to the Pew survey, "Black Catholics are a minority in the United States in numerous ways. They comprise a small share of Black adults (6%) and an even smaller share of Catholic adults (4%). . . . Just 25% of Black Catholics who attend Mass at least a few times a year report that they typically go to a Mass where most other attendees are Black." "Black Catholics in America," Pew Research Center, March 15, 2022, https://www.pewresearch.org/religion/2022/03/15/black-catholics-in-america/.

Afterword

1. "Chronology of the Diocese from 1945–1970: A Year by Year [sic] History of the Events of the Past 25 Years," *North Carolina Catholic* (November 1, 1970), 5.

2. Blank parish stationery, Archives of the Roman Catholic Diocese of Raleigh, Raleigh, North Carolina (hereafter ARCDR), box 3, Newton Grove—Our Lady of Guadalupe.

3. Vincent S. Waters letter to Most Rev. Apostolic Delegate, December 16, 1953, ARCDR, box 3, Newton Grove—Our Lady of Guadalupe.

4. Monsignor Gerald Lewis, eighty-six-year-old white man, interviewed by the author, in person, North Carolina, July 25, 2019.

5. For an early history of the movement of Latinx Catholics into North Carolina, see Susan B. Ridgely, "Sweet Tea and Rosary Beads: An Analysis of Catholicism in the South at the Millennium," in *Religion in the Contemporary South: Changes, Continuities, and Contexts*, ed. Corrie E. Norman and Don S. Armentrout (Knoxville: University of Tennessee Press, 2005), 191–220, and Chad E. Seales, *The Secular Spectacle: Performing Religion in a Southern Town* (Oxford: Oxford University Press, 2013).

6. Father James Garneau, sixty-eight-year-old white man, interviewed by the author, in person, North Carolina, July 24, 2018.

7. Eighty-three-year-old white woman, interviewed by the author, telephone, July 19, 2019.

8. For more on the early years of Latinx migration to North Carolina, see Seales, *The Secular Spectacle* and Susan B. Ridgely, "Sweet Tea and Rosary Beads: An Analysis of Catholicism in the South at the Millennium," in *Religion in the Contemporary South*, 191–206.

9. Father James Garneau, sixty-eight-year-old white man, interviewed by the author, in person, North Carolina, July 24, 2018.

10. Dennis Rogers, "Catholic Church in Sampson County Works to Ease Farmer's Plight," *Raleigh News & Observer*, November 21, 1985, 47.

11. Father James Garneau, sixty-eight-year-old white man, interviewed by the author, in person, North Carolina, July 24, 2018.

12. Cindy A. Adams and Angela Godwin Page, *Road to the Cross: A History of the Catholic Church in Newton Grove, 1871–2019* (self-published, 2019), 55.

13. Father James Garneau, sixty-eight-year-old white man, interviewed by the author, in person, North Carolina, July 24, 2018.

14. Eighty-nine-year-old African American man, interviewed by the author, telephone, July 17, 2021.

15. Eighty-nine-year-old African American man, interviewed.

16. Father Kevin Moley, seventy-five-year-old white man, interviewed by the author, in person, North Carolina, July 18, 2018.

17. Sixty-two-year-old African American woman, interviewed by the author, telephone, July 22, 2019.

18. Monsignor Gerald Lewis, email to the author, October 22, 2023.

Index

Page numbers in italics refer to illustrations.

abolitionism, 32, 35, 38
African Americans: and "Black codes," 36–37; Catholic and Protestant involvement of, 58–59; in Catholic Church, 7, 54–55, 65–67, 90, 139, 180n42, 182n64; Catholic outreach to, 63, 67–68; Great Migration of, 7, 46; involuntary servitude of, 37; land ownership of post–Civil War, 37–38, 43–44, 56–57; loss of land of, 145–46. *See also* enslaved persons; segregation
agriculture: commercial, 152; cotton industry, 86–87, 100; difficulty of in twentieth century, 146; and land ownership, 145–46; and rural farmers, 100; sharecropping, 38, 99
altar servers, 117–19
Anderson, Bentley, 40–41
anti-Catholic sentiment, 66, 67–68, 89, 107–8; and interfaith marriages, 102; and opposition to integration, 128; and public schools, 88; softening of, 59, 139–40
author's methodology: analysis, 10; chapter outlines, 18–20; online interviews, 14–15; oral histories, 7, 9, 12–18; personal experiences, 10–12

Barron, James, 95–96
Bassett, John Spencer, 27
Battle of Cold Harbor, 34
Battle of Fort Sumter, 33
Battle of Gettysburg, 34
Battle of Spotsylvania, 34
Benedict the Moor, Saint, 86

Benton, Alexander, 25
Benton, Celia M., 97
Benton family, 33
Black Americans. *See* African Americans
"Black codes," 36–37
boll weevils, 86–87, 100
Brown v. Board of Education of Topeka (1954), 4
buses: integration of, 142; service to Mass, 117, 138–39; as symbol of desegregation, 109; as transportation to school, 108–12, *118*, 138–40

Cameron, Mary Charles, 140
Catholic Board of Colored Missions, 89
Catholic Church: African American parishes, 7, 139, 177n64; African American priests, 90; altar servers, 117–19; as Body of Christ, 8; conversion to, 21, 49, 54–55; "cradle Catholics," 21, 77; and Democratic Party, 41; integrated parishes, 40–41, 95; Mass, 119; and missionary outreach to Black and Native communities, 62, 120; parochial schools, 79–81; in Protestant-dominated South, 1–3, 47–50; and racial justice, 10; restrictions on Protestant involvement in, 58–59; segregation of in twentieth century, 101–3; segregation in orders of, 82–84; spiritual care of African Americans in, 65–67; and unity, 39–40, 42, 125–26; as universal church, 9, 10. *See also* Plenary Councils

187

Catholic Foreign Mission Society of America, 70
Catholic Interracial Council, 4, 95, 174n5
Cavagnaro, Josita, 72–76, 74, 87
Cecelski, David, 13
Charles, Mary, 17–18
Civil War, 31, 32–34, 36, 38, 42
Cold Harbor, Battle of, 34
Cole, Abram, 37
Cole, Hinton, 30–31, 33, 37, 48
Cole, Martha. *See* Monk, Martha Cole
Cole, Sarah Elizabeth Williams. *See* Williams, Sarah Elizabeth (Cole)
Cole, Willis, 30
Cole family, 23
cotton industry, 86–87, 100
Cox, Beatrice, 79–81, 123
Cox, J. Blackman, 25
Cox, Lula Monk, 79
Cox, Moses, 25
Cox, Nathaniel, 123, 125
Cox, William E., 35–36
cross-racial relationships. *See* interracial relationships

Democratic Party, 41, 165n58
desegregation. *See* integration; segregation
Disciples of Christ Church, 31, 48
DNA testing, 6
Dominican Sisters, 67, 69, 72–73, 81–82, 87, 101
Drexel, Katharine, 9, 62–64, 66–68, 73–75, 79, 84–85, 89–90
Driscoll, Joseph, 122, 178n75, n1, 182n65
DuBois, W. E. B., 43

Eason, Elizabeth, 33
Eason, Euphemia Alice. *See* Monk, Euphemia Alicia Eason
Eason, John, 33
Ellis, John Tracy, 53
emancipation: of Archibald Monk farm, 23, 28; white support for and backlash against, 35–36

Emancipation Proclamation, 36
enslaved families: and marriage prior to emancipation, 30; reunification of during Reconstruction, 37; separation of during enslavement, 23
enslaved persons: on Archibald Monk farm, 25, 26–27; family identity and kinship patterns of, 29–31; and free household members, 18, 22; labor of, 23; marriage of, 30; in popular culture and romanticization of, 26; rape of enslaved women, 18, 25, 30. *See also* slavery
enslavement. *See* plantation system
Eucharist, 63–64
evangelization efforts, 62, 120

families. *See* enslaved families; kinship bonds
farming. *See* agriculture
Federated Colored Catholics (FCC), 4, 90, 94–95, 174n5
Fifteenth Amendment, 43
Finding Your Roots (Gates), 5
First Plenary Council (1852), 70
Foner, Eric, 37
Fort Sumter, Battle of, 33
Fourteenth Amendment, 43
Freedman's Bureau, 37

Garneau, James, 56, 152–55
Gates, Henry Louis, Jr., 5
Gettysburg, Battle of, 34
Gibbons, James, 9, 41–42, 47, 50–51, 53, 168n36
Glick, Dolores "Dolly," 137
Godwin, Amanda (née Gregory), 53
Godwin, Enoch David, 40, 46, 53, 78, 116
Godwin, Julia, 13
Godwin family, 59–60
Goldsboro Messenger (newspaper), 59
Gone with the Wind (Mitchell), 26
Goshen Methodist Church, 39, 45
Great Migration, 7, 46
Gregory, Amanda Godwin, 53

Gregory, John T. "J. T.," 53, 78
Gregory family, 23, 33, 151; and music at St. Mark's, 59–60
Gross, Mark, 41, 47, 53
Gummer, Thomas, 93, 94

Hadden, Thomas, 138
Hafey, William J., 80–81; and Dominican Sisters, 87; and St. Benedict Hall, 90–91
Hahn, Steven, 30
Hamilton, William D., 34
Han, Steven, 23
Hargrove, Harriet (Monk). *See* Monk, Harriett Hargrove
Hargrove, Jane Carr, 24
Hargrove family, 33
Harvest Day celebrations, 119, 178n69, 183n79
Herring, David, 106
Herring, Menus, 45, 46, 55
Holden, William Woods, 44, 45
Holy Redeemer Parish, 113, 116; African American parishioners' unease in, 135–36, 137–38; Harvest Day, 119, 178n69, 183n79; and integration, 128–30. *See also* St. Mark's parish; Trinity Sunday (1953) integration

Institute of St. Francis de Sales, 80
integration: of schools in North Carolina, 139–42; of US military, 143. *See also* segregation; Trinity Sunday (1953) integration
interfaith marriages, 102, 114, 137
interracial relationships, 3; as goal of Catholic Church, 4; kinship, 5–7, 162n14; marriages, 37
involuntary servitude, 37
Irwin, Michael A.: aging and retirement of, 91–92; on anti-Catholic bias, 88; background and views of, 70; building projects and leadership of, 69–70, 72; and Dominican Sisters, 87–88; on foundations of St. Mark's, 49; and fundraising for St. Benedict Hall, 88–90; impact and legacy of, 64, 66; and Dolores Jackson, 81–84; race relations and leadership of, 72–78, 98–99, 113, 116; and St. Mark's expansion efforts, 84–85; and white violence, 85–86

Jackson, Dolores, 81–84
Johnson, Andrew, 44
Johnson, Guion Griffis, 26

Kilde, Daniel, 32
kinship bonds, 9–10; in enslavement, 23; spiritual, and baptismal sponsorship, 55–57; between Black and white families, 127–28
Knights of Columbus, 132
Ku Klux Klan, 44, 45, 111; terrorism and threats of, 65, 116, 141

Ladies' Altar Societies, 132, 144
LaFarge, John, 9, 95, 134, 174n5
land ownership: Black loss of, 145–46; by Black persons after Civil War, 37–38, 43–44, 56–57; as heritage, 24
Latinx Catholics, 151–55
Lee, Pharaoh, 169n46
Lee, Robert E., 96
Lee family, 23
Lewis, Gerald L., 131
Logan, Frenise, 46
lynching, 45, 46, 56, 66

Markoe, William, 9, 95
Maryknoll Fathers, 70
Masters of Science (Willoughby), 31
Mathews, Donald G., 45
McCloskey, John, 39–40
McGreevy, John, 10
McGuinness, Eugene J., 116–17
McMahon, Robert E., 138
McQuaid, Joseph J., 96–97, 100–101, 102, 113; and school bus transportation, 108–11
Mexico, 153

Meyer, Edward, 62–63, 67–68
migrant farm workers, 152
Migrant Ministry, 152–54
missionary programs, 62, 120
Mitchell, Margaret, 26
Moley, Kevin, 157
Monk, Archibald, 6, 21, 24; on education, 163n24; emancipation of slaves of, 29; and neighbors, 23; and plantation crop inventory, 26; political activity of, 24–25; as slaveholder, 25–28
Monk, Catherine Currie, 24
Monk, Claudius Buchanan, 34
Monk, Euphemia Alicia Eason, 33, 165n46; as baptismal sponsor for Mary Delia Monk, 55–56; conversion of to Catholicism, 51
Monk, Harriet Hargrove, 24
Monk, Henry Clay, 33, 34
Monk, Hinton, 30–31, 33, 37, 48, 164n37
Monk, James, 24
Monk, John Carr: and abolitionism, 32; as baptismal sponsor for Mary Delia Monk, 55–56; and Black community, 48–49; Catholic conversion of, 21, 39–42, 43, 50–51, 51; and Catholic theology, 41–42; childhood and background of, 1, 26–27; emancipation of enslaved persons of, 33–36, 165n50; farm of, 165n48; impact and legacy of, 23–24, 155–58; and kinship patterns, 22; and Klan, 45; marriage of, 33; Mass held in home of, 53–54; medical school and practice of, 31–32; and neighbors, 23–24; and parochial school, 61–62; political and personal activity before and during Civil War, 33–38; and Republican Party, 35; school founded by, 72; as slaveowner, 33; social rejection of, 51–52, 60; and Solomon, 50; and transportation to church, 57–58, 138–39; and unity, 39–40, 42, 97–98, 127–28, 148–49
Monk, Julius, 49, 54
Monk, Kaplan, 162n13
Monk, Martha Cole, 37; conversion of to Catholicism, 54; daughter with Solomon Monk, 79; exclusion of from home Mass, 54; founding vision of, 125–29, 148; sacramental record for, 56
Monk, Mary Delia, 56
Monk, Rufus, 33, 39, 56
Monk, Solomon: background and childhood of, 1, 26–27; daughter with Martha Cole Monk, 79; descendants of, 28–29, 30–31; after emancipation, 28–29; exclusion of from home Mass, 54; founding vision of, 125, 129, 148; kinship patterns of, 22, 162n14; and land acquisition post–Civil War, 37–38; and slavery, 25; and twin brother Kaplan, 162n13
Monk, William, 24
Monk family: background of, 5–6; family tree, 21–22, 164n37; plantation and slavery, 24–28; relationships between siblings, 26–27
Mueller, Francis X., 61

Native Americans, 63, 116
Nelson, Scott Reynolds, 44
New Bern Daily Journal (newspaper), 46
New Orleans, 40–41
Newton Grove, NC: anti-Catholic sentiment in, 58–59, 84–85; Catholic Church in, 7–8; and economic challenges during Great Depression, 99–101; financial stress due to cotton collapse in, 86–87; Klan activity in, 46; rural nature of, 75–76, 95–96; segregation in, 5–6, 8; social pressure in, 51–52; St. Mark's parish, 65–67; Union and Confederate troop presence in, 34–35

North Carolina: "Black codes" in, 36–37; Catholic Church in rural areas of, 47–48; census data on slavery in (1860), 25–26; cotton industry in, 86–87; Klan activity in, 45–46; map, 2; pre–Civil War history of, 22; public education for African Americans in, 85; rural culture in, 72–73; school integration in 1970s, 4; secession of, 33; segregated education in, 72, 159n4

North Carolina Catholic (newspaper), 119, 131, 151

North Carolina Catholic Layman's Association (NCCLA), 120, 132

North Carolina State Constitution, 171n14

North Carolina State University, 148

November Harvest Festival, 142

Oblate Sisters of Providence, 171n9

"Old South," 1–3. *See also* Southern life and culture

oral histories, 7, 9; author's use of, 12–18; online interviews, 14–15; as reconstruction of past, 13–14

O'Rourke, J. H., 51–52, 67

Our Lady of Guadalupe, 151–52; contemporary interest in heritage, 153–56; Latinx parishioners, 151–56; Migrant Ministry, 152–54

Page, Angela Godwin, 169n43

Parish Boundaries (McGreevy), 10

"Perpetual Help Motor Chapel," 102–3

Phifer, George W., 26

Philadelphia, PA, 32

plantation system: dismantling of, 36–37; romanticization of, 26

Plenary Councils: First (1852), 70; Second (1866), 48; Third (1884), 62, 90

Plessey v. Ferguson (1896), 4, 41, 68

Price, Thomas Fredrick, 67, 70

Protestant congregations and segregation, 7–9

racial terrorism, 75. *See also* Ku Klux Klan

racism: in medical practice, 31–32; prejudice and emotion, 131. *See also* white supremacy

Raleigh Christian Advocate (newspaper), 60

Raleigh News and Observer (newspaper), 123

rape of enslaved women, 18, 25, 30

Raynor family, 23

Reconstruction, 37; backlash against, 43–47; Black labor during, 38; Black land ownership during, 37–38, 43–44; Black political participation in, 44

Redemptorist Order, 92, 94–95, 96–97; Holy Redeemer, name change to, 116; and "Perpetual Help Motor Chapel," 102–3; racial issues and challenges, 98–99; removal of, 140

Redmond, Jeanette, 83

Republican Party, 35; and emancipated Black men, 44

Rialls, Gabriel, 45

Robinson, Bennie, 144

Robinson, Betsy Lee, 57

Robinson, Cora, 98–99, 130

Robinson, John, 57, 169n46

Robinson, Mamie, 73

Robinson, Margaret, 61–62

Robinson, Paul, 111

Rosenwald, Julius, 104

Rosenwald Foundation, 104

Rudd, Daniel A., 9

Salisbury North Carolina Evening Sun (newspaper), 59

Sampson County, NC, 1–3; during Civil War, 34–35; Klan activity in, 45–46. *See also* North Carolina

"scalawag" (term), 35–36

schools: African American, 48–49; African American parochial, 68–69; Johnston County public, 49; parish schools, 101, 103–8; public schools and anti-Catholic bias, 88

Index 191

Second Plenary Council (1866), 48
segregation: on buses, 111–12; in Catholic Church, 82–84, 99, 101–3; in Catholic church choirs, 59–60; dual church doors, 55, 113, 133, 136; gendered contexts of, 75; as missionary method, 93–94; North Carolina State Constitution, 72, 159n4; in parochial schools, 69, 72, 106–7; in Philadelphia, PA, 32; in Protestant congregations, 7–9, 39; Protestant vs. Catholic approaches to, 7–8; during Reconstruction era, 44; religious elements of, 45; during school recess, 85–86; of St. Mark's parish seating, 63–64, 73–74
sharecropping, 38, 99
Sherman, William Tecumseh, 34–35
Sisters of Mercy, 101, 140
Sisters of the Blessed Sacrament, 63–64; and St. Benedict Hall contract, 90–91
Sisters of the Mission Helpers of the Sacred Heart, 137
slavery: family separations during, 23, 29; kinship ties during, 23; labor shared between plantations, 30; marriages of enslaved persons, 29–30; on Monk Plantation, 24–28; plantation system, 26, 36–37; relationships between slaveholder and enslaved families, 26–27; slave rebellions, 24–25; and Whig Party, 25. *See also* enslaved persons
Society for the Propagation of the Faith, 116
Southern life and culture, 6–7; corn shuckings, 97; foodways, 53; hospitality, 97, 100; norms, 65; white supremacy, 96–97
Spotsylvania, Battle of, 34
St. Benedict's Church and Hall, 88–91, 93, 105; removal of, 151; social events at, 119–20; white parishioners' use of, 98

Stevens, John, 45
St. Francis's School (St. Benedict's School), 62, 72–76, 79, 85, 175n17; student experiences at, 103–6, 107–8
St. Mark's parish, 115; African American lived experiences at, 156–57; African American parochial school, 68–69; background and overview of, 1–3; Black converts in early years of, 54–55; building architecture of, 55; cemetery, 5; and children and young people, 147–48; contemporary interest in history and heritage of, 153–56; contemporary situation of, 148, 151–58; and conversion to Catholicism, 50–61; economic challenges of, 75–76; and educational opportunities, 78–80; and Eucharist, 63–64; holiday celebrations at, 73, 89, 142; impact of, 148–49; integrated parish schools (1950s), 139–42; and integration, 15–16, 74–75, 133–34, 117–21, 127–28, 142–45; interfaith families and inclusivity in, 49–50; interracial vision of, 97–101; as model of Christianity, 9–10; motivations of parishioners of, 11–12; music and choir, 59–60; 150th anniversary of, 156; and orphans, 78; overview of, 3–4; parochial school, 61–62, 101; Redemptorist Fathers, 96–97; Holy Redeemer, name change to, 113, 116; Our Lady of Guadalupe, name change to, 151–52; resegregation with St. Benedict's, 93–94; segregated schools, maintenance of, 72–77; segregation of, 3, 4, 55, 63–64, 99, 113, 133, 136; segregation and integration, tension between, 82–84, 113–17; stained glass windows in, 52; unique nature of, 60–61; and unity, 8

192 *Index*

St. Mark's Parochial School, 69–72, 71, 175n17; student experiences at, 106–7
Sullivan, Timothy, 107, 112, 120–21; house diaries of, 128; on integrated schools, 140; on Trinity Sunday (1953), 126–27

Tentler, Leslie Woodcock, 41
Theusen, Sarah Caroline, 177n56
Third Plenary Council (1884), 62, 90
transportation: and African American school attendance, 110–11; to church, 111, 117, 138–39; to school, 79–80, 108–11, 177n56. *See also* buses
Trinity Sunday (1953), 122–26, 124; criticism of, 136; impact of, 126–30, 134, 137–39; press coverage and public opinion of, 134–36; protest of, 145–49
Truman, Harry, 143
tuberculosis, 87
Turner, Nat, 24
Turner, Thomas Wyatt, 9, 90, 95
Tuscarora tribe, 30

Union Army, 34
University of Pennsylvania, 31

violence: lynching, 45, 46, 56, 66; rape of enslaved women, 18, 25, 30; threats of white, 85–86

Virginia Commission on Interracial Cooperation, 120
Virgin of Guadalupe, 151–52
Voss, Henry, 139, 140

Wall, John, 144, 146
Washington, Booker T., 104
Waters, Vincent Stanislaus, 4, 95, 119–20, 122–23, 158, 178n3; commitment to interracial Catholicism, 130–34; John Carr Monk's influence, 130; pastoral letters of, 126, 151
Wells-Oghoghomeh, Alexis, 28
Whig Party, 25, 32
White Oak Disciples of Christ Church, 48, 138; school, 104, 176n37
"white purity," 83
white supremacy, 129; in Catholic orders, 82–84; and community pressure, 133; and Confederacy, 96–97; in medical training, 31–32; in Reconstruction era, 44, 47; shifting standards and rules, 9; varying expressions of, 3; white violence, threats of, 85–86
Williams, Isaac, 60
Williams, Sarah Elizabeth (Cole), 30, 37
Willoughby, Christopher, 31

Xavier University, 79

Zwilling, Diana, 13

www.ingramcontent.com/pod-product-compliance
Lightning Source LLC
Chambersburg PA
CBHW031437160426
43195CB00010BB/761